JOURNEY TO MEXICO

Antonin Artaud

JOURNEY TO MEXICO
REVOLUTIONARY MESSAGES
& THE TARAHUMARA

Translated by Rainer J. Hanshe

Edited, introduced, and with notes & a chronology
by Stuart Kendall

Contra Mundum Press   New York · London · Melbourne

*Journey to Mexico:
Revolutionary Messages &
the Tarahumara*
© 2024 Rainer J. Hanshe;
introduction © 2024
Stuart Kendall

First Contra Mundum Press
edition 2024.

All Rights Reserved under
International & Pan-American
Copyright Conventions.
No part of this book may
be reproduced in any form
or by any electronic means,
including information storage
and retrieval systems, without
permission in writing from the
publisher, except by a reviewer
who may quote brief passages
in a review.

Library of Congress
Cataloguing-in-Publication
Data

Artaud, Antonin, 1896–1948
Journey to Mexico:
Revolutionary Messages &
the Tarahumara /
Antonin Artaud

—1st Contra Mundum Press
Edition

532 pp., 5 × 8 in.

ISBN 9781940625645

   I. Artaud, Antonin.
  II. Title.
 III. Hanshe, Rainer J.
 IV. Translator.
  V. Kendall, Stuart.
 VI. Editor, introduction.

2023947852

CONTENTS

Life is Elsewhere by Stuart Kendall					0

Chronology										XXXVIII

JOURNEY TO MEXICO:
REVOLUTIONARY MESSAGES & THE TARAHUMARA

THE CONQUEST OF MEXICO

    The Conquest of Mexico							4

PREPARATORY WRITINGS

    The Awakening of the Thunder Bird					16
    Mexico and Civilization							26
    The Eternal Treason of the White Man					33
    Notes on Cultures								38

LETTERS (1935–36)

    To the International Congress of Writers…				46
    Jean Paulhan, 19 July 1935						51
    Jean Paulhan, 6 August 1935						56
    Jean Paulhan, 15 August 1935						58
    To the Minister of Foreign Affairs, August 1935			60
    To the Minister of National Education, August 1935		63
    Jean Paulhan, September 1935						66

Mrs. Paulhan, September 1935	67
To the General Secretary of AF, 14 December 1935	68
Jean Paulhan, 6 January 1936	72
Dr. Allendy & Ms. Nel-Dumochel, 10 January 1936	73
Jean Paulhan, 25 January 1936	75
Jean Paulhan, 31 January 1936	77
Jean-Louis Barrault, 31 January 1936	78
Balthus, 31 January 1936	79
René Allendy, 7 February 1936	81
Jean Paulhan, 26 March 1936	83
René Thomas, 2 April 1936	85
Jean Paulhan, 23 April 1936	87
Jean Paulhan, 21 May 1936	95
Jean-Louis Barrault, 17 June 1936	100
Balthus, 18 June 1936	103
Jean-Louis Barrault, 10 July 1936	104

REVOLUTIONARY MESSAGES

Three Lectures Presented at the University of Mexico
Surrealism and Revolution	110
Man Against Fate	123
The Theater and the Gods	135

Mexico
Post-war Theater in Paris	148
Open Letter to the Governors of Mexico	167
Universal Foundations of Culture	170
First Contact with the Mexican Revolution	174

A *Medea* Devoid of Fire	181
Young French Painting and Tradition	186
French Theater Searches for a Myth	192
What I came to Mexico to Do	195
The Eternal Culture of Mexico	202
The False Superiority of the Elites	209
Eternal Secrets of Culture	215
The Occult Forces of Mexico	220
The Social Anarchy of Art	225
I came to Mexico to Escape European Civilization ...	228

Franz Hals — Ortiz Monasterio — Maria Izquierdo

Franz Hals	240
A Technician Who Works in Stone: Monasterio	242
The Painting of Maria Izquierdo	248
Three Notes on Maria Izquierdo	253
Mexico & the Primitive Spirit: Maria Izquierdo	254

THE TARAHUMARA

Texts Published in Él Nacional *&* Voilà

The Land of the Magi	266
Note	271
A Principle Race	272
The Rite of the Kings of Atlantis	277
The Race of Lost Men	283

Journey to the Land of the Tarahumara

The Mountain of Signs	288
The Peyote Dance	294

LETTERS (1937)

Jean Paulhan, 4 February 1937 — 312
Jean Paulhan, 27 February 1937 — 321
Jean Paulhan, 13 March 1937 — 322
Jean Paulhan, 28 March 1937 — 323
Jean Paulhan, 13 April 1937 — 325
Jean Paulhan, 27 or 28 May 1937 — 326
Jean Paulhan, early June 1937 — 327
Jean Paulhan, end of June 1937 — 328

LATER WRITINGS ON THE TARAHUMARA

Two Letters

Henri Parisot, 10 December 1943 — 334
Dr. Gaston Ferdière, 11 December 1943 — 338

Later Writings

Supplement to the Journey to the Land of the Tarahumara + Appendix — 344
Letter to Henri Parisot, 7 September 1945 — 357
Indian Culture — 360
The Peyote Rite Among the Tarahumara — 365
A Note On Peyote — 393
Tutuguri, Rite of the Black Sun — 394
Tutuguri — 397

Notes — 404

INTRODUCTION

LIFE IS ELSEWHERE

Stuart Kendall

> ... I do believe
> that
> nature
> is about to speak
>
> Antonin Artaud, *50 Drawings to Murder Magic*

On 10 January 1936, the poet, actor, and dramatic theorist, Antonin Artaud (1896–1948) departed Europe on a journey to Mexico that would take him from the streets, cafés, and lecture halls of Mexico City to the remote mountains of the Sierra Tarahumara where he participated in indigenous rituals. The journey would last only ten months, culminating in some six to eight weeks spent among the Tarahumara (Rarámuri), but it was to be a profound turning point in his life.[1] Within ten months, after returning to Europe, he would begin a period of internment that would last almost nine years.

Despite the claims of some critics & biographers to the contrary, Artaud was quite specific about the motives and intentions for his trip. Artaud didn't just leave Europe. He fled it. "I came to Mexico to escape European civilization, born of seven or eight centuries of bourgeois culture, & out of hatred for this civilization

& this culture. I hoped to find here [in Mexico] a vital form of culture" (228). "I have come to the land of Mexico to seek the foundations of a magickal culture that can still burst forth from the forces of Indian soil" (122). The vital form of culture that he sought was one wherein individual & communal behaviors were rooted in the soil of a place, wherein the rituals of religion, conceived in its tri-partite forms of belief, action, and experience, reinforce a connection in human lives between the earth & the sun. By connecting the environment, individual life, & communal life through ritual, religious or mythological consciousness becomes ecological consciousness.

Artaud's search for a vital form of culture, however, would not be a simple one. Aside from the emotional, physical, and financial challenges of the journey, he would have to confront and attempt to untangle the legacies of Christian conquest & colonialism & the imposition of modern European forms of government & economy, both Capitalism and Marxism. In contemporary terms, his appeal to indigenous culture would first require an intense and intricate effort at aesthetic, religious, political, and philosophical decolonization. This intellectual work would not be without a psychological cost. The very structure of his identity, the borderline between self and world, between mental and physical space, would come to be in question, as would the modern European notion of subjectivity itself. His search for a vital form of culture would ultimately require him to grapple with altered states of his own consciousness. To think in other terms requires one to become an other. In 1936, Antonin Artaud was far from the ideal candidate to undertake such a journey.

To say that Artaud is a paradoxical and difficult figure is to understate the matter considerably. As a dramatic theorist, his influence on the theatrical arts in the twentieth century, particularly through his book *The Theater and Its Double* (1938), has been second only to that of Bertolt Brecht. His work as an actor includes roles on the stage with some of the most significant dramatic companies of his era, as well as in at least two classic films, Abel Gance's *Napoleon* (1927) & Carl Dreyer's *The Passion of Joan of Arc* (1928). But he was also a poet and *homme des lettres* who wrote with tremendous energy, force, and fierce originality. His greatest works may be his poems and letters, *Correspondence with Jacques Rivière, The Umbilicus of Limbo, The Nerve Meter,* and later, *Artaud the Momo* and *To have done with the judgment of god*. But also, in his final years, as he filled hundreds of notebooks with written matter, he used his pencil to draw, shattering the distinction between writing and drawing, producing a haunting and virulent body of work as a visual artist that has been exhibited in galleries and museums around the world.

Despite the renown of Artaud's work as a poet, actor, dramatic theorist, and visual artist, the events of his life all too often eclipse our experience of that work.[2]

It is another profound understatement to say that Artaud's life as a writer and artist was complicated by his addiction to opiates and his struggles with mental health. Having been prescribed laudanum as a palliative to his mental and emotional suffering as a young man, he remained an unrepentant but desperate addict for the rest of his life. "I am an opium addict the way that I am myself [,] without healing myself. To stop taking drugs is to die."[3] Even as he struggled with addiction, attempting detoxification cures again and again, he wrote about his drug use and railed against drug laws throughout his career. "Let the lost lose themselves," he wrote in 1925.[4] His drug use and defense of drug use would contribute to his mystique among readers across subsequent generations, particularly readers interested in the Beat Generation and the counterculture in the 1960s. If one views Artaud primarily through this aspect of his life, it is tempting to see his journey to Mexico as being motivated by an interest in taking peyote among the Tarahumara. An early English translation of some of these materials was titled *The Peyote Dance* undoubtedly in an effort to appeal to this reading.[5] This association is particularly and indeed painfully misleading since peyote is a sacred plant and sacrament in a religious rite. It also produces a completely different kind of chemical impact on the body than opiates do. Opiates are sedatives, taken to relieve mental and physical pain. Peyote is a hallucinogen, taken to open one's perception.

Even more significantly though, at the far edge of Artaud's experience, in a delirium of dreams and visions, signs and symbols, enchantments and spells perceived to be immanently and aggressively at work in the world, lies madness, where the self truly is an other. Artaud's almost nine years of internment in psychiatric hospitals testify, as a simple fact, to the depth and extremity of his daily combat with perception and reality during those years of his life. His œuvre cannot be considered without taking account of the problem and possibility of madness, of the relationship between madness and meaning, madness and civilization. This is also to say that his œuvre inevitably and inexorably tempts the edge of radically distinct discourses, the critical and the clinical, where the question is not that of signs & symbols but that of signs or symptoms.

But even at that edge, as an argonaut of the soul and cartographer of consciousness, Artaud was also and perhaps finally & foremost a modern mystic. His most persistent struggle — etched in myriad forms — was the struggle to exist, the drama of consciousness caught between emptiness & existence, being and the void. While his most frequent and familiar references might be fellow *poètes et artistes maudits* — Baudelaire, Poe, Lautréamont, Rimbaud, Nietzsche, and Van Gogh most often — the deep core of his thought derives from the classic works of religion, myth, and the esoteric tradition. The *Vedas*, the *Upanishads*, the *Bhagavad Gita*,

Milarepa, *The Tibetan Book of the Dead, The Egyptian Book of the Dead*, the *Zohar,* the *Popol Vuh* and *Chilam Balam* were among books he read, re-read, and recommended, essential points of reference. Much of his later work in particular maintains a combative dialogue with the Gospels. Heraclitus, Pythagoras, *&* Plato were important to him, as were writers in the alchemical tradition, like Paracelsus and Robert Fludd, and more recent figures associated with esotericism and the occult, like Fabre d'Olivet, Saint-Yves d'Alveydre, *&* René Guénon. In this light it is telling that the first name Artaud mentions among people who might help him find his way to Mexico was Louis Massignon, a specialist in comparative religious studies who had had his own mystical experiences.

Given this range of reference, work, *&* experience, it is unsurprising that Artaud has been a fecund focus of theatrical, literary, and philosophical criticism. Susan Sontag, Michel Foucault, Jacques Derrida, Gilles Deleuze and Félix Guattari, Julia Kristeva and the other writers *&* critics associated with the journal *Tel Quel* are only some of the most prominent critics and philosophers whose work shaped the reception of Artaud's œuvre even as it shaped the direction of theirs.[6] Given the breadth *&* depth of this legacy, in literature, philosophy, and the arts, in some senses, whether we know it or not, we are always already reading under the influence of Artaud, and we have been for a long time.

The territory traversed by Artaud, the motives and methods, the problems & limits articulated by his life and œuvre, anticipated our own.

One contemporary critic, Olivier Penot-Lacassagne, summarizes the challenge facing readers of Artaud: "The temptation is great — and it remains — to divide up this unique œuvre and to privilege this or that moment in order to exhume what one believes is the truth of Artaud's discourse."[7] The temptation, in other words, is to read Artaud selectively, to prioritize one's own interests, to find oneself in this or that aspect of Artaud's vast corpus; to prioritize Artaud's career as a poet, an actor, a dramatic theorist, or visual artist, or his life as an addict, madman, or mystic; to read Artaud through the lens of literature, theater, philosophy, religion, or even anthropology.

By gathering together writings related to Artaud's journey to Mexico, the current collection is symptomatic of both sides of this temptation. It presents only a selection from Artaud's vast corpus but in assembling that selection, it brings together an almost impossibly wide range of materials: the scenario for a tragedy; essays, lectures, and notes on Mexican and European arts, religion, and civilization; poetry written in reflection of ecstatic and visionary experiences of indigenous rituals; as well as letters written before, during, and after his journey to Mexico. The writings span fifteen years, from early 1933 to February 1948, only weeks before Artaud's death. The majority of them were nevertheless written between 1935 and 1937, as he prepared for, embarked upon, and returned from his journey to Mexico.

One might say that the book falls into four acts: the rising action shows Artaud as he prepares for his journey to Mexico, sketches his initial ideas, takes notes, proposes himself to people who might be of assistance to him on his way. The second act reveals Artaud in Mexico City, at the podium and in print, hurling his revolutionary messages past his audience. By the third act, something has happened, Artaud has already been to the Sierra Tarahumara. Though at least two of his reports were filed from the field, the action itself has taken place off-stage and the hero has been profoundly changed. The final act takes place years later, in a different country. After eight years and eight months of confinement, Artaud returns in thought and vision to the land of the Tarahumara, sifting through his memories for messages that have become still more revolutionary in their virulence and intent.

In another way though, this book collects at least three books, none of which was realized by Artaud. Only two of them were even suggested by him. In a letter written on 21 May 1936 to his erstwhile supporter, Jean Paulhan, editor of the *Nouvelle Revue Française* (*N.R.F.*), Artaud boasted that a publisher in Mexico was interested in a collection of his "writings about the autochthonous cultures of Mexico" as well as some of his writings on theater. He proposed the title *Revolutionary Messages*. Perhaps inevitably the volume failed to appear, if indeed it had ever really been discussed. Artaud may have been using the idea of it as a lure to convince Paulhan that he was being taken seriously in Mexico. Real or unreal, decades after his death, Paule Thévenin, the editor of Artaud's *Œuvres Complètes* at Gallimard, would use his proposed title for her own assemblage of his writings about Mexico, granting the project posthumous verity.

The gathering nevertheless should not be mistaken for the book Artaud might have had in mind. In the interest of completeness, Thévenin's collection attempted to present all of Artaud's texts from Mexico, his lectures as well as the articles, essays, and reviews he published in newspapers and journals. Some of these pieces were indeed focused on autochthonous Mexican cultures and topics on the theater. But there were other pieces as well, articles Artaud may have been asked to write by editors in Mexico who believed he had something to say on a particular topic that might have interested their readers. Would Artaud have retained all of these pieces in his own collection of these writings? Which of his other writings on theater might also have been included? There is no way to know: none of Artaud's letters and notes provide an outline for the volume.

When he returned to Europe at the end of his journey, he pressed Paulhan to publish some of his writings from Mexico in the *N.R.F.* &, after some delays, he was successful. Two essays were published together as *Journey to the Land of the Tarahumara* (D'un voyage au Pays des Tarahumaras) in *N.R.F.* No. 287 (1 août 1937). The first of these, "The Mountain of Signs," had been written and published in Mexico. The second, "The Peyote Dance," was newer, the precipitate of months of consideration, writing, and revision over the spring and summer of 1937. These two pieces would be republished with a supplementary letter as a small book in 1945 & gather additional supplements & addenda as Artaud shifted through the meaning of his journey to Mexico in other essays, letters, and poems written during the final years and even weeks of his life. A book collecting this material was ultimately published posthumously as *The Tarahumara* (Les Tarahumaras, 1955).

But even that collection did not precisely represent an assemblage organized as Artaud might have intended: several manuscripts had been recovered in the years since his death. Still later, when Thévenin came to present the material on the Tarahumara in Artaud's *Œuvres Complètes*, she expanded the collection even further, including essays that Artaud had published in Mexico but subsequently either lost or abandoned, or both, as well as letters related to the journey.

By presenting the letters alongside the other writings, a third book emerges, one that in some ways overwhelms the other two. This third book is a book about the other two; it tells the story of the journey to Mexico.

INTRODUCTION

This is less a book of ideas than a narrative of events, the story of a man's life, his successes and failures, his needs and ambitions, the things that happen to him along the way.

Revolutionary Messages and *The Tarahumara,* then, and a life in letters, but much else besides. Reading either one of these collections on its own reveals only part of the story. Nor do any of these collections themselves coincide with a clear outline presented by Artaud himself. Rather, they are loose assemblages of essays and articles, poems & letters that circulate around at least two potential and quasi-mythic collections. The current volume expands this frame even further by including writings Artaud prepared prior to his journey to Mexico, a wider range of poems and essays written about his experiences during the final years of his life, as well as letters written prior to, during, and following the journey. Though large, this remains only a selection of Artaud's writings on these topics. A great many passing references to the journey are to be found throughout his final works, including his later letters and notebooks.

The current collection consists of essays, articles, reviews, poems, notes, lectures, letters, and a scenario for a tragedy. This list of forms, however, says nothing of the contents or of the disciplinary lens through which one might read and understand these writings. One temptation might be to relegate these writings to the realm of the literary, to understand them as an episode in the history of French literature, or perhaps literature and the arts. And there are indeed poems here and writings on literature, theater, and the visual arts. Another temptation might be to read them as a kind of travel writing, since the book does after all recount a journey to Mexico. Some of the essays here were intentionally written and presented as the record of a journey, most notably the two pieces presented as the *Journey to the Land of the Tarahumara*. Others are specifically concerned with exploring what might be called the spirit of place, the connection between a place, a people, and the culture that arises from this connection and maintains it. It is also tempting to read those pieces through the disciplinary lens of anthropology, or the more recent field of indigenous studies, and within these two fields, to highlight moments like the peyote rite, in which Artaud is concerned with the connection between religion & mind-altering substances.

But what set Artaud on this path? The origin of his interest in Mexico remains both impossibly obscure and overdetermined. We may never know why he went there, as opposed to somewhere else, at that moment in his life and career. It may simply have been his fate. A decade earlier, in August 1926, he had been told by Madame Sacco, a fortune teller, that: "in order to write, to set myself free, in order to reach the high life [*la vie plane*], I would have to leave France, Europe; in Africa or in America I will write major works."[8]

INTRODUCTION

Regarding Mexico, Artaud biographer Florence de Mèredieu cites his childhood interest in the *Journal des Voyages* as a possible first source of Artaud's fascination with Mexico.[9] The stories of Cortés & Montezuma figure among many other clichés of myth and legend in children's books of exploration and adventure as well as the most basic schoolbook lessons in world history.

More directly though, the first large exhibition of Pre-Colombian art had been held in Paris in 1928. A catalog of essays related to the show, *L'Art Précolombien: L'Amérique avant Christophe Colomb,* included contributions from, among others, Paul Rivet, Jean Babelon, Alfred Métraux, Paul Morand, François Ponceton, and Georges Bataille.[10] Artaud and Bataille knew one another, "to some extent," according to Bataille, who wrote about Artaud in his memoir of Surrealism, "Surrealism from Day to Day."[11] They had both been part of the extended circle of artists, writers, and intellectuals who frequented André Masson's studio at 45, rue Blomet in the 1920s. Other figures in the group included Michel Leiris, Jean Dubuffet, Roland Tual, and Georges Limbour. In a brief memoir of the group, André Masson admitted their shared fascination with travel:

> A few words on reading travel books, from the imaginary travels of Cyrano up through those of the explorers of Tibet passing through those of Captain Cook. This remark is not so trivial if

> one wants to really consider that most of us became eminent travelers. Michel Leiris' *Phantom Africa*, Antonin Artaud's *Journey to the Land of the Tarahumara*, the hieroglyphs of his wandering adventures that are the marvelous novels and stories of [Georges] Limbour testify to this.[12]

Masson's remark obviously reminds us to read Artaud's writings about Mexico alongside those of Michel Leiris on Africa.

But there were many other sources as well. In the early 1930s, alongside his roles for film and theater, Artaud acted in a number of plays recorded for radio broadcast. Among these was a production of Paul Claudel's *Le Livre de Christophe Colomb*. The play had been published in *Commerce* XXI (automne 1929) & again in 1933 as a book with illustrations by Jean Charlot. Charlot was himself of mixed Russian and Mexican descent. He lived in Mexico in the 1920s and 1930s and was part of the burgeoning modern art scene surrounding Diego Rivera. In the late 1920s, he participated in the excavations of Chichén Itzá, making copies of the bas reliefs and carvings as they were uncovered. His work brought pre-Columbian & indigenous themes and motifs into modern art in a profound and influential way. Though not directly linked to Mexico, other than through Charlot's illustrations, as an evocation of the meeting of Europe and the New World, *Le Livre de Christophe Colomb* nevertheless undoubtedly fed into the compost of Artaud's mounting obsession.[13]

Another tangential source for Artaud's interest in Mexico might have come about during his brief relationship with Anaïs Nin. Though born in France, Nin was of Cuban descent and had spent her childhood in Cuba and Spain. Artaud had met her in March 1933 through mutual friends, René and Yvonne Allendy. Artaud had recently written his scenario for *The Conquest of Mexico*, intending it to be the first production of his Theater of Cruelty, and it is easy to imagine Nin's Latin-American heritage playing a role in Artaud's fascination with her. Nin had at that time also recently published her first book, *D.H. Lawrence: An Unprofessional Study*. Lawrence was among her major obsessions and Lawrence himself had been deeply affected by his own journey to Mexico. The English author and his wife, Frieda, travelled through & lived in Mexico — primarily Taos, New Mexico, but with notable time spent in Oaxaca & Lake Chapala — between September 1922 and mid-1925. His novel *The Plumed Serpent* (1926) was set there, and he also devoted a volume of travel essays, *Mornings in Mexico* (1927), to his experiences in the region. A French translation of those essays, *Matinées mexicaines*, was published in 1935 just as Artaud was preparing for his embarkation. The plot of *The Plumed Serpent* concerns a political conspiracy that replaces Christianity with a paganism rooted in indigenous beliefs, a theme echoed in Artaud's interests. Lawrence's syncretistic perspective in *Mornings in Mexico* is also similar to Artaud's, particularly in passages devoted to indigenous culture and religions. For Lawrence, as for Artaud, "The American aborigines are radically, innately religious. The fabric of their life is religious. But their religion is animistic, their sources are dark and impersonal, their conflict with their 'gods' is slow, and unceasing. This is true of the settled pueblo Indians and the wandering Navajo, the ancient Maya, and the surviving Aztec. They are all involved at every moment in their old, struggling religion."[14] It is easy to imagine Artaud and Nin talking passionately about Lawrence, Mexico, and the dark forces of religion. Artaud referred to Nin as a "plumed serpent" in evocation of Lawrence's novel.[15]

A still more direct source of Artaud's interest in Mexico — and in the Tarahumara specifically — might be found in a poem by one of grand masters of 20th century Mexican literature, Alphonso Reyes. Reyes' poem *Yerbas del Tarahumara* (Tarahumara Herbs) was published in a French translation by Valery Larbaud in *Commerce* XX (été 1929). The poem evokes the peyote rites of the Tarahumara as synesthetic vehicles of metaphysical transcendence. According to Reyes' account, written years later, Artaud wrote to him during the early months of his journey to Mexico requesting information about ways to contact indigenous groups, what he called members of a "pure race."[16] The Tarahumara were not the only indigenous people in Mexico whose rites included the use of peyote. Had Artaud's primary purpose been simply to partake of peyote among indigenous people, he could have done so more easily, among the Huichol, for example, who lived closer to Mexico City. Artaud may have believed that peyote was not a native plant in that region, and that therefore the peyote rites practiced there were likely to have been derivative of some earlier rites imported, like the peyote itself, from elsewhere.[17] By traveling to the Sierra Tarahumara, Artaud may have been in search of the most remote forms of these rites, remote in space as well as in time, the oldest forms of these rituals.

Significantly though, Artaud does not mention peyote in his earliest references to his journey to Mexico. Rather, his interest had been piqued by a far more general movement and purpose: "For some time," he wrote to Paulhan on 19 July 1935, "I have heard of a substantive movement in Mexico in favor of a return to the civilization before Cortés" (51). Once again, the precise source of this notion remains obscure, but it is nevertheless telling. Artaud wasn't interested in modern Mexico; he was interested in indigenous Mexico, Mexican cultures dating back to the period before Columbus and Cortés.

In the mid-1930s, Mexico was a state struggling with its identity. The Mexican revolution of the 1910s had occasioned the beginnings of a massive transformation of the economy beginning with a redistribution of land and reallocation of resources, away from the hacienda system that had been imposed during the colonial era, toward more modern forms of social and economic organization. Mexican intellectuals were keenly interested in the debate on the world stage between Capitalism, Socialism, and Communism while also grappling with the legacies of colonialism, colonial Catholicism, and the indigenous heritage of Mexico. A violent anti-clerical war on Catholicism in the 1920s had left churches in Chiapas and elsewhere in ruins and sent clergy on the run or into hiding for several years.[18] Meanwhile, even as the historic forms of indigenous civilization were being celebrated and promoted as the common heritage of the nation, contemporary indigenous communities were seen as a barrier to the unified cohesion of the modern state.

Artaud was not wrong in perceiving Mexico as being at an important inflexion point in its history, but he was out of step with the times. He met Diego Rivera, for example, but showed little interest in the work of *Los Tres Grandes* of the celebrated muralist movement, Rivera, José Clemente Orozco, and David Alfaro Siqueiros. Even though they incorporated ancient Mexican images and symbols in their work, that work was, in Artaud's eyes, too modern and too European, associated as it was with Marxism and modern Mexico. For Artaud, this too was a question of colonization, not of the legacy of the colonial past, but of that of a contemporary mode of colonialism, the colonization of the contemporary mind with European ideas and ideals. While these artists were indeed *living*, they were, in Artaud's view, living embodiments of European rather than indigenous Mexican culture.

Unfortunately, to the extent that Artaud was welcomed in Mexico City, his lectures well-attended, his writings commissioned and published, it was as a representative of the latest trends in European art and thought. This was the furthest thing from what he intended. The situation might have been ironic were it not for the very real consequences that it wrought in Artaud's life. He had come to Mexico to celebrate indigenous culture. But his audiences came to hear him celebrate European civilization, a civilization that he had fled. "For me, the culture of Europe has failed [,] and I believe that in the unbridled development of its machines Europe has betrayed true culture; and myself, in turn, I want to be a traitor to the European conception of progress" (167). By turning away from European civilization, Artaud hoped to be the handmaiden to a new phase of the Mexican revolution, a phase in which indigenous culture could be reborn. In a personal note he wrote: "Came to Mexico to flee the civilization *&* culture of Europe which bring us all back to Barbarism [,] yet I find before me the corpse of the civilization *&* culture of Europe, / against the utilitarian Imperialism of Europe a revolution is necessary [,] and I ask the Mexicans what they want to do" (43). Elsewhere Artaud insists on the essentially political, rather than literary, nature of his interest in Mexico: "I came to Mexico in search of politicians not artists" (195).

The point here is significant but subtle. Whereas Artaud had previously conceived of himself primarily as an artist, who might change culture through the arts, he now sought to have an effect on culture directly. In a letter to Paulhan, he stressed the importance of publishing *The Theater and Its Double* not only so that he could claim credit for the ideas expressed in the book, which he believed were important and timely, but also so that he could "be free from [his] literary past" (84). At the same time, it must be said that Artaud also had no interest in studying Mexican indigenous cultures objectively, from the scholarly perspective of an anthropologist. Though he attempted to secure funds and some kind of legitimating endorsement for his journey from Paul Rivet, then director of the Musée d'Ethnographie du Trocadéro and an expert on Latin American cultures, Artaud had an entirely different purpose in mind. He wrote in his "Open Letter to the Governors of the States of Mexico":

> Archæologists have spoken of [indigenous rites] as scholars, that is to say very badly; artists have spoken of [them] as artists, which is to say even

> more badly... I do not want to study them either as an archeologist or as an artist, I will study them as a scientist, in the true sense of the term; and I will try to let myself be consciously penetrated by their healing virtues for the soul. When human magnetism is exhausted, one must return to the earth to regain one's strength. (168)

Artaud's use of the word "scientist" here should not be mistaken for an endorsement of science in the sense of modern Western rationalism. When he uses the word science here, "in the true sense of the term," he means the esoteric, alchemical, and occult traditions whose master is Paracelsus.

Nor, obviously, was Artaud interested in indigenous Mexico in the way a tourist might seek quaint souvenirs, whether memories or mementos, of the exotic other. Tourists are essentially unchanged by their travels. Artaud made no effort to visit archeological sites. He mentions some of them in his writings & lectures — Palenque, for example — but he went to Mexico in search of *living* culture, not vestiges of an ancient one. Artaud wanted to escape the reaches of modern European civilization and find evidence of a vital culture, a culture whose rites and rituals, whose stories and structures, were rooted in place but linked to the life of the sun. As he later wrote to Henri Parisot, "I did not go to Mexico on a voyage of initiation or for a pleasure trip, the kind that is recounted later in a book that one reads by the fireside; I went there to find a race of people who could follow me in my ideas. If I am a poet or an actor, it is not in order to write or recite poems but in order to live them."[19] Artaud's language here is complicated but precise, layered with reference, but also very specific and consistent. He went to Mexico in search of a true culture, a vital culture, in order to regain his health, in order to live.

This purpose had already been present in his writing on the theater, in the essays, manifestoes, and letters that he would eventually publish as *The Theater and Its Double*. One of the central axes of that collection had been the contrast between what Artaud referred to as the Oriental theater and the Occidental theater. He had been deeply affected by the performance of a troop of Balinese dancers at the Colonial Exposition at the Bois de Vincennes in Paris in 1931. His review of the performance begins with language that reflects many of the concerns that would motivate his journey to Mexico: "The spectacle of the Balinese theater, which draws upon dance, song, pantomime — and a little of theater as we understand it in the Occident — restores the theater, by means of ceremonies of indubitable age and well-tried efficacity, to its original destiny which it presents as a combination of all these elements fused together in a perspective of hallucination and fear."[20] In notes he later appended to the review, he was even more insistent on the paradoxically material and spiritual purpose of the Balinese theater as he understood it:

> The Balinese productions take shape at the very heart of matter, life, reality. There is in them something of the ceremonial quality of a religious rite, in the sense that they extirpate from the mind of the onlooker all idea of pretense, of cheap imitations of reality. This intricately detailed gesticulation has one goal, an immediate goal which it approaches by efficacious means, whose efficacy we are even meant to experience immediately. The thoughts it aims at, the spiritual states it seeks to create, the mystic solutions it proposes are aroused & attained without delay or circumlocution. All of which seems to be an exorcism to make our demons FLOW.[21]

Needless to say, the Balinese theater, for Artaud, stands in for all of what he calls Oriental theater in his essays "On the Balinese Theater" and "Oriental and Occidental Theater" in *The Theater and Its Double*. And his interest in the indigenous peoples of Mexico and their rites extends this same interest. Like Columbus before him, Artaud seems to have gone West to reach the East. More importantly though, his interest in Mexico, his purpose in going there, was a mystic one.

Artaud makes another distinction in his lectures, letters, and essays between what he claims are the two centers of true or vital culture, Mexico and Tibet. This distinction rests on his previous dismissal of Occidental culture but contrasts Mexico and Tibet as cultures fit for the living and for the dead, respectively. In his lecture on "Surrealism and Revolution," after dismissing Surrealism and Marxism, Artaud encourages his audience to see Mexico as a land of the living: "True culture helps to explore life, & the young, who want to reestablish a universal idea of culture, think that there are predestined places to bring forth sources of life and they look toward Tibet & toward Mexico. The culture of Tibet is valid only for what in the *Egyptian Book of the Dead* one calls the corpses, the Overturned. On the contrary, the ancient culture of Mexico serves to make burst forth the inner senses from their barrier. Ancient culture creates resurrections" (122). He makes a similar claim in his "Open Letter to the Governors of the States of Mexico": "Present-day Tibet & Mexico are the nuclei of the culture of the world. But the culture of Tibet is made for the dead; this is where we can still learn, to detach ourselves from life, the technical means of dying well. The eternal culture of Mexico was always made for the living" (168).

Artaud didn't go to Mexico as either an anthropologist or an artist. His journey to Mexico was a mystic one, a search for life in the very heart of matter, a search for reality and immediacy through religious ritual, an attempt to return to the earth to regain his health and strength, a search for resurrection.

Artaud arrived in Mexico City with only 300 francs, confidence inspired by the augury of a favorable horoscope, and a deep determination to "risk everything to change [his] life" (72). The voyage at sea had occasioned a forced detoxification, but as the days and weeks wore on, and his clothes and conditions wore out, it was perhaps inevitable that he should slip back into his laudanum habit once again, scouring the city for doctors willing to help and scoring in Chapultepec Park after dark. This of course only exacerbated his financial concerns.

Artaud was paid for a series of lectures, three at the Universidad Nacional Autónoma de México, one at the Alliance Française, as well as others later that spring. But he primarily lived by his pen, publishing articles in *Él Nacional Revolucionario* and other newspapers and journals. These pieces were often translated into Spanish by friends more or less on the spot, in the café where Artaud wrote them. The cheap rooms in which he lived, passing from one to another and eventually staying with friends, weren't the sort of accommodations that supported collaborative work. By the end of the spring, his untimely messages having fallen flat, he was looking for a way out of the city.

Of his trip into the Sierra Tarahumara, nothing is certain. His likely route has been traced: a train to

Chihuahua, then another train to Bocoyna, where he could obtain the services of a mestizo guide near the Jesuit Mission at Sisoguichi. From there he would have had to travel on horseback into the mountains to Norogachi.[22] But everything about this remains speculation. It is possible that he might have obtained the services of a guide who could translate from Rarámuri into Spanish, but Artaud could not speak Spanish.

As the years passed, a variety of stories and theories have come to light purporting to explain how Artaud might have been able to reach the Tarahumara. Luis Cardoza y Aragon mentions a mission sponsored by the Palace of Fine Arts for the Universidad Nacional Autónoma de México suggesting that Artaud might have accompanied that mission. Artaud had delivered a series of lectures at the University, after all, and published in journals that were supported by it. Looking into the matter years later, though, J.M.G. Le Clézio couldn't find a record of any such mission in the University archives, nor did anyone there know anything about Artaud.[23] Another suggestion is that Artaud had been part of a government-sponsored project to promote children's theater throughout the country. Artaud mentions giving a lecture to people associated with this project in a letter to René Thomas from 2 April 1936. But this too seems unlikely. Yet another rumor is connected with another government-sponsored effort to promote literacy. In connection with this theory, a researcher,

Christian Baugey, encountered an instructor, Felipe Armendariz, who remembers the project and, without knowing anything about Artaud, claimed that the only person who was successful in reaching the indigenous people of the region was a "French poet" for whom the "Indians had a great veneration." The story continues with the detail that the poet held them spellbound with the power of his voice and manner while declaiming poems in French.[24] The anthropologist Lars Krutak also offers yet another account of an interview he conducted with a Rarámari elder who claimed to remember Artaud, "who said the truth was with the Tarahumara."[25]

In her preface to the Folio edition of Artaud's writings on the Tarahumara, Thévenin admits her deep skepticism about many of the more recent "discoveries" regarding his time in Mexico City and in the mountains: "The more the memory becomes uncertain with time, the more the Latin-American imagination works on it; strangely, the memories flow."[26] Having devoted her life to cultivating Artaud's reputation, it is unsurprising that Thévenin might dismiss the more outrageous stories as they began circling his grave. But her caution is well-advised, particularly in a situation like this, wherein fact & fiction may so easily become entwined.

In considering Artaud's journey to the land of the Tarahumara, we are asked to imagine a man, once again wracked with withdrawal, riding on horseback into remote mountain villages in the company of a guide with whom he most likely did not share a common tongue. Having reached his destination, he was to have participated in an indigenous rite, the origins of which are lost in the depths of time. How did he gain the trust of the Tarahumara enough to be permitted to participate in their sacred rites? How could he have understood what was happening if he did?

All things considered, Krutak is probably correct in his thorough and well-reasoned contention that Artaud did not in fact participate in the peyote rite but rather witnessed a minor funerary ritual.[27] He was, quite simply, there at the wrong time of the year. But he *was* there, and moreover, the mountains and valleys, the rock formations that he describes in "The Mountain of Signs," correspond, roughly speaking, to the formations found in the rock art site near a cave called *rehebahuéami* (Rarámuri for "signed" or "marked rock"). Krutak even sees parallels between the "anthropoid figures, spoked wheels, and skeletal beings" among the petroglyphs at the site and the drawings animating the pages of Artaud's later notebooks, a selection of which are presented in *50 Drawings to Murder Magic*.[28]

Krutak also convincingly demonstrates the extent to which Artaud constructed his descriptions of the peyote rite in terms borrowed from anthropologists who had preceded him in the region, Carl Lumholtz & Wendell C. Bennett and Robert M. Zingg. The details of his descriptions of the rite paraphrase similar descriptions in the writings of the anthropologists to such an extent as to almost beg the question of plagiarism.[29] As Le Clézio also suggests, Artaud most likely borrowed the terms "tutuguri" & "ciguri" from Carlos Basauri's writings about the Tarahumara.[30] But Artaud borrowed language from other sources as well. His description of the rite of the Kings of Atlantis derives, as he himself observes, from Plato's *Critias* (277).

What are we to make of this? Weston La Barre, the eminent anthropologist and author of an enduring account of the peyote rite, dismissed Artaud's writings with a withering remark: "It is unreasonable to treat the fantasies of a gifted psychotic once in Rodez Asylum as authentic ethnography."[31] This is a strangely overstated remark, though, given the fact that Artaud never presented his writing on the Tarahumara as authentic ethnography. To the extent that he published that writing at all, he did so most often in newspapers in Mexico & in literary journals like *La Bête noire,* the *N.R.F.*, and *L'Arbalète* in France, not in *L'Année sociologique.*

On this point, two texts that Artaud wrote for another French review, *Voilà*, in the early 1930s, are important to remember. These essays, one on the Galapagos, one on Shanghai, appear to be travel pieces, but they are in fact fictional, or at least derivative of other people's writings. Artaud never visited either place. He also published the final essay that he wrote on the Tarahumara in that same journal. The photographs accompanying the piece seem genuine enough but they in fact depict an entirely different group of indigenous people.[32]

These issues only become more acute when reading Artaud's later writings on the Tarahumara, the pieces he produced at Rodez and after, following years of harrowing internment. It is unsurprising that these writings reveal more about Artaud's obsessions with and interpretations of the Cross, among other things, than they do about the Tarahumara. These later writings are perhaps even more fragmented than his earlier ones. They circle back on themselves as Artaud writes and re-writes his way through his memories of Mexico, supplementing and supplanting text after text, tackling his tropes in different genres: essays re-written as letters, re-worked as poems, repeated right up until days before his death.

Le Clézio, for his part, sweeps aside the question as to whether or not Artaud actually visited the Tarahumara, or rather, he shifts the focus of it. For him, what matters is the act of writing. Writing about the rite, writing through the rite, is itself sufficiently transformative. Le Clézio: "The question of the authenticity of Artaud's experience has no meaning. For him, describing the peyote ritual was to be aware of an enchantment, a spell which completely transformed him, which turned him into an other."[33]

Artaud returned to Europe as a visionary but broken man. He had passed through the mountain and the valley of signs, crossed over to the other side of life, wherein every object is revealed to be both real and imbued with symbolic meaning. "I am not dead, but I am set apart," he wrote in *The New Revelations of Being* during the summer of 1937. "I am therefore going to say what I have seen and what is."[34] He also corrected the proofs for *The Theater and Its Double* during that summer. He reworked the preface, "Theater and Culture," in light of his experiences in Mexico: "In Mexico, since we are talking about Mexico, there is no art: things are made for use. And the world is in perpetual exaltation. ... For the Mexicans seek contact with the *Manas,* forces latent in every form, unreleased by contemplation of the forms for themselves, but springing to life by magic identification with these forms."[35] His journey to Mexico, since we are talking about Mexico, had been a journey from art to life. Artaud fled Europe on the strength of his work as an artist in search of a vital form of culture. He returned gripped by a magical identification with a world in perpetual exaltation.

Artaud's journey to Mexico, then, might be considered in terms of both success and tragic failure. He clearly failed to spark a revolution in contemporary consciousness rooted in indigenous rituals and modes of life. But in abandoning the outward forms of that quest, the very quest for outward forms, he discovered its inner force and necessity. Artaud's later writings, drawings, & final performances, with their glossolalia, scratches and tears, and screams, would explore and exploit the materialization, the very matter of that force with a delirious fury.[36]

But finally, there is deep irony too, at the end of the journey, in the fact that Artaud — or anyone — should have to travel so far from home in search of a sense of place, an ecologically rooted and, one hopes, sustainable culture. Life is elsewhere.

ENDNOTES

1 Tarahumara is the Spanish name for the Rarámuri people.

2 For biographies of Artaud in English, see Stephen Barber, *Antonin Artaud: Blows and Bombs* (Faber and Faber, 1993), and David A. Shafer, *Antonin Artaud* (Reaktion Books, Critical Lives, 2016). For an exhaustive treatment in French, see Florence de Mèredieu, *C'était Antonin Artaud* (Librairie Arthème Fayard, 2006).

3 Antonin Artaud, *Œuvres Complètes,* Vol. 8, éd. Paule Thévenin (Gallimard, 1971) 25. Hereafter Artaud, OC volume (year) page number.

4 Artaud, OC 1 (1970) 320.

5 See Antonin Artaud, *The Peyote Dance*, tr. Helen Weaver (Farrar, Strauss, Giroux, 1976). *The Peyote Dance* is a translation of some of the material published in French under the title *Les Tarahumaras* (The Tarahumara).

6 Needless to say, the critical literature on Artaud is immense. For a survey, see Olivier Penot-Lacassagne, *Antonin Artaud: L'Incandescent perpétuel* (CNRS Éditions, 2022), or, for a detailed engagement with this critical tradition in English, see Jay Murphy, *Artaud's Metamorphosis: From Hieroglyphs to Bodies without Organs* (Pavement Books, 2016).

7 Olivier Penot-Lacassagne, "Singularité d'Antonin Artaud," *Europe*, 873–874 (janvier–février 2002) 104.

8 Antonin Artaud, *Oeuvres*, éd. Évelyne Grossman (Gallimard, Quarto) 212. Hereafter *Quarto*.

9 Florence de Mèredieu, *C'était Antonin Artaud*, 543.

10 Jean Babelon, et al., *L'Art Précolombien: L'Amérique avant Christophe Colomb, Cahiers de la République des lettres[,] des sciences et des arts* XI (Les Beaux-Arts, 1928).

11 Georges Bataille, "Surrealism from Day to Day," in Bataille, *The Absence of Myth: Writings on Surrealism*, tr. Michael Richardson (Verso, 1994) 42.

12 André Masson, "45, rue Blomet," in Masson, *Le Rebelle du surréalisme,* éd. Françoise Levaillant (Hermann, 1994) 80. The "explorers of Tibet" referenced by Masson undoubtedly include Alexandra David-Néel, whose celebrated memoirs *Voyages d'une Parisienne à Lhassa* and *Mystiques et Magiciens du Tibet* were published in Paris in 1927 and 1929 respectively.

13 Florence de Mèredieu, op. cit., 486–7.

14 D.H. Lawrence, *Mornings in Mexico* (William Heinemann, 1927) 148.

15 Anaïs Nin, *Incest: The Unexpurgated Diary of Anaïs Nin (1932–1934)* (Harcourt Brace, 1993) 185.

16 See Alphonso Reyes, "Artaud: No se juega infamemente con los Dioses," *Universidad de México: Revista de la UNAM* (Junio) 6. Quoted in Lars Krutak, "(Sur)real or Unreal? Antonin Artaud in the Sierra Tarahumara of Mexico," *Journal of Surrealism and the Americas*, 8:1 (2014) 33.

17 On the origins and transmission of peyote rites, see Weston La Barre, *The Peyote Rite*, 5th edition (University of Oklahoma Press, 1989) 35.

18 On this, but from a perspective radically opposed to that of Artaud, see Graham Greene, *The Lawless Roads* (1939) and *The Power and the Glory* (1940).

19 Artaud, "6 October 1945," *Lettres de Rodez, Quarto*, 1019.

20 Antonin Artaud, "On the Balinese Theater," in Artaud, *The Theater and Its Double*, tr. Mary Caroline Richards (Grove Press, 1958) 53.

21 Ibid., 60.

22 On this route, see Luis M. Schneider, "Power & Devotion: Artaud ~ Tzontémoc," in *Tiempo Suspendido: Fotografía sobre La Ruta de Antonio Artaud en la Sierra Tarahumara* (Casa de Las Imágenes, 1995).

23 J.M.G. Le Clézio, *The Mexican Dream, or the Interrupted Thought of Amerindian Civilizations*, tr. Teresa Lavender Fagan (University of Chicago Press, 1993) 168.

24 See Alain and Odette Virmaux, "[Note]" in *Europe*, 667–8 (novembre–décembre 1984) 120. They are referencing an article published in *Ailleurs*, No. 5 (1964).

25 See Krutak, op. cit., 40.

26 Paule Thévenin, "Préface," in Artaud, *Les Tarahumaras* (Gallimard, Folio, 1987) 12.

27 Krutak, op. cit., 37.

28 See Krutak, op. cit., 49, note 72. A description of the petroglyphs can be found in William B. Murray, "Tres sitios de pinturas rupestres en la Alta Tarahumara de Chihuahua," *Anales de Antropología*, Vol. 20 (1981).

29 See Krutak, op. cit., 37–40. For Artaud's sources see, Carl S. Lumholtz, *Unknown Mexico: A Record of Five Years' Exploration Among the Tribes of the Western Sierra Madre* (Charles Scribner's Sons, 1902), *Symbolism of the Huichol Indians* (Memoirs of the American Museum of Natural History, 8, 1900), and Wendell C. Bennett and Robert M. Zingg, *The Tarahumara: An Indian Tribe of Northern Mexico* (University of Chicago Press, 1935).

30 See J.M.G. Le Clézio, op. cit., 170, and Carlos Basauri, "The Resistance of the Tarahumaras," *Mexican Folkways*, 2: 4 (1926), and *Monografía de los Tarahumaras* (Talleres Grafico de la Nación, 1929).

31 Weston La Barre, op. cit., 300.

32 See "The Race of Lost Men" (herein) as well as "Galápagos, les îles du bout du monde" and "L'Amour à Changhaï" in Artaud, OC 8 (1980) 25-46.

33 J.M.G. Le Clézio, op. cit., 170. Translation modified.

34 Artaud, *Quarto*, 789.

35 Artaud, *The Theater and Its Double*, 11.

36 On Artaud's later works considered from this perspective, see in particular Allen S. Weiss, "Libidinous Mannerisms and Profligate Abominations," in Weiss, *Breathless: Sound Recording, Disembodiment, and the Transformation of Lyrical Nostalgia* (SUNY, 2002) 115-38, and Jay Murphy, *Artaud's Metamorphosis*, op. cit.

CHRONOLOGY

1896

Antonin Artaud born in Marseille on 4 September.

1901

Contracts a severe case of meningitis. He is eventually cured, but his childhood will be marked by a nervous disposition & stuttering. He does poorly in school.

1910

Publishes his first poems and stories under the pseudonym Louis des Attides. Baudelaire, Rimbaud, and Poe are influences.

1914

Experiences a depressive crisis. Becomes extremely pious, intends to enter the priesthood.

1915

Diagnosed with acute neurasthenia, symptoms include headaches, fatigue, lassitude, & irritability. Artaud will be in & out of convalescent and rest homes in France & Switzerland for the next five years. He reads, writes, and draws extensively during this period.

1916

February: publication of first poems under the name Antonin Artaud.

August: conscripted into the army. Artaud is stationed in Digne, in Alpes-de-Haute-Provence, but discharged after a few months due to his unstable mental health.

1919

While staying in a clinic near Neuchâtel, Switzerland, Artaud is prescribed laudanum for the first time. He will become a life-long addict.

1920

Moves to Paris. Begins working in the theater, initially under the tutelage of Lugné-Poe. Continues writing. Serves as co-editor of a small literary review, *Demain*.

1921

Meets Max Jacob and, through him, Charles Dullin, whose theater company he joins. Meets actress Génica Athanasiou, entering into a romantic relationship with her that will last six years.

1922

Meets André Masson, Michel Leiris, Jean Dubuffet, Georges Limbour, and Joan Miró, among others, while continuing to act in Dullin's company.

1923

Begins correspondence with Jacques Rivière, editor of *Nouvelle Revue Française* (*NRF*), which will later be published. Begins writing essays on theater.

1924

September: death of Artaud's father.

October: meets André Breton and joins the Surrealist group. Struggles with his opium addiction. First film roles.

1925

Active in the Surrealist group. Publishes *The Umbilicus of Limbo* and *The Nerve Meter* through *NRF*. Plays Jean-Paul Marat in Abel Gance's *Napoleon*.

1926

September–November: founds Alfred Jarry Theater with Roger Vitrac, Robert Aron, & Yvonne & René Allendy.

November: expelled from the Surrealist group.

1927

Gance's *Napoleon* released to great acclaim. Artaud portrays Jean Massieu in Carl Dreyer's *The Passion of Joan of Arc*. Writes the scenario for *The Seashell and the Clergyman*, which will be filmed by Germaine Dulac.

1928

Continues acting in films while also participating in Alfred Jarry Theater. Definitive break with Athanasiou.

1929

Violently attacked by André Breton in *Second Manifesto of Surrealism*. Publishes collection *Art and Death* through Robert Denoël, who becomes a significant supporter of Artaud's work over the next eight years.

1930

Alfred Jarry Theater dissolved. Artaud continues writing for & about, as well as acting in films. Acts in the French version of G.W. Pabst's film of *The Threepenny Opera* among other roles this year. He also translates a version of Matthew Lewis' gothic novel *The Monk*, "as told by Antonin Artaud," which will be published by Denoël in 1931.

1931

July: deeply affected by a performance of a Balinese theater group at the Colonial Exhibition in Paris. Robert Denoël, Jean Paulhan, and René Allendy emerge as crucial supporters of Artaud's work. Paulhan publishes Artaud's essays frequently in *NRF*, of which he is the editor. Denoël publishes several of Artaud's books and translations through the 1930s. And Allendy sponsors Artaud's lectures in the series he directs at the Sorbonne. Artaud nevertheless suffers grave financial difficulties, primarily due to his ongoing opium addiction.

1932

Publishes in the *NRF*, including essays that will later be included in *The Theater and Its Double*. Beginning of friendships with Roger Gilbert-Lecomte and René Daumal, both associated with *Le Grand Jeu*. Attempts to cure his opium addiction.

1933

January: completes writing the scenario for *The Conquest of Mexico*, which he intends as the first production of his projected Theater of Cruelty.

March: beginning of friendship with Anaïs Nin. Roles for film and radio productions. Conducts extensive research on ancient cultures and religions while writing *Heliogabalus, or the Crowned Anarchist*, on the suggestion of Robert Denoël, who will publish the book in 1934.

April: lectures at the Sorbonne on "The Theater and the Plague."

1934

January 6: presents *The Conquest of Mexico* along with a reading of one act of his adaptation of Shakespeare's *Richard II* at the home of Lise & Paul Deharme in hopes of obtaining funding for the Theater of Cruelty.

June–July: travels to Algeria for a role in the film *Sidonie Panache*. This is Artaud's first trip outside of Europe.

October: another attempt at detoxification.

1935

Writes and stages *The Cenci*, based on versions of the story from Shelley and Stendhal. The production, with sets and costumes by Balthus, closes in May after only 17 performances. Artaud also performs in what will be his final two films. Amid serious financial difficulties, he begins planning and attempting to raise funds for his journey to Mexico, while also attempting to end his opium addiction once again.

1936

January 10: embarks for Mexico from Antwerp on the S.S. Albertville. The voyage will entail a forced detoxification while at sea.

January 30–*February* 2: during a stopover in Havana, Artaud attends a voodoo ceremony and is given a small decorative dagger that will become a talisman for him.

February 7: arrives in Vera Cruz, travels to Mexico City. While in Mexico City, Artaud meets writers and artists including Luis Cardoza y Aragón, Diego Rivera, and Maria Izquierdo. He lives itinerantly in cheap rooms, including a room in a brothel, as well as occasionally staying with friends. He writes in cafes & begins to take drugs again after the detoxification he endured at sea.

February 26, 27, *and* 29: delivers three well-attended lectures at the University of Mexico: "Surrealism and

Revolution," "Man Against Fate," and "The Theater & the Gods."

March 18: delivers a lecture entitled "Post-War Theater in Paris" at the Alliance Française. The lecture is attended by the French Ambassador.

April–July: publishes a series of articles, including the texts of his lectures, in translations often done on the fly, in a government sponsored newspaper, *Él Nacional Revolucionario*, as well as other periodicals. This is his primary source of income while he is in Mexico. He begins to conceive of these articles as a book which he proposes to Gallimard through Jean Paulhan under the title *Revolutionary Messages*. He sends Paulhan the manuscripts of the three lectures he delivered at the University of Mexico in February hoping they will be published in the *NRF*.

August: Artaud's visa is extended for an additional six months.

August 10: an exhibition of paintings by Maria Izquierdo and sculptures by Eleanor Boudin opens in the Wells Fargo building. Artaud contributes to the exhibition catalog and writes a review of the show.

End of August: departs Mexico City, first by train for Chihuahua, then on horseback into the Sierra Tarahumara. He abandons his remaining supply of heroin before crossing into the mountains.

August–September–October: spends six to eight weeks in Norogachi, among the Tarahumara (also known as the Rarámuri). He participates in their festivals and rites, though accounts differ as to the precise ritual he attended. Most likely he attended a funeral rather than the traditional peyote rite.

October 7: returns to Mexico City via Chihuahua. He publishes accounts of his journey in *Él Nacional*: "The Mountain of Signs" and "The Land of the Magi." "The Rite of the Kings of Atlantis" and "A Principle Race" will appear after his departure from Mexico. He collects the texts that he hopes will be included in *Revolutionary Messages* and leaves them with a friend, José Gorostiza, entrusting him to see them into publication. The manuscripts will be lost.

October 31: departs from Vera Cruz on the steamship *Mexico*, arriving in Saint-Nazaire on 12 November.

November 1936–*August* 1937: Artaud will later claim in letters to Henri Parisot & Gaston Ferdière to have written a 200-page manuscript entitled *Journey to Mexico* that he subsequently lost along with his other papers and belongings when he was interned.

1937

January–February: Artaud is in an exalted state, consumed by prophetic pronunciations but also insulting people in the street. His extreme financial difficulty is complicated by deepening drug addiction. During this period, Artaud stays with friends & even occasionally in the street, refusing help from anyone.

Artaud studies astrology as well as the Tarot, with Manuel Cano de Castro, and pursues a romantic relationship with Cécile Schramme, a young woman he met in 1935. Schramme is also an addict.

Artaud helps organize an exhibition of gouaches by Maria Izquierdo at a gallery in Montparnasse. He also continues writing about his journey to Mexico, in letters to Jean Paulhan, but also in additional texts, like "The Peyote Dance," which he hopes Paulhan will publish in *NRF*.

February 25–March 4: Paulhan pays for a detoxification cure, but it is again unsuccessful.

March–April: becomes engaged to Cécile Schramme. Around this time, he receives a knotted cane, covered in spikes, from the painter Kristians Tonny. Artaud comes to believe that the cane is the lost cane of St. Patrick & that he must return it to the Irish people.

During this period Artaud is also correcting the proofs for *The Theater and Its Double*. He rewrites the preface substantially in light of his experiences in Mexico.

April 14–29: attempts another detoxification at a different clinic, again with the financial help of Paulhan.

May: travels to Brussels to deliver a lecture at the Maison d'Art. He is accompanied by Cécile Schramme and they stay with her parents. Artaud's lecture, ostensibly concerning the "decomposition of Paris," ranges widely, from his journey to Mexico to pederasty. It causes a scandal that results in Schramme's parents insisting that the anticipated plans for marriage be abandoned.

Artaud informs Paulhan that he has decided that he will not sign the account of his journey to the land of the Tarahumara, by now forthcoming in the *NRF*, saying, "My name must disappear."

June–July: Artaud writes *The New Revelations of Being* based on a reading of his horoscope from 15 & 19 June. The small book is published by Denoël in July. The author is listed as "The Revealed One."

August: *Journey to the Land of the Tarahumara* is published in the *NRF* with three stars in place of the author's name. This same month Artaud writes to the Irish Legation in Paris requesting support for a journey to Ireland. He hopes to "rediscover in Ireland the living sources [...] of a very ancient tradition." He also mentions the importance of visiting the places where the playwright John Millington Synge lived. Borrowing money from friends, he departs for Cobh on 14 August.

August 14–September 9: Artaud travels from Cobh to Dublin, from Dublin to Galway, and from Galway to Inishmore, the largest of the Aran Islands, where he spends a few days in Kilronan. He often slips away from his lodgings without paying his bills. His letters to friends like Paulhan and Breton alternate between asking for money and proclaiming the prophetic and mystic purpose of his journey. Artaud returns to Dublin on 9 September.

September 23–October 16: arrested in Dublin for disturbing the peace and vagrancy. Incarcerated at Mountjoy Prison through 29 September when he is repatriated to France on the steamship *Washington*, via Cobh. During the voyage, Artaud attacks a mechanic and a steward who had entered his cabin, either to perform maintenance work or to ask him to be quiet. He is placed in a straitjacket and taken to the General Hospital when the boat arrives in Le Havre on 30 September.

October 16: after being held for 17 days in a state of violent delirium, suffering from severe hallucinations, Artaud is moved to the Quatre-Mares psychiatric hospital and officially incarcerated. He claims to be Greek and to be named Antoneo Arlanapulos. He will spend the next eight years & eight months in psychiatric asylums.

December: "The Race of Lost Men" is published in *Voilà* under the pseudonym John Forester.

1938

February: Gallimard publishes *The Theater and Its Double*.
April: Artaud is transferred to Sainte-Anne in Paris.

1939

February: Artaud is transferred to the psychiatric hospital at Ville-Évrard in Neuilly-sur-Marne, 20 km from Paris.

1939

September 3: World War II begins.

1940

May 10: Germany invades France.

1940

June 22: France signs armistice with Germany, which divides the country into occupied and unoccupied zones. Conditions at Ville-Évrard, in the occupied zone, deteriorate due to severe rationing.

1941

December: Artaud begins signing his letters Antonin Nalpas, after his mother's maiden name.

1943

February: Artaud is transferred to the psychiatric hospital in Rodez, in the unoccupied zone of France. Conditions for him improve markedly. There is adequate food, and he is encouraged to write and draw. While interned at Rodez, Artaud also receives 58 unanesthetized electroshock treatments, from June 1943 through December 1944.

September: renounces the name Antonin Nalpas and returns to using the name Antonin Artaud.

End of year: writing on behalf of publisher Robert Godet, Henri Parisot proposes publishing Artaud's two articles on the Tarahumara from the *NRF* as an illustrated volume. Frédéric Delanglade, an artist Artaud encountered at Rodez, is suggested as the illustrator.

December 14–19: Artaud writes the first version of "The Peyote Rite Among the Tarahumara" to accompany the texts in the volume proposed by Parisot.

1944

January: Artaud writes "Supplement to the Journey to the Land of the Tarahumara" to replace "The Peyote Rite Among the Tarahumara" in the proposed collection.

February: at the suggestion of Delanglade, Artaud begins drawing again.

May: Gallimard reissues *The Theater and Its Double*.

May 23–*June* 16: Artaud undergoes another series of 12 electroshocks. Two additional series of shocks will be administered during the second half of the year.

August 25: mentions intestinal hemorrhages in a letter to his mother.

1945

February: begins writing in the small notebooks typically used by students. Over the next three years, he will fill 406 notebooks with writings and drawings.

April 1: violently rejects Christianity and all religion. Begins writing the word god in lower case.

July 6: since Robert Godet has not pursued the project, Henri Parisot proposes publishing *Journey to the Land of the Tarahumara* through Éditions Fontaine. Artaud accepts this proposition and writes a letter to Parisot that will serve as a new appendix to the text in place of the "Supplement" written in January 1944.

November: *Journey to the Land of the Tarahumara* is published in the collection L'Age d'Or, directed by Henri Parisot at Éditions Fontaine.

September 17–*December* 9: continued correspondence between Artaud & Henri Parisot. Artaud's letters will be published as *Lettres de Rodez* (G.L.M., 1946).

1946

Discussions throughout the winter and spring regarding Artaud's release from Rodez to another clinic, closer to Paris, where he will have greater freedom. Arthur Adamov organizes an auction of donated paintings and manuscripts in order to raise money on his behalf (the auction takes place on 13 June).

Among other projects at this time, Artaud plans a book with the title *For the Poor Popocatepel*, named after the volcano in central Mexico. He consistently and intentionally misspells Popocatepetl, suppressing the second *t* for rhythmic purposes.

May 25: Artaud is released from Rodez. He travels by train to Paris with Dr. Ferdière where he moves into a room at a clinic in Ivry-sur-Seine. A few months later he moves into a small building on the grounds away from the main house. Artaud writes almost incessantly, while also continuing to produce drawings.

June 7: "Hommage à Antonin Artaud" is presented at the Théâtre Sarah-Bernhardt. Presentations and readings by André Breton, Arthur Adamov, Jean-Louis Barrault, Roger Blin, Alain Cluny, Charles Dullin, Louis Jouvet, Colette Thomas, & Jean Vilar, among others.

September 6: signs contract with Gallimard for the publication of his *Œuvres Complètes*.

November 25: writes *Here Lies* and *Indian Culture*, two poems that will be published together by Henri Parisot through K. Éditeur in January 1948.

1947

January 13: Artaud presents "Histoire vécue d'Artaud-Mômo. Tête à tête par Antonin Artaud" (The Story Lived by Artaud-Momo: Head-to-Head by Antonin Artaud) at the Théâtre Vieux-Colombier. The evening consists of a free-form lecture recounting his life since his internment as well as a dramatic reading of recent poems.

February: writes *Van Gogh, The Suicide of Society*.

May: publication of *L'Arbalète 12*, edited by Marc Barbezat, which includes two texts by Artaud, "L'Arve et l'aume, tentative anti-grammaticale contre Lewis Carroll," Artaud's adaption of chapter VI of Carroll's *Through the Looking Glass*, and "The Peyote Rite Among the Tarahumara."

June: signs contract with Marc Barbezat for *The Tarahumara*, a collection of previously published and new writings on his journey to Mexico.

July 4–20: exhibition of "Portraits and Drawings" by Artaud at the Galerie Pierre.

October: writes "Tutuguri, Rite of the Black Sun." Initially intended for publication in *The Tarahumara*, it will be including in *To have done with the judgment of god* when Artaud begins work on that sequence of texts recorded for radio broadcast the following month.

December: *Artaud the Momo* is published by Bordas. *Van Gogh, The Suicide of Society* is published by K. It will be awarded the Prix Sainte-Beuve in January.

1948

January 30–31: completes *50 Drawings to Murder Magic*.

February 1: *To have done with the judgment of god* is suppressed by the director of its sponsor, Radiodiffusion française, causing enormous controversy. The text will be published by K in April.

February 16: writes "Tutuguri," his final text on the Tarahumara. It is among his last writings.

March 4: Artaud is found dead in the morning, seated at the foot of his bed. Though suffering from advanced inoperable rectal cancer, Artaud died of an overdose of chloral hydrate, likely to have been accidental, given his lack of familiarity with the drug.

1953

Publication of *Vie et Mort de Satan le Feu* suivi de *Textes Mexicains pour un Nouveau Mythe* (Arcanes), edited by Serge Berna.

1955

Publication of *The Tarahumara* (L'Arbalète), edited by Marc Barbezat. The volume includes the writings on the Tarahumara that Artaud published in *NRF* in 1937 alongside many of the supplements, letters, and additional texts he devoted to the Tarahumara & the peyote rite between 1943 and 1948.

1956

Gallimard publishes the first volume of Artaud's *Œuvres Complètes,* edited and annotated by Paule Thévenin. 25 further volumes will follow, through 1994. Additional volumes will continue to appear, including collections of letters, notebooks, & drawings.

1962

Luis Cardoza y Aragón undertakes a systematic search for articles published by Artaud in newspapers & journals in Mexico. He publishes the collection in Spanish as *México* (Universidad Nacional Autónoma de México). François Fricot, J.-F. Azaïs, and other researchers will later discover additional texts.

1971

Publication of volumes eight and nine of Artaud's *Œuvres Complètes* in France. These volumes include the majority of Artaud's writings from and about his journey to Mexico, the texts of his *Revolutionary Messages* and *The Tarahumara*. These texts include many of the articles that Artaud published in *Él Nacional Revolucionario* in 1936.

2002

Creation of the Premio de Narrativa Antonin Artaud, a literary prize awarded by the French Embassy and the Association of French Companies in Mexico for literary works written in Spanish & published in Mexico.

JOURNEY TO MEXICO

REVOLUTIONARY MESSAGES
& THE TARAHUMARA

THE CONQUEST OF MEXICO

THE CONQUEST OF MEXICO

The Conquest of Mexico will stage events presented in their multiple & most revealing aspects, and not men. Men will take their right place with their passions, with their personal psychology, but as a harmonization of certain forces and in the light of the events and of the historical fatality in which they have played their part.

This subject has been chosen:

1) *Due to its topicality* and all the analogies it offers regarding problems of vital interest for Europe and for the world.

From a historical point of view *The Conquest of Mexico* raises the question of colonization. It revives in a brutal, bloody, implacable way, the still living fatuity of Europe. It makes it possible to devalue the idea that Europe has of its preponderant superiority. It contrasts Christianity with much older religions. It reveals the false conceptions that the West may have of paganism and other natural religions and emphasizes in a pathic, burning way, the splendor & ever-present poetry of the old metaphysical foundations that are at the base of these religions.

2) By raising the terribly contemporary question of colonization and the right that one continent believes it has to enslave another, it questions the problem of the supremacy, this time real, of some races over others and shows the inner filiation linking the genius of a race with particular forms of civilization.

Thus, it contrasts two concepts of life & of the world:

a) The misdirected dynamic conception of the races that call themselves Christian.

b) The static conception of races who appear contemplative and marvelously hierarchical within. It contrasts the tyrannical anarchy of the colonizers with the profound moral harmony of the future colonized.

And this despite the human sacrifices that are not ultimately a derogation from a principle and which if they were in the true tradition of the Aztec civilization, they should already be considered for what they possess as moral and intrinsically purifying.

Further, by contrast with the disorder of the European monarchy of the time, based upon entirely unjust & vulgar materialistic principles, light is shed on the organic hierarchy of the Aztec monarchy established on indisputable spiritual principles.

From a social point of view, it shows the concord of a society that knew how to feed itself and that from its inception had carried out the Revolution.

In this clash of Catholic moral disorder & anarchy with pagan order, this subject can provoke unprecedented conflagrations of forces and imagery in which brutal dialogues suddenly appear, and this through man-to-man combat between men bearing within themselves the most contradictory ideas, like stigmata.

Once the inner moral background and topical interest of such a spectacle have been sufficiently delineated, emphasis can be given to the *spectacular* value of the conflicts that it has to stage.

First there are the internal struggles of Montezuma, the astrologer king whose motives history has been unable to clarify.

Two characters could be found here:

1) The one who obeys, in an almost holy way, the orders of fate, who passively complies, armed with his conscience, the fatality that binds him to the stars.

We can show almost pictorially, objectively at least, his struggles and his symbolic dialogue with the visualized myths of astronomy.

Beautiful examples of dances, pantomimes, and all kinds of scenic objectifications.

2) The sparagmatic man who, having completed the external gestures of a rite, the rite of submission, internally wonders if by chance he has not made a mistake, revealing himself in a kind of superior confrontation in the regions where the ghosts of being hover.

Although he has the security of the magician, it is permissible that, for the needs of the stage, for the justification of life & the theater, he is made to doubt humanly.

Aside from Montezuma, there is the people, the diverse strata of society, the rebellion of the people against fate, represented by Montezuma, the clamors of the incredulous, the wiles of the philosophers & the priests, the lamentations of the poets, the treachery of merchants & bourgeois, the duplicity & sexual profligacy of women.

The mentality of the crowds, the spirit of events, will move in material waves over the spectacle, suddenly determining certain lines of force, and within these waves and above them, the diminished, rebellious, or despairing consciousness of some men who will be carried aloft like straw.

The theatrical problem consists in determining and harmonizing these lines of force, concentrating them and extracting suggestive melodies from them.

These images, this movement, these dances, these rites, this music, these truncated melodies, these mutilated dialogues, will be carefully noted and described in words as far as possible, especially in the non-speaking parts of the spectacle. The principle being, to succeed in writing down or giving keys to what cannot be described in words, as on a stave.

Let us now see the structure of the spectacle according to its order of development.

Act One. — Signs of Prediction.

A tableau of Mexico in anticipation, with its cities, its countryside, its troglodyte caves, its Maya ruins.

Immense objects that evoke certain Spanish ex-votos & the strange landscapes that they contain inside bottles or under glass domes.

Through this principle, cities, monuments, countryside, forest, ruins & caves will be evoked; the lighting will show their appearances, disappearances, & reliefs.

The musical or pictorial way of emphasizing these elements, of showing their roughness, will be built within the spirit of a secret melody, invisible to the spectator and which will correspond to the inspiration of a poetry overloaded with whispers and intimations.

Everything trembles, moans as if inside an abnormally rattled vitrine. In the landscape the storm can be sensed: objects, music, fabrics, lost clothing, shadows of wild horses pass through the air, like distant meteors, like lightning on a horizon full of mirages, as the wind touches the earth due to a lighting that presages rain and vehement storms. Then the total illumination begins to dance; to the shrill conversations, to the disputes of all the echoes of the population, respond the mute, concentrated, terrorized confrontations of Montezuma and his priests gathered in council before the signs of the zodiac, severe forms of the firmament.

On Cortés's side, a staging of rough seas and dwarfed caravels, and Cortés & his men are larger than them and as firm as rocks.

Act Two. — Confession.
Now Mexico seen by Cortés.
Silence covers all these secret struggles, apparent stagnation, & everywhere magick, the magick of an immobile, unusual spectacle, with cities like walls of light, palaces over canals of stagnant water, a heavy melody.

Then, with a single stroke, a single sharp and piercing tone, heads crown the walls.

Then a low roar full of menace, an impression of terrible solemnity, holes in the crowd like hollows of calm in the air embraced by the storm; appearance of Montezuma all alone heading toward Cortés.

Act Three. — Convulsions.

At every level of the country, revolt.

In every strata of Montezuma's consciousness, revolt.

Battleground in the mind of Montezuma, who argues with fate.

Magick, magickal stagings evoking the gods.

Montezuma cuts living space, cleaves it in two like a woman's sex to make the invisible spring forth.

The stage wall is teeming unevenly with heads and throats; cracked, strangely mutilated melodies, & the responses to these melodies seem like stumps. Montezuma himself seems split in two, divided; pieces of his body are half-illuminated; others are set in blinding light; multiple hands emerge from his garments, painted faces appear on his body like a manifold portrait of consciousness, but from within Montezuma's consciousness all questions shoot toward the crowd.

The Zodiac that roared with all its beasts in the head of Montezuma is transformed into a crowd of human passions embodied in wise heads, brilliant at disputation, of official orators: secret motives which the crowd, despite the circumstances, does not forget to mock.

However, the real warriors make their sabers resound, waving them over the houses. Rapid ships traverse a Pacific of purplish-indigo, laden with the riches of fugitives and smuggled weapons arrive, landing on other rapid ships.

An emaciated man eats soup at full speed, feeling that the city will soon be besieged, and as the rebellion breaks out, the stage is filled with a kind of howling mosaic in which men or compact troops whose units, tightly clustered together, clash frantically. The space is rife with whirling gestures, horrible faces, wild eyes, clenched fists, manes, armor, and at every level of the stage fall shells, limbs, heads, stomachs, bombarding the earth with supernatural explosions like hail.

Act four. — The Abdication.

As a counterpart Montezuma's abdication causes a strange & evil loss of assurance on the part of Cortés and his warriors. A concrete bewilderment in which the discovered treasures appear as illusions in the corners of the stage. (Effect to be achieved by multiple sets of mirrors.)

Lights, sounds that seem to melt and unravel, grow and crush like watery fruits on the ground. Strange couples emerge, the Spaniard over the Indian, horribly crowded together, swollen and black, oscillating like carts about to be upturned. Several Hernán Cortés' enter at the same time, showing that there is no longer a leader. The Indians massacre Spaniards, while before a statue whose head turns to the sound of music, Cortés seems to dream with his arms hanging down. Betrayals are not punished and forms germinate that never exceed a certain height in the air.

This upheaval and the approach of a rebellion among the defeated will manifest themselves in a thousand ways. And in this fall, the decline of the brutal force that is exhausted, no longer having anything to devour, the first indication of a passionate affair will be drawn.

The weapons fall, feelings of luxury appear. Not the dramatic passions of so many battles, but calculated feelings, a drama wisely plotted so that for the first time the head of a woman will appear in the spectacle.

And as a consequence of all that, it is also the time of miasmas, of diseases.

On every level of expression, species of muted blooms appear: sounds, words, poisonous flowers that explode at the level of the earth. Then a religious breath bends the heads, fearsome sounds seem to bray, guillotined according to the baroque whims of the sea that falls on a vast expanse of sand, of a cliff torn apart by rocks. It's Montezuma's funeral. Footsteps, murmurs. The crowd of indigenous peoples whose footsteps echo the noise of a scorpion's jaws. Then whirlpools before the miasmas, gigantic heads with noses swollen from the smells, and only immense but crippled & malevolent Spaniards. And like a tidal wave, like the sudden eruption of a storm, like the whipping of the rain on the sea, the revolt that pushes the populace in ranks toward the body of the dead Montezuma, rocking over their heads like a ship. And the sudden spasms of the battle, the foam from the heads of the cornered Spaniards that are crushed like blood on walls turning green again.

PREPARATORY WRITINGS

THE AWAKENING OF THE THUNDERBIRD

It is a fact that civilization wakes us up. A civilization where the sky is agitated while men sleep is a civilization that has missed its aim.

This is why, much more than the Italo-Ethiopian war, what is currently happening in Mexico is of vital interest for civilization.

THE REBIRTH OF AN INSPIRED RACE

The Indianist policy of the current Mexican government doesn't only indicate a revival of indigenous nationalism.

It is not a state policy; it is a race policy. It is not just a nation that is being formed: it is a real civilization that is being born.

A DIRECTED CIVILIZATION

This rebirth of civilization is conscious. If one speaks here, in Europe, of directed economy, we think that one can speak in Mexico of directed civilization.

It is necessary to insist on the point that this rebirth is not artificial. Mexico is in reaction against Europe. It wants to rediscover its tradition. That doesn't mean it retains the superstition of the past.

12 AGAINST 5

The race over there has been kept two-thirds pure and one-third mixed.

On one side, twelve million Indians are there and they are waiting. On the other hand, five million Spanish mestizos who own land and privileges dispose of the wealth of the country; and they control everything. But the twelve million are terribly strong. They are patient. They have the strength of silence. Their patience is millennial, and the silence of the Indians is a terribly eloquent silence. We will endeavor to describe this silence, and to speak of all that it can hide of conscience and of lucidity. Soon, the five million half-breeds will be overthrown by this silence.

THE REVOLUTIONS OF MEXICO

It is very important to know here in France that this impression of instability and insecurity, of a world in perpetual turmoil and change, which the new Mexico gives us, comes from the five million Spanish mestizos and not from the twelve million pure Indians.

In Mexico, as elsewhere, it is the white man who has perverted the race.

The revolutions of Mexico are a revolt against this state of things. As long as the government does not belong to the true Indian race, Mexico will be in a state of revolution.

This has already been said, but what has not been described is the new social state dreamed of by the true Indian race and which would impose a new spirit.

IN THE LAND OF TALKING BLOOD

Again, the blood of the old Maya-Toltec race begins to speak there.

Under the guidance of its painters, its poets, its intellectuals, who constitute a living and even virulent elite, Mexico as a whole begins a marvelous journey through its own blood.

For the blood of the race speaks, and it is by following the inspirations of the blood and of the race that the Mexicans seek to remake their civilization.

If above the facts and the oppression of history it is now the Indian blood that speaks, we propose to question this blood and to detect its mysterious language.

A SYMBOLIC JOURNEY THROUGH INDIAN BLOOD

We will search throughout the country for the still living vestiges of the ancient Maya civilization.

In all the places that modern progress has not definitively begun, it is the Indian blood itself that we will question.

PERSISTENCE OF ANCIENT MAGICK

And this pure blood, we believe it to be magick, and we want to say that we believe it to be magick.

MEXICAN PAGANISM

We will dwell extensively on Mexican paganism. We will describe the dance of water, fire, corn, and serpents. We will say that the Mexicans have the idea of a black sun that is at the center of the earth; and the serpents that crawl on the earth partake of the spirit of the earth; they are the subjects of this black sun.

A DESCENT OF GODS

We will bring down the gods. We will describe them in their familiar attitudes. We will say how the Mexicans go about making their gods appear.

We will describe the entrance of gods, half-red, half-black, with feet and hands of blue feathers; and we will show in the middle of the dances the red of the fire that, by concentric movements, gradually wins over the blackness of the night until it completely eliminates it.

And then the feathery feet reach the upper parts of the air in a sort of staggered theater. And it is thus that in the long run & with patience the myth is completely realized.

MEXICAN TOTEMISM

We know or we do not know this magickal process that consists in linking the fate of an individual, of a clan, of a country or a sect with the life of a beast, the duration of an animal species.

We will seek in Mexico the persistence of totemism, insisting on the point that Mexico is the only country in the world where this identification has been made on a large scale; that they drew from it a system of life and of culture and that their kings, their magicians, their initiators, their priests, who have become birds or serpents, figure in the foreground of their rites, of their myths, and consequently of their magick. Not only was totemism admitted, exposed to the light of day, but until the hour of the conquest it constituted the basis of Mexican civilization, and it took on the value of a belief in a sort of State institution.

By this identification, by this symbolism that is not imaginary but real, the Mexicans acknowledge and proclaim the living forces, the violent blood, the active and magnetic fluid that they have drawn from their trade with animals.

But this belief, to be effective, must be collective: entire crowds must form a chain from time to time.

Can modern Mexicans still create collective totemism?

ONE SOURCE OF ORIGINAL INSPIRATION

Be that as it may, it appears almost certain that the land and air of Mexico have sources of original inspiration.

The old theogonies prove it with the exalted, furious images, the superabundant metaphors of their poems or migrating animals.

The air that scratches the bodies & brings out their organs contorts the images of the great Mexican poems.

THE SECRET OF INDIAN BLOOD

There is the blood that speaks and the blood that is shed; and the two are in reality one.

The blood speaks in tortured images, which, in turn, have become torturous.

It speaks in human sacrifices.

It indicates the presence of a hidden force, but which emerges when called upon; and everything proves that the ancient Maya knew how to invoke it.

THE MEXICANS AND WAR

Since we are talking about blood it would be appropriate to speak of war; and it is not well enough known that in Mexico human sacrifices were a means of exorcising war, of driving out blood with blood.

MAGICK AND THEATER

Faced with the ravages of the modern scientific spirit, and the impossibility of reviving from scratch, and all at once, the old civilization of the bird that flies in an intense desire for space and for liberation, we will ask painters, poets, intellectuals of all kinds if they do not believe that the theater, which uses the symbol and allows all allegories, is not the last religious and sacred means which remains for us to revive the magick channel in the crowds, and to favor this poetic and fluidic emission of the forces contained in the metaphors, the gestures, the signs, the allegories.

MEXICAN HIEROGLYPHS

An important idea that can be reborn is that of contempt for art.

In the sculpted or painted imagery of the Mexicans, art does not exist. Neither does beauty. It is a European and modern idea. Pleasure in the face of beauty does not exist. The shapes, the lines, are not beautiful; they are useful, they serve. But they serve neither to eat nor to drink, nor to support the material comforts of life. They serve to capture forces, or to make them capable of capturing forces. They are not separated from magick.

They have a life content, which, in turn, releases a science. Mexican hieroglyphs are at the same time an art & a language and they must be understood in several senses.

MEXICO AND JUSTICE

All theogonic civilizations had an antisocial idea of justice.

And if theft didn't exist in Mexico, it wasn't just because social laws were such that everyone had enough to eat.

We will try to make people understand a social state where the individual is perpetually sacrificed to the masses, accepts it and even rejoices in it.

There is a latent heroism among Mexicans that stems from a contempt for human personality.

A whole social order ensues from it, notably with regard to war, property, love.

Ancient Mexico did not know individual love, which is a European and Christian idea.

It is very important to know what the new civilization, if it is born, proposes to do with love.

THE MUSIC OF THE INVISIBLE

We will look for what remains of ancient quartertone music, which had up to 60,000 notes.

We will describe instruments such as those whose cry echoed from peak to peak and which drowned out the noise of the sea.

A METAPHYSICAL LIFE

But we propose to go even further.

We will research to what extent the emerging civilization intends to become aware of the metaphysical spirit that is behind the myths and the forms of the ancient gods, and what living forms it thinks it can presently give to it.

If Indian blood means anything, it has the power to revive and capture this metaphysical spirit. Not to resuscitate a reality of this order is to put the gods of the ancient pantheon of Mexico and the cult of the sun itself on the level of a veritable carnival.

The suns that turn like vast cogwheel gears, the serpent-god with its meanderings, its abstract convolutions, the god of Fire, the multiple gods of the Waters, the god of Thunder, the Serpent-Woman, the Thunderbird, and the old old god responsible for all this creation, all this roaring imagery, which slides and flows with the force of a primitive deluge, all this which is for us a more or less sacred & ritual imagery, all this slides, thunders, rolls, and actually flows. Because the Mexicans did not know of detached creation, we mean the image that one contemplates and which is detached from the spirit, as if there were the image on one side and life on the other. Everything that is spirit is blood, that is, living operation. What is thought & created, the act and the thought communicate, and we would even say that it

is the act that forms the thought. As regards spirit &
matter, the Mexicans know only the concrete. And the
concrete never tires of operating, of drawing something
out of nothing.

MEXICO AND MADNESS

For the Mexicans, the madman is the one who has rediscovered the divine and who returns to nature, the one whose unconscious has rediscovered the movement of nature. For them, the madman is right, and the truth like death does not scare them.

We will finally show how the ancient civilization of Mexico knew how to tame celestial catastrophes, and to recognize in madness and earthly crimes the words of a mysterious stranger.

This is the secret in connection with totemism, astrology, the bloodshed in purity and in a detached and ritual way to spare greater blood, — the secret from which the Thunderbird can be reborn in an uproar of volcanoes.

MEXICO AND CIVILIZATION

It is perhaps a baroque idea for a European to go to Mexico in search of the living foundations of a culture of which the notion seems to collapse here; but I admit that the idea obsesses me; in Mexico there exists, connected to the earth, lost among the flows of volcanic lava, vibrant in the Indian blood, the magick reality of a culture that undoubtedly requires very little to revive materially its fires. And it is not by chance that, when speaking of Mexico, I am taken to speak of fire. If all civilization began with fire, the idea of fire feeds from below and for life all Mexican reality. Fire, the image of civilization, has been preserved in Mexico, through the ages, as something more than an image; it has been actively incorporated into the Myths through which the civilization of Mexico manifests its vivacity.

Earth,
water,
air,
fire,
I outline a kind of inverse hierarchy,
I return to the list of elements within an order of values opposite to that given by Heraclitus;
fire,
air,
water,
earth,

I take the list of elements according to the hierarchy of Heraclitus;

I release this philosophy into action, I reconstitute those four mythical images; and all of Mexico stripped bare is framed in those four images.

Not like you find them in other places. I certainly do not remake an elementary alchemy. But just as any existing matter passes at a given moment through these four points; in the same way that modern physics has rediscovered the energies & principles that correspond in clear language to the symbols of ancient alchemy;

and mercury corresponds to movement,

    sulfur   "   to energy,

    salt   "   to stable mass,

thus the activity of the principles in Mexico manifests in image its perpetually renewed powers.

If there is a culture, it is red hot and it burns the organisms. Because there is no culture without a hearth. And for what remains, the land & air of Mexico seem to hold the form of limitlessly renewing living hearths of culture. And that is why we may still be interested in the ancient Toltec Maya civilization.

A constant irrigation of nerves runs under the Mexico of the conquest, makes boil the blood of the old Indian race, hidden and covered, certainly, but which time does not destroy.

And where material progress, or the conquests of a totally external perfection, to which neither the heart nor the body of man have participated, there where everything that rests, *refines itself* on comfort, *to the exclusion of all interior progress*, it can be said that true culture has stopped developing.

As our progress evolves, as our control over external nature gives us deserts that can be measured, it would seem that the sky is escaping us and this expression is not an image without consequences for reality.

We know nothing of Mexican civilization. A beautiful occasion undoubtedly to dream hypothetically.

[D.H.] Lawrence got the idea from there; nothing prevents us from advancing ours, launching this idea of a mass culture that lacerates individuals. A culture that is a vast & tenacious impregnation. Because the danger of myths, however lofty & tenacious they may be, is that they die out.

And the Myths of Mexico, no matter what you think of them, still rekindle in us, in each one of us, ideas of mass, rapacious needs for flight.

A civilization in which only so-called cultivated people participate in culture, and which possesses a supposedly restricted idea of culture, but which anyone on the other hand can disrupt as long as he learns about books, is a civilization that has broken with its primitive sources of inspiration. For it recognizes a duality of culture, a dualism in reality. A civilization for which the body is on one side and the spirit on the other, runs the risk in brief of seeing how the lives that unite these two extreme realities are disjointed.

For a long time now there have been no myths in Europe in which communities can believe. We are all on the lookout for the birth of a valid and collective Myth.

And I think that as Mexico is reborn it will be able to once more teach us to revitalize those Myths. Because Mexico is also on the lookout for the Myths that are beginning to be resuscitated.

But contrary to what has occurred among us, Mexico has not had time to see its old Myths die.

The Spanish Conquest suddenly destroyed Myths whose strength had not ceased to grow. It extinguished the gods that its subsoil still fed, and it extinguished them at the moment when they were preparing to transform themselves. The barbaric, non-evolved appearance of the gods of the old Mexican Pantheon is the appearance of gods that did not have time to humanize themselves. Yet the gods of a thunderstruck culture, I'm speaking of the Toltec Maya culture that seems to have returned to the earth, which the subsoil of Mexico had one day suddenly absorbed, those gods, who could reappear, because the new Aztec culture did not sufficiently draw them up (and if you think that all of this is extravagant, absurd, capricious, imaginary, and irrational, don't forget that from the beginning I took care to mention that this is a dream that I dreamed) I want to believe that they are preparing to be reborn but to an even more rapacious and concentrated life.

Now these gods-connections of the earth, which the water and air have reconciled, these gods-emanations of the fires of the earth and of the water of the sky, of the feathered water of the sky, from which the rain unwinds the plumage, these gods iridescences of life, trembling with the water of life bent by the wind of the sky that plays in the four sonorous corners of the atmosphere, in the four magnetized knots of the sky (and I know well that for an indigenist sage all of this is nothing but verbiage and poetry, but for a sage, whoever he is, true poetry is nothing but verbiage and this is what separates every true sage from life), these gods are the unquenched vibration that speaks from the ear of the soul to the heart of the spirit.

These gods are a way of life, an inextinguishable testimony of life. A civilization that has lost its gods and that only appreciates its material comforts is one in which the representation of its gods has lost all contact with the real. And gods linked to the real never lose their power, because life would perish with them. Wherever the gods become effigies, it is because their symbolism was transitory and illusory; gods that signify creation are spasmodic manifestations of being, and one of the aspects of the spasms of this being is that there is no human or inhuman force that can ever dispossess them.

What we want to say is that the gods of Mexico have never lost contact with force, since they were and are in themselves active natural forces. This is what gives us hope in the civilization of Mexico, which is an image of the world, the revelation of a system of forces. It has known the balance of two worlds (its relationships, even the most intimate, the most hidden).

The macrocosm and the microcosm, whose tenacious reality Paracelsus, once again in fashion, was the first to clearly formulate.

And yet the civilization of Mexico lives on a nightmare of organs.

It is a tetanizing idea, fertile in obsessions of all kinds. Fertile and difficult perhaps, but close to all sensateness. Outside of this organic burn it does not seem that any Mexican individual can escape or ever wake up. We want to say that for the Maya race whose blood is beginning to speak again, the means of coming out of their dreams, or of entering the dream again, of an inexhaustible fecundity, are of the nature of a mythical force whose bite has never been exhausted. — Neither the images of its thunderous poems which bring out the inside of its organs and return their sensibility like a glove, nor the hieroglyphics of its always armed, always thundering gods, have exhausted its nervous undertakings; it is the same blood which continues to speak. Now we search in vain among ourselves for some poem where the Mexican individual talks of blood, some image, some statue where some violent allegory is expressed. Our world has lost its magick. If magick is a constant communication from the interior to the exterior, from the act to the thought, from the thing to the word, from matter to spirit, it can be said that we have long since lost that form of sudden inspiration, of nervous illumination, and that we have the need to immerse ourselves anew in living & unaltered sources. It is all very well to distribute the lands, and that wealth can still circulate, but it is known that in Mexico at the same time that the indigenous people recover the lands of which their race was dispossessed, an active school searches for its gods and it is not improbable that it will find them underground. We want to say that it is through black forces that the new civilization could start again down there.

Before concluding we would like to draw a picture of Mexican civilization, as it could be reconstituted.

It is certain that, although we are few in number, civilization is in the process of looking for itself in Europe,

and if it is true that no sign can convert European civilization,

we must help by attempting to discover their ideal of life there,

and this brings me to the end of the page,

but see again Massignon's letter.

THE ETERNAL TREASON OF THE WHITE MAN

Tired of being gods, humans periodically remember that they are human, and begin to exalt this condition of humans as if it were superior to that of the gods.

I don't know if it has ever been observed that, in every age, the moment men simply recognize themselves as men and nothing else, civilization in its turn crumbles around them, as if the life of the world needed the exacerbated imagination of men to be able to keep up with the superiority of their destiny.

The crises of humanism always correspond, with a remarkable parallelism, to the crises of civilization. It must be confessed that the coincidence is strange. When the state of civilization is already desperate, when the idea of culture is in a phase of total regression, then men begin to speak of humanism, as if man could escape from Nature, as if the ruling anarchy had not been provoked above all by that narrow-minded and demeaning idea of man which, over the centuries, has been camouflaged under the term humanism: from the humanism of the Renaissance to the materialistic humanism of today.

Humanism has always meant that man has reduced Nature to his measure, that he has made the model "Man" a kind of common measure, both physical and moral, to which, periodically, all things in the world had to be referred.

And this is always the moment in which the cult of a specifically human faculty, reason, spreads, and in which the double point of view of human morality and psychology extends its cruelties in all directions.

It is disconcerting to note that morality does not exist outside of man, and that the materialist point of view, which seeks to make human reason a kind of universal model, has as its only result the slavery of man before Nature, because man makes himself a slave to his own morality and a prisoner of the taboos that he himself has created.

In turn, this moral conception of nature and of life, according to which man feels his own life in himself as distinct from Nature, corresponds to a dualistic idea of things. Humanism has always been born in times that separated spirit from matter & consciousness from life.

This conception is European. The white world has always had, over the centuries, the specialty of this particularization.

When there have been wars of religion in Europe, they have always been waged against the eternal unity of the spirit. The Albigensian War was waged against the advocates of unitary life, while in India's religious wars it was the advocates of the duality of life and the pre-existence of matter that invariably ended up crushed.

Over the centuries, the Hindu world has manifested an unshakable faith in its monistic view of man, Nature, spirit, & life.

And heresiarch Buddhism was extirpated from India by the Brahmins in wars that lasted two or three hundred years.

Buddha, the great Buddha, was a traitor. In India he is considered a traitor & the Brahmins do not hesitate to proclaim him so.

The enviable infantilism of this diminution of man and this anarchic idea of life does not belong to the Renaissance of the 16th century. Even in Greece, in the 4th century B.C., there was a school of skeptical philosophers who reduced life to a human scale and qualified as childish tales the divine myths on which the authentic civilization of Greece had been built, those myths whose underground and magickal life had fermented the Aeschylean drama.

From Aeschylus to Euripides the Greek world follows a downward curve. In schools it is said that man, thanks to Euripides, was able to acquire a more just & rational idea of Nature. The truth is that Euripides lowered the consciousness of Nature, with his petty & humanized conception of life. The ignorant speak of the eternal culture of Greece and put Aeschylus, Sophocles, and Euripides on the same level, without seeing the world that separates them and without seeing that these three names represent the three stages of a fatal curve which, from century to century, has brought *man to relinquish his powers.*

The term "humanism" really means nothing more than an *abdication* of man. For the divine myths man is equal to Nature, which he understands synthetically; but when the analytical mind is born, man imagines he can penetrate Nature and dissect its secrets just like a surgeon dissects a muscle or separates the organs of the body; only, from this moment on, just as the surgeon ceases to understand the body, man loses contact with Nature, because only by instinct can one penetrate the soul of Nature. Say what you will against instinctive knowledge, but it is this that has made all of man's great inventions possible. It is man's *boundless imagination* that has always fueled civilizations. When the rational mind reappears, its reappearance indicates the death of a world. There is a taint in the mind of the white race that periodically causes it to deny that the understanding of the world can be limitless, and to collect into knowledge that is clear, perhaps, but useless because based only on dead objects, the scattered & inanimate limbs of Nature.

The struggle today is located between the precise and dead Western knowledge and the confused but eternally alive knowledge of Eastern monism.

P.S. — We must not confuse the high metaphysics of the East, as it has been transmitted to us in the written versions of the Vedas, starting from the 7th century A.D.

(a metaphysics which unites spirit and matter in an indissoluble whole which, in turn, is reflected in pieces in the world of Samsāra, or the domain of universal illusion), one must not confuse, I repeat, this high monist metaphysics with the falsifications offered to us by the English theosophy of H.P. Blavatsky & Annie Besant. The theosophical school is English and represents the effort of the secret services to stick its nose into the doctrines of the East as well.

NOTES ON CULTURES

TOLTEC CULTURE

Matter	water
	earth
	gas
idem	radium
idem	???

Ether	elastic transmission
Energy	heat, light, electricity
Energy	Mental, psychic phenomena
Energy	Life

Form produced by vibration,
forms   of the physical plane,
            of the Astral plane,
            of the Mental plane,
for the last 2 planes win the related concept.

Location: One,
a locating faculty of geographical classification
                of things,
                  exploring research (interpersonal
                  skills give the coarsest of the thing).

Color.
The astral body emerges with its particular colors. The Buddhas and the Spiritual also have theirs. Manas that operate in some parts of the brain, organs corresponding to faculties of Observation carried in the Manas   Contingency.
Manas — Mahat — Mahatic Faculties or Gods.

7 Hermetic Principles	7 Planes
1° of mentalism	1° of the mineral mind
2° of correspondence	2° id. id. elemental A
3° of vibration	3° id. id. vegetal
4° of polarity	4° id. id. elemental B
5° of rhythm	5° id. id. animal
6° of cause and effect	6° id. id. elemental C
7° of type	7° id. id. human

Change your vibration. Break the vibration through Reverse Polarity.

Father Mother. Madre. Compensation. El Kybalion.

To dominate the Polarity means to dominate the principles of transmutation.

One does not step out of the circle of cause and effect, but one can escape the evil effects of one plane by the laws of another.

Turquoise encrusted snake mask,
coat of feathers, symbols of the god.

Tula, city of the Toltecs.

Two-headed serpent mask, attribute of Tlaloc.

[N]

Tezcatlipoca

[W]　　Quetzalcoatl　　　　　Tonatiuh　　　[E]

Huichiloboch

[S]

※

Guilds.
College of Craftsmen.
Collective lordship.

Organization of the profession in a collective and hierarchical form enjoying professional and territorial competence,
 privilege but control by higher authority.

Protection,
egalitarian regulation.
All bosses, same rights & same obligations,
apprentices,
servants, sergeants, companions,
masters,
exact reflection & institutions of Time.

Corporate economics repudiates individualistic & anarchic liberalism.

Professional specialization,
no innovations,
fraud led to the stake,
craftsman works on the ground floor under the eyes of the public,
private professions, hierarchy of large & private,
privacy confers the official guarantee of the Monopoly,
private corporations integrated constitutional frameworks of the kingdom,
corporation, discipline;
Production eliminates competition, achieves social peace.

Corporation will be flexible, it will evolve.
Monopoly, privileges.
From democratic becomes aristocratic, seeks honors.

SIX CORPS: drapers, grocers, furriers, haberdashers, money changers, goldsmiths.

Reform.

※

A CIVILIZATION

This civilization does not abdicate
a civilization, which does not maintain relations, or the life of kinships fades away, is a civilization that abdicates.

All true civilization excoriates the soul, maintains the concern for revival.

Expose the means of revival of the high civilization of Mexico.

Delimit in the civilization of Mexico the influence of Barbarism,
differentiate the currents:
Maya,
Toltec,
Otomis,
Anaxtec,
Nahuatl,

Totonac,
never affirm anything except for points of high principle.

෴

Came to Mexico
to flee Barbaric Europe,
last example of European Barbarism: Marxism,
if it interests Mexico.

Came to Mexico to flee the civilization & culture of Europe which bring us all back to Barbarism yet I find before me the corpse of the civilization and culture of Europe,
against the utilitarian Imperialism of Europe a revolution is necessary and I ask the Mexicans what they want to do,
to analyze the faces of this barbarism,
Europe speaks of progress,
and its progress is purely material and mechanical,
the human race has not been improved.

On the contrary,
here is a description of the state of affairs to which industrial civilization has led us.

LETTERS (1935–1936)

TO THE INTERNATIONAL CONGRESS OF WRITERS FOR THE DEFENSE OF CULTURE

(*Draft letter*)

[*End of June 1935*]

Dear Sir,

Your invitation was delivered to an old address and has just arrived and it [is] too late to send you my support.

First of all, I would say that I consider excessive & misplaced the honor that is being done to me by asking me to join a congress that is called: For the Defense of Culture. I don't believe the International Writers' Meeting can expect much from my suggestions about something that isn't to me what it is to them.

Because if I see in culture a reality to be defended, it does not seem to me that this reality currently exists.

Moreover, I consider it absolutely necessary, before elucidating this idea of the spirit opposed to culture, & which nothing has ever been able to establish, because only material formalists can consider that they have reached, by gestures against culture, what is above all culture and which the cultural forms that change are only responsible with representing, I consider it absolutely necessary to insist on the reasons that provoked this congress & that make the culture believe that it has been reached and I will say right away that it is perhaps good that a certain culture be reached, however barbarous the means that may have been employed for this.

I will never give any fascism the honor of believing that it can harm my culture or any culture by burning books in which shines this hybrid mixture that I accuse of our abasement.

It would also be a question of defining what we mean by culture and what we want to defend in culture: and if it is the spiritual heritage that is at the origin of the present civilization, I reject such a culture.

True culture has never had a homeland, it is not human but spiritual, and it is not insignificant to note that, in this congress convened for the defense of culture, we seek by devious means a justification of the utilitarian and base idea of the fatherland.

For me, there is no heritage to defend, nor wealth to safeguard, insofar as they are particularized; and the fatherland of the craftsman disgusts me like that of the banker.

That we imprison a few contemporary thinkers, that we burn the writings of ten centuries among those to which [...] I can clearly see that we want to restrict culture, I do not see for this that Barbarism threatens us, nor that the spirit is diminished.

Because insofar as one is not interested in the spirit and because culture is linked to an idea of the spirit developed in man, I will always say that the material fate of man is not a side of culture that should above all interest us.

Because this debate in favor of culture seems to me above all a debate in favor of the conveniences of man who has always called culture that which prevents him from thinking.

Apart from the fact that it is not with protests that one can save a culture threatened by guns or force, I personally do not feel ready for any war to save a culture that on all sides relies only on force and on guns.

The life that escapes what is written and the poetry that is its violent expression, the metamorphosis in perpetual action, are not linked to the preservation of a culture that has resulted in the materialisms that we know.

If culture is a form of spirit, it is also a form of life, and I do not separate from it the sinister spectacle that this life has unanimously resulted in.

Culture was not born today and I cannot forgive it for the use that has been made of it here, in France, in Germany, in Italy, in the name of the more reasoned and more logical use than is done for example in Russia, because it is the same culture that reigned in all these countries. And if we pretend that it is not the same, why do we want to unite in the defense of a mixture whose elements are at odds.

Moreover, it is not true that the forms that help us to think are linked to the use of such and such a culture, & that if we burn all the written themes, all the forms that are fixed, I say that true culture will not cease to survive the disappearance of all these forms, of all these petrified signs.

If systems of thought replace each other, all the more reason life forms replace each other, and there are times in History when it is not useless to burn these life forms.

True culture has never been linked to the preservation of individual freedom, and to believe that culture has been affected by the loss of a few men or the destruction of a few writings is in my opinion to underestimate it.

And I would even say that the sense of historical fatality, the knowledge of the return of certain cycles, and of the catastrophes in which forms of life and of thought disappear, are part of a haughty culture that the organizers of this congress did not think of.

I will appeal to this universal culture that has always ignored the particularism of fatherlands and that separates the fate of the spirit contained in such and such a culture from the fate of man on whom such and such a culture has raged.

The poetry that escapes culture, and whose manifestations remain unscathed, within any absence of freedom, is a notion to which our era of complete spiritual disarray has long since lost the key. And it seems important to me never to speak of the spirit, which I consider absolutely foreign to the systematizations of culture, without adding to it this notion of pure poetic energy which has become the very flame of the spirit.

The question of culture indeed poses for me, it reawakens the old antagonism between spirit and matter, it allows me to attempt a definition of the spirit that escapes forms, it allows me to oppose passing materialism, this hideous imprisonment of poetry through language, the notion of something which lasts, the preservation of a subtle quality, the duration of which is capable of nourishing a hundred cultures, of surviving the burning of a hundred stakes.

And I ask that we not confuse this spiritual attitude which can give rise to the appearance of a more certain and more authentic concrete world with I do not really know what confused and neutral spiritualism which has also lost contact with real energies.

Because if all that we agitate which is concrete, certain, and natural and which gives us the illusion of living fears nothing without the presence of a subtle virtue which must be called the spirit, in turn the spirit can do nothing without the envelopment of a palpable dynamism that must also be called material.

It is in a suitable destination, the most pressing, in a lost differentiation between an element coming from the spirit, & the same transformable, thick, sonorous, and resistant element and that [...]

TO JEAN PAULHAN

My new address:
Antonin Artaud
12, rue Victor Considérant
(Place Denfert-Rochereau)
Paris

19 July 1935

Very dear friend,

I don't know if you remember that one day I came to talk to you about a project to travel to Mexico — for which I feel the urgent need, and I told you: Louis Massignon is very capable of directing me on that side and of providing the means; and you said to me: What does Louis Massignon have to do with Mexico?

It happens that this project is coming together & you can do a lot for me, actually almost everything — and this time it is enough to want, and surely you can do far more than Massignon.

For some time I have heard of a substantive movement in Mexico in favor of a return to the civilization before Cortés. This has seemed impressive to me, so much so that I have done research specifically with

Robert Ricard, who has just returned & has done a rotation at the École Française in Mexico.

I have woven a vast *research project* and I think I have found a way, a means of doing it, and here it is. All this, Jean Paulhan, must remain a secret, limited to you, me, and the people who will be able to help me.

Perhaps I am very wrong, but the civilization before Cortés is metaphysically based, which is expressed in religion and in acts through a kind of active totemism, disseminated everywhere, and which creates symbols which allow all kinds of application.

I don't think this pre-Cortésian movement is aware of the magick that it seeks, but when I explained my project and my ideas to Robert Ricard, who is a student of Paul Rivet, he told me: Those people don't really know what they are looking for. You can help correct their ideas. But you have to go there and this is what I have gathered: Professor Rivet, to whom Ricard spoke about me, told him: There is no money, nobody has money. So I have a series of lectures that I could give in Mexico and in other cities. These lectures would be about the relationship which theater has with civilization and culture, which is, it seems to me, very topical. And I would say that theater could help us find a culture and *immediately* give us the means. Culture is not in books, nor in paintings, nor in statues, nor in dance, it is in the nerves and in the fluidity of the nerves, in the fluidity of the sensitive organs, in a kind of sleeping *manna*, and it can place the spirit in an attitude of very high receptivity and of immediate total receptivity, and allow it to act in the most dignified, highest, and also most penetrating and fine sense; this *manna* is awakened by the theater as I conceive it — and *this is what is thought in France*.

You know no doubt that the last Congress for the Defense of Culture invited me to present my point of view, but I felt that these people were so far removed from such an *essential* notion of culture, that I was totally displaced in the midst of them. This is to tell you that I have an idea of culture and that it doesn't seem bad to me to go and expose it to a country that surely, compared to France, has an idea of theater in its short pants, & on the other hand, it doesn't seem bad to us here that someone go *investigate* what remains in Mexico of a naturalism in full magick, of a kind of natural effectiveness scattered here and there in the statuary of the temples, in their form, in their hieroglyphics, and above all in the subterranean elements & in the still undulating avenues of the air. There is nothing better than sinking into a country to remove the shifting vestiges and to directly detect its strength. And I believe that in Mexico there are still forces that boil & hinder the blood of the Indians. Yet, since the government has no money, neither it, nor the services for French works abroad, I went to present my project at *Paris-Soir* and I met one of the directors, who seemed to me *amazed* (I am not exaggerating this, you know), and who told me: Get a more or less official assignment & *Paris-Soir* will commission an extended series of articles on Mexico & will give you a sum of 5 to 10 thousand francs in advance. So I went to see Massignon, who I thought was influential in certain circles, & he is, but he told me: Your literary titles may in fact entitle you to a *mission*, but if there is a man who deals with French works for foreigners, it is *Jean Paulhan*, with his friend *Jean Marx* from the Quai d'Orsay, go see him.

I'm coming to see you, Jean Paulhan. I feel at an important crossroads in my existence and it turns out that you can suddenly do a lot for me. You know very well what I can do as a speaker. As a speaker, the theater that I imagine, that I contain, perhaps, is expressed directly without the interposition of actors who can betray me. It seems to me that it must be easy to get a series of lectures commissioned from me. That the Quai d'Orsay, through propaganda or otherwise, can give me an official title. It is all the easier since it costs them nothing, since that's how I'll also be entrusted with the series of articles and the money for the Journey. In principle, this should not be more than a formality. If you can do it, and I know that you can get Jean Marx to give me the official designation I'm talking about, telling him that something important, perhaps something sensational can come out of all this.

If you were in Paris it would be simple, but you are not in Paris. If you could phone someone, it would fix things faster than a letter. If you can't do it, tell me so that I can do what needs to be done and see whoever needs to be seen with a written recommendation from you, but it is also necessary that a letter from you precede me. I think Gide can support that request. You know well that I am still SEARCHING for *my path*. The theater (Cenci) has left me materially & socially on the outskirts. I have the chance to find a social utility and it turns out that you can help me. Surely you will. But this time it is necessary for me to succeed, Jean Paulhan, and if Jean Marx is to be seen it is important that he be forewarned and inclined in my favor. You know deep down, very deep down, what I think. You would guess if this letter did not sufficiently explain it. Thanks for what you can do, and apologies.

ANTONIN ARTAUD

Faithfully to you, 3 times thank you.

TO JEAN PAULHAN

Paris
6 August 1935, Tuesday

Dear friend,

I have just seen Jean Marx who told me, even before I had been able to explain my project to him, that was absolutely contrary to the principles of the Quai d'Orsay of giving anyone a certificate, an official document, an approval or any assignment whatsoever; that all he could do was refer me to his agents in Mexico, but without any letters that I could present. He claims that the less official *National Education* could perhaps do it, or even better, the Museum of Ethnography, under the auspices of Professor Rivet. I'm going to see Professor Rivet, but without an official document I won't get my assignment. He later asked me about the background of my project, and he was kind enough to tell me that the ideas I presented to him were very interesting *&* new, and yet that has not changed his decision. I have spoken to you, among other things, of the notion of a living *&* non-written culture that could be extracted from the true subterranean activity of the best minds, here, in France, and of everything that only posterity will retain. And that is what will be the object of my Lectures in Mexico!!!

Apart from our insipid literature, our critics' essays, our sad theater embedded in its lifeless dialectic, without true virtuosity even from an intellectual point of view, the boiling spirit of what is called the French School of painting makes our time a kind of diminished "Quattrocento." Under the contempt of natural representations, a kind of geometry of creation can be deduced, a skeleton of visible and invisible aspects where the living tremor of thought sometimes appears as if alive — in medicine, homeopathy, which is gaining more influence every year, about this notion of a universal cure that Paracelsus had dreamed of and perhaps himself applied. In this new conception, the disease does not deprive the patient, but adds a security, a wealth that makes him ascend a level. In short, this dynamic notion of poetry that Rimbaud bequeathed frees poetry from the text & from writing and gives us back a magickal idea of life. All this developed, embellished with examples, enriched and full of details, can serve to show that under the despair of Europe, the spirit continues its dramatic fate in the midst of a reassuring mobility and, I think, this is an exciting lecture topic. Having seen Rivet, I believe it is better that I wait for your return, in order to take to the Ministry of Education a piece of paper that will inspire confidence in the newspaper that will pay for my trip. I am affectionately yours.

Antonin Artaud

P.S. — What happened to the article on Barrault? The last sentence was missing! The most beautiful of many!!!

TO JEAN PAULHAN

15 August 1935, Thursday

Dear friend,

It seems decided that I will not be able to do anything before September and rather toward the end than at the beginning of the month. I will then wait for your return to act.

I was told that Professor Rivet would not be in Paris before the middle of next month.

No matter how unwilling Marx is, it is *necessary* that I have for my assignment a *real title*. Without this, no newspaper will give me the report. Since these assignment titles exist and the government will not have to spend any money on my case, there is no reason for me to be refused, and Marx's reasons have seemed fuliginous and non-existent to me. Perhaps it is necessary to put someone who is in a very high place into action and it is necessary that in my case the objection that I am a revolutionary be given up.

For the rest this will go down well, since my birthday is on 4 September after which astrologically speaking, there is a regeneration.

The hard thing is to live absolutely without resources, which I would so like, among other things, that this trip to Mexico take place, with the report paid in advance which will get me out of trouble for a while. I live only on my wits and it is necessary for me to display constant ingenuity in anguish at all times in order to be able to eat every day. Truly my fate is curious!!!

A friend gave me a book by Claude de Saint-Martin on *Numbers*: it is at your disposal. Do you want me to send it to you?

Affectionately yours.

ANTONIN ARTAUD

P.S. — The magazine is still delivered to 4, rue du Commerce. It will eventually go astray. Couldn't we have it sent to 12, rue Victor-Considérant.

Thanks, and apologies.

Benjamin Crémieux, to whom I wrote, if he does not like *The Cenci*, seems to do me justice for the rest and he offers to give me a hand for what I could ask.

TO THE MINISTER OF FOREIGN AFFAIRS

(Fragment from a letter)

[*August 1935*]

. . . .
. . . .

No theogony is more burning & effective than that of the three great gods:

TEZCATLIPOCA — HUICHILOBOCH — QUETZALCÓATL.

I mean to say that a country in which the living forces of the subsoil can be seen naked, where the air bursting with birds vibrates with a higher timbre than anywhere else, creates, by that very fact, & by the force of things, gods.

And those gods in turn get a science where astrology speaks its own word.

We have a lot to learn from the secrets of Mexican astrology, read in situ and interpreted through hieroglyphs that have not yet been revealed.

We have a lot to learn from a kind of diffuse consciousness that belongs to everyone over there, in a time in which all the countries of the world, taking Russia at the head, are trying to find a collective dynamism.

My mission, if it comes to be, will consist of obtaining and fixing that dynamism, where, as in the philosophy of Heraclitus,

EARTH, symbolized by Volcanœs & Serpents;

WATER, symbolized by multiple gods; the infinite faces of Tlaloc, & the feathers of the birds of the storm;

AIR, symbolized by bird shawls — from the bird of Thunder to the Quetzal bird, the most precious of the birds in the sky;

FIRE, symbolized by the bird of Thunder and by the volutes of the volcanœs;

the four ELEMENTS reveal a magickal naturalism, are perpetually animated, *and clear*.

It is a spasmodic civilization, the living and concrete realization of a philosophy.

I do not believe that any other civilization in the world offers us such clear & lively examples. It seems that the flayed organs show the soul perpetually.

The civilization of the VEDAS among others maintains within itself & in an extra-organic way a similar idea of heaven.

Therefore, there is everything to find in reality in the example of Mexican civilization. It is in this sense that we will work.

If the civilization of Mexico offers a perfect example of primitive civilizations with a magickal spirit, we will obtain all the forms of primitive and magickal culture that this civilization can propose: from totemism to enchantment, passing through astrological hierarchies, rites related to water, fire, corn & snakes; healing through music & plants, apparitions in the woods, etc., etc.

We will tell you why Mexicans are so afraid of the shadows and of the night in the woods.

I will not dwell further on all these points. I think that I have said enough to show what the mission I ask for could consist of and I hope that you will support it and that you will make it happen.

In this sense, Mr. President, believe in the sentiments of my consideration.

ANTONIN ARTAUD

"*Nouvelle Revue Française*," 5, Rue Sébastien-Bottin, Paris

P.S. — An example: description of totemism converted to the state of allegory. Kings turned into birds. Birds with the names of men. And men moved by a dissonant vibration attract or reject the influences of the stars that dictate their hierarchies.

TO THE MINISTER
OF NATIONAL EDUCATION?
(Fragment from a letter)

[*August 1935*]

. . . .
. . . .
. . . . . it's the act that forms the thought. About spirit and matter, Mexicans know nothing but the concrete. And the concrete never tires of operating, of extracting something from nothing: here is the secret that we want to investigate among the descendants of the high civilizations of Mexico.

On lost plateaus, we will question the healers and the sorcerers, and we hope to make ourselves say of the painters, of the poets, of the architects, and of the sculptors, that they possess the entire reality, the images that they have created and which capture them. Because the secret of high Mexican magick lies in the strength of the signs created by those who in Europe we still call artists and who, in evolved civilizations that have not lost contact with natural sources, are only performers and prophets of a speech to which the world must periodically come to drink. Mexico has yet to teach us the secret of a speech and a language, in which all words and all languages come together in one.

If the civilization that is beginning to be born in Mexico does not manage to become aware of this multitude of expressions gathered around a unique center, & that participate in the speech, the line, the gesture, the form and the cry, it would show that it has managed to find the line of its true tradition.

In order to recognize oneself in language, in all languages, and to avoid a universal confusion of languages, there is a key that opens all means of expression.

The Maya knew the hieroglyphic that speaks, and which is understood in various ways. And currently liberating the Indians from Spanish oppression does not mean anything if they are only liberated materially, if the return to pre-Cortésian civilization does not mean a return to cultural sources from which the ancient Maya civilization arose.

The old Mexicans did not separate civilization from culture, and culture from personal knowledge, distributed throughout the entire organism. In their organs and in their senses, the Mexicans, like all the pure races, had learned to embody their culture, which in its last point and in its highest title came to be a refinement of sensibility.

It must be said that the last Maya barbarian, the most distant Indian peasant, embodies this culture as an atavism; and with this culture that arms him with internal knowledge in an exacerbation of all its nerves, the uneducated Indian is before us, Europeans, similar to a highly civilized person; and this is the truth which seems to us of all importance to affirm.

The conclusions of all this can only be drawn in situ; and it is important to recognize what in modern rites can subsist from ancient magick and ancient divination.

Are there still forests that speak, and in which the sorcerer, with the burning fibers of Peyote or of Marijuana, finds again the terrible old man who illuminates the secrets of divination?

If the Mexicans attribute a high importance to the sky, if the flying birds represent their violent desire for liberation and space, and their contempt for ordinary reality, and, to say the least, for life, if a prophecy promises them for a long term next to the awakening of the Thunder Bird in a flurry of volcanoes, the question arises of knowing to what extent this marve[lous] . . . .

. . . .
. . . .

TO JEAN PAULHAN

[September 1935]

Dear friend,

I have been granted the *mission* as far as the Ministry of National Education is concerned. Therefore, it is settled. It arrived with a delicious letter from your friend Planté, who seems to have been enthusiastic about the project and has shown it by acting immediately. On the other hand, as far as the Mexican Legation is concerned, I think they will be able to organize lectures for me there and perhaps other people will find me a room in Mexico.

All I need is to get the money for the trip. Maybe I can get it through a newspaper and friends. But here in Paris I *literally don't have a penny*. Is there no way to make *the notes about the Balinese Theater* appear and immediately obtain a little money? I really don't know how I can live these days.

Pardon me & see you soon.

ANTONIN ARTAUD

12 rue Victor-Considérant
Paris

TO MRS. PAULHAN

[*September 1935*]

Dear friend,

Things are working out admirably. Not only do I not have to pay for the entry visa, but I have been told by the Mexican Legation that a note regarding me had been sent to Mexico & that people there in the government milieu are interested in seeing what I could do in the theater. They have asked me for my complete works, that they be sent to them in Mexico. Can I have another copy of "The Theater and the Plague" (October 1934) and a copy of "Mise en scene & Metaphysics" (February 1932) and could I ask you to send them to Mr. Jaime Torres Bodet at the Legation of Mexico, 9, rue de Longchamp (XVIe).

Thanks and apologies.

ANTONIN ARTAUD

TO THE GENERAL SECRETARY OF ALLIANCE FRANÇAISE?

(*Draft letter*)

Paris
14 December 1935

Sir,

In reference — — — — —

I wrote a screenplay for a talking film that was distinguished by the fact that it contained only one spoken line around which the entire text was written. The *N.R.F.* of October '32 published my "Manifesto for the Theater of Cruelty" which proposed an alternative form of theater inspired by Chin[ese], Hind[u], and Bali[nese] Theater, and in which image, gesture, and movement take precedence over the written text. Not that speech is despised, but it is taken in its concrete state, for its vibratory and sonorous value. It gives rise to gesture and gesture has given rise to it; and gesture has ceased to be conditioned by it. And in this way a kind of new poetry appears in space.

This Manifesto has practical principles. New actor founds Theater on these principles. Then there was *Heliogabalus*, published by Denoël.

The life of Heliogabalus is theatrical. But his theatrical way of conceiving existence strives to create a true magick of the real. Indeed, I do not conceive of theater as separate from existence. Not that life appears to me as illusory and overdone. But on the contrary I am seeking to do away with the illusion of theater itself &, by poetic & technical means that are fundamental to the old art of theater as it was practiced in the beginning, to introduce into the theater the notion of reality. If dreams are the underside of life, if reality appears in dreams in a bewitching and magickal form that the mind completely accepts, it is this non-illusory acceptance that I seek to force on the spectator. Thus it is that in *The Cenci* the arrangement of the Loudspeakers maintains a public bath of sound, and a diffused thunderstorm *as* terrible [as the] disturbing power [of an] authentic natural thunderstorm.

The lectures will mainly deal with theater,
one on
    traditional theater in France.

I will search for what has been preserved & what seems to be the old mythical tradition of theater, where theater is understood as therapeutic, a means of healing comparable to that of certain dances of the Mexican Indians.

Going from this artistic and psychic therapy to the new modern therapy inspired [by] Paracelsus, by spagyric doctors, occultists like Jerónimo Cardan, Robert Fludd, etc.,

from which I will draw a lecture on
Mexican Medicine and the French Middle Ages
and on
    The Animist Spirit in France,
I will show new spiritual currents that cross consciousness of the youth *&* are expressed in poetry, Surrealism, medicine, Psychoanalysis and Homeopathy, Universal Myth Healing, which is actively talked about here; in painting, Surrealism, Cubism, Picasso, Chirico, Balthus, who are nothing more than the old animist spirit of the totems of Mexico and the high magickal and metaphysical poetry of the *Popol Vuh*, of the *Rabinal-Achi*, of the *Apu Ollantay*, of the Pyramids of Chichén-Itzá, of the Maya hieroglyphics, etc., etc.

 Likewise, I will be able to give a lecture on
the poetic and magical Spirit [of the] *Popol Vuh*
compared to the *Zend Avesta*, the Bible, the Zohar, *Sefer Yetzirah*, the Vedas, the Rajah Yoga and I will finish with the
    Universal Healing Myth
seen in the light of elements, Symbols, Psychoanalysis, naturally. All these lectures will seek to explain to Mexicans what is happening in France, a viewpoint of the evolution of spirit and of mind, and to establish an inner musical concordance between Mexican Metamorphoses and Metamorphoses [of the] French mentality. As unofficial as this may be, the point of view must please Mexico, moreover it is true that Mexico corresponds

[to a] profound transformation [of] youth that evolves, intense spirituality is sought, and this word is given [a] concrete, dynamic, exalting, renewed meaning.

ANTONIN ARTAUD

LETTERS (1935–36)

TO JEAN PAULHAN

Paris
6 January 1936

Dear friend,

As I wrote to you, I am leaving Paris these days to go to Mexico. My ship leaves Antwerp on the 10th in the morning for Havana. I would like to find a time to drop by on Tuesday, as I am taking the train for Antwerp on Wednesday morning, but anxious for what I have to do.

You know that in recent days I have had my bond removed, and I have also obtained with a simple letter from myself to the Transat Company, and superseding all the people who claim to be influential and who have not done anything, a reduction of 50%. This has made my voyage possible. I leave, however, with just enough money for the trip. Determined to risk everything to change my life. But the Embassy of Mexico has given me two letters: one for the Undersecretary of State for Foreign Affairs, the other for the Minister of Fine Arts, announcing my theater lecture: *The Conquest of Mexico*. I also have letters for the Mexican newspapers. So I leave with the best wishes & with great opportunities to work there.

ANTONIN ARTAUD

TO DOCTOR ALLENDY AND MISS COLETTE NEL-DUMOUCHEL

Antwerp
10 January 1936

Dear friends,

A few words from Antwerp where I am staying for twenty-four hours longer than I had thought. My ship was delayed.

I leave on a very large cargo ship of the Transat, a ship of 9 to 10,000 tons, very modern, with imposing shapes, with a high and wide chimney. The chimney is very important to me on ships.

I could not telephone you before my departure. You cannot imagine the innumerable amounts of things that have to be done, and the last-minute obligations, when undertaking such an important journey, and in the circumstances in which I have undertaken it. But I take advantage of these twenty-four hours of waiting in Antwerp to write to you. It is a true adventure for me and it is also what I like, since I am also starting with very limited funds. And I must count in every way on what will be presented to me there to live. And fate, it seems to me, cannot stop speaking. You would give me immense pleasure, and it is a courtesy of the ultimate service that I ask of you, if you could consult my celestial bodies, and extract from my horoscope some detailed information about what will happen to me there. Since some parts of your predictions have already come true, I think this should give you precious indications as to how to interpret the rest. If you see an event outstanding as a fact, obviously I'd be very happy to hear about it, but in general you know well how I regard astrology: not as a means of low analytical and objective guessing. But as a series of interior indications. Paths and affective modifications. A synthetic orientation of the virtues of the stars. These are the movements concerning me that I would like to learn of based on a departure that has taken place. I will arrive in Mexico around 8 February. You can write to me immediately at the *French Legation* in Mexico where I will go to get my mail, since as you know, I have an excellent relationship with the French Ambassador. And on the other hand, if you make a fortune, think of me since the early days will be very hard. I have to earn enough to sustain myself for 3 months and I only have enough for a few weeks.

 I hug Colette & I shake your hand affectionately.

ANTONIN ARTAUD

TO JEAN PAULHAN

Havana
25 January 1936

My dear friend,

I believe I have found the right title for my book.
It will be:

THE THEATER AND ITS DOUBLE

because if theater doubles life, life doubles true theater and that has nothing to do with Oscar Wilde's ideas on Art. This title will correspond to all the doubles of theater that I thought I had found over so many years: metaphysics, plague, cruelty,

the reservoir of energies that constitute the Myths, which men no longer incarnate, is incarnated by the theater. And by this double I mean the great magickal agent of which the theater, through its forms, is only the figuration on its way to becoming the transfiguration.

It is on the stage that the union of thought, gesture, & action is reconstructed. And the Double of the Theater is reality *untouched* by the men of today.

I apologize for once again not being able to notify you of the time of my departure. But the last day was terribly chaotic. You can write to me at the *French Legation in Mexico*. I'll go there to get my letters.

I affectionately shake hands with you and Madame Paulhan.

ANTONIN ARTAUD

TO JEAN PAULHAN

Havana
31 January 1936

Dear friend,

I am writing to you from a small port in North America to send you the final title of my book, *The Theater and Its Double*.

Having arrived in Havana I saw intellectuals and artists and I already feel I am in the current that I was looking for. I still wonder if this time the illusions will not differ from reality. A single black spot: I will have money until what must happen happens. It is beautiful to have confidence in your own star as I have done and to play my luck to the end but it is necessary to help yourself and to be helped. If you can get me even an advance of 500 francs for my book, this time I'd be high for life.

Yours affectionately,
ANTONIN ARTAUD

P.S. With all the expenses, taxes, incidentals, I arrive with 300 francs in Mexico!

TO JEAN-LOUIS BARRAULT

Havana
31 January 1936

My dear Barrault,

As soon as I arrived in Havana I entered a new current, to believe that there are never any illusions & that one can only dream of what exists. So far, both the horoscopes and my intimate faith, which have never deceived me, prove that Mexico will give me what it must give.

A single black spot: will I endure? unforeseen taxes proliferate, and an obligatory change of class under penalty of not entering Mexico force me to ask you, if you can, something more, if only at least 500 fr. Send them in this case as a matter of urgency, and by the quickest route, to the *French Legation* in Mexico, with which I am and will be continually in touch. If things continue to flare up as they have started since the beginning of January, I will send everything back at the end of March.

I thank you and embrace you.

ANTONIN ARTAUD

P.S. I will write to you at greater length & better from Mexico.

TO BALTHUS

Havana
31 January 1936

My dear Balthus,

Arrived yesterday in Havana where I could see a multitude of signs that a new and different world sends its discharges here.

If things continue to manifest as they have been up to now, I could say for once that I had no illusions: on the contrary. Everything in this adventure seems to have a miraculous character. A black spot that may not be black at the end of the day, but at this moment it is: money. Unforeseen taxes, duplicate travel expenses will make me reach Mexico at this point like an exhausted wave. I need to urgently find more money. I have already written to two or three people who had done a lot. If you see others, send them to me as quickly as possible, and by extra-fast means, so that I do not lack money at my destination. I often thought of you at sea & the sketch of my portrait. Your terrible unconscious knew how to situate me exactly with the lassitude & disgust of the left female profile which leaves behind me a disgusting past, with the burning, awake, watchful side of the right profile which is about to devour my future. It is very beautiful, in addition to the surprising & secret inner & physical resemblance.

I thank you and shake your hands affectionately.

ANTONIN ARTAUD

TO DOCTOR ALLENDY

Friday, 7 February 1936
Mexico

Very dear friend,

I arrive in Mexico on a Friday, the 7th, and we are in February 1936. Your letter overwhelms me with its attentive friendship and the moving clarity of its views, which rejoins all the marvelous things that surprisingly surround me. There is not a single word that you say that does not corroborate what is happening.

Havana is a country of black African rites, and a man there told me what I should listen to in life so that the world of images that is in me moves in a certain direction, and you say that the past must be allowed to die. I can't say more. I don't have the right to speak but you know that *from now on*, in effect, things are decided by nameless tortures.

I detoxified again on the boat, and now after a month has passed, the fundamental pains, descending, in terrible probes, cease, and the terribly hardened man, black of air and of light, begins to manifest.

It seems that from the material point of view I *should no longer* worry, whatever the difficulties that assail me. I know those difficulties and I know how long they will last.

LETTERS (1935–36)

We will see each other again and I will remember the support, the frequent support that you have given me many times. Know that Yvonne, Colette, and you are linked. And that Pain pays us back one day, and because each one of us in our own way has suffered horribly.

I had a symbolic dream the night before I landed in Veracruz.

A woman I had had a vague feeling for at the age of 18 presented herself to me as a widow and offered herself and I had never thought of her again, neither in life nor in dreams, but at the moment of carrying out the act the husband returned from the shadows and a child had previously physically blocked the way.

Hug Colette for me.

I am yours with all my heart.

ANTONIN ARTAUD

TO JEAN PAULHAN

26 March 1936

Dearest friend,

Thank you for the letter and for the check. The money arrived just in time; but from hereafter I think my finances are about to settle. With the Mexican government, things are starting to go well.

I was invited as a delegate to a small conference on Children's Theater. The proposals and suggestions I made caused a kind of scandal in the company, I should say in the rabble, of the Schoolteachers. They claimed that I was talking to them about things *they had never thought about in their life*. And they appointed a five-member commission to explain my ideas about theater to an audience of professors.

By now you must have received the text of my 3 lectures made at the University of Mexico. I'm doing a new one these days, at the Mexican L.E.A.R. (Liga de Escritores y Artistas Revolucionarios). I will speak against Marxism and in favor of the Indian Revolution, which everyone here forgets. This population of Whites (Creoles) and mestizos would no longer want to hear about the Indians. From a cultural point of view, they are behind America and Europe. It is painful to have come to Mexico to discover this.

However, *the Indians exist*. My ideas have caused a scandal in all sorts of circles. But a lot of people come to them individually and soon I'll join the Indians, most of the Indians, and with them I hope to be understood.

I am leaving these days for Cuernavaca, a small town 2 hours from Mexico City.

The famous teponaztli, a ritual drum, is beaten there. Then I will try to see the people who flay the bulls alive and who are overcome with laughter (Yaqui Indians).

I found in the Undersecretary of State for Foreign Affairs a young man who understood me, and all the doors of the government were opened to me.

But this is the exoteric side. There is certainly an *esoteric* world in Mexico. I made contact with that world *as early as* Havana. We will see.

Cordial greetings to Madame Paulhan.

For you all my sincere affection,

ANTONIN ARTAUD

I am sending you a corrected text of "The Theater of the Séraphim" and of "An Affective Athleticism." Please make your observations to me by return post, so that this text can appear as soon as possible, and that I can finally be free from my literary past.

It seems that this is the condition for success.

Fondly,

A.A.

TO RENÉ THOMAS

2 April 1936

My dear Thomas,

I plan to leave Mexico City shortly for the interior of Mexico. I leave in search of the impossible. We'll see if I can still find it.

When you know what it is and how in the official circles here you have been able to seriously listen to me when I have said what I wanted to do, you will think that *the Gods* exist, and that they are on my side.

It is a *kind* of expedition, but I am not looking for a city or a race. As of now, my material situation here seems safe, since I do not bear the costs of the expedition. I cannot say anything, but know that I am helped by particular means & it is likely that I will be in danger. Maybe I won't be leaving until a month later, and I hope I haven't wasted my time coming to Mexico.

Here the Government invited me to participate in a Children's Theater Conference. The government sends puppet theater companies to every region. And these, at times, are received with a rifle. I have been invited to give a report on the dynamism of the puppets. All my suggestions have been adopted & will be applied. So it seems that things are going well.

On my return from the expedition, I plan to return to France to rest.

I hug you and ask my friends to think of me.

ANTONIN ARTAUD

TO JEAN PAULHAN

Mexico City
23 April 1936

Dear Jean Paulhan,

There is something miraculous about my life here: I can well say it. What I got from the Compagnie Transatlantique to leave, I get here from the government, from different groups, from the University, etc., etc., to continue my journey, to enter the interior of Mexico. I *hope*, on returning home, to be able to tell you many amazing things that will be able to show everyone that in fact the world is double and triple & that everything proceeds by plans & by regions. I am guided and protected. Here is what I can say. I had some frightening material difficulties, they didn't last very long, & I was pulled out of them by a combination of circumstances that demonstrate the presence of an active & alert force around me. When one knows the facts, one will have no doubts.

Mexico is an amazing country; it keeps its forces in reserve, and keeps them, so to speak, bare. I certainly wasn't wrong in trying to come here. Only here: as everywhere there is the official world and the other. But the other is so strong that the *official* world itself is shocked.

Please *insist* with Gallimard that my book on theater finally appears, and appears without delay: there are many articles there that all those who should have read them have not read because they were published in a magazine and not in a book. And then the Wheel of Time is turned. And many things that that book contains have become topical. Still others are about to come to the fore in this same moment, because the consciousness of the world changes, and it is never the same objects that affect people's consciousness. What was subtle and impermeable to the abstract side of its nature, without changing its appearance, shape, suddenly becomes concrete. You will understand, dear Jean Paulhan, how it matters to me to set a date and that I am a bit tired of seeing my ideas used by others. What I see in Mexico proves to me that I have always been on the right track. I must not be cheated, for purely commercial reasons, of the benefit of what I have thought first of all in this time. This seems immoral to me. I tell you: I ask you again. Tell André Gide, André Malraux, about this book. It is not possible, when one has told them about it, that one will not find allies in them.

Here the Government has my texts translated and publishes them in a volume. These are new things that I have written here about culture, Tradition, Magick, Mexico, and Fate. In short, in Paris I had nothing but failures. I left some texts with you when I left Paris: none have been published. They will be published in ten years, when the whole world has sucked up the substance and I will have the air, saying what I say, to continue imitating myself. This is not possible. I dare to say that my book: *The Theater and Its Double*, the two texts destined for *Mesures*, contain essential ideas, regenerated ideas, the foundations of a true science, a way of reconnecting relationships, in a *small way*, but they contain it, with a whole lost tradition. A moment in which the world is seeking foundations is not the moment to hold back books, works that suggest the basis for publishing in place of God knows what that will make money right away but won't have a future, and whatever Gallimard thinks a book like *The Theater and Its Double* can make money if, through judicious promotion, one knows to send it where it should be sent. Several hundred copies could be sold in Mexico alone. May Gallimard not pay me, if he wants, but good God let this book be printed.

I can't tell you how irritated I am by this absurd resistance.

Gallimard must know that the Revolution is brewing *everywhere* and that it is a Revolution for culture, *within* the culture, and that there is only one traditional magickal culture, and that madness, utopia, irrealism, the absurd are about to become reality. Let him take a tour of Mexico: he will understand that a state of affairs is dead and that it outlives itself and that it is useless to cling to a dead body. And that it would be very clever to cling to the works that contain the foundations of this sort of enduring madness. I hope, dear Jean Paulhan, to receive a letter from you telling me that *The Theater and Its Double* has been published, or is about to be, and finally set me a publication date.

I had some serious, terrible financial difficulties here, but I'll tell you again: Heaven has miraculously helped me. Thus, it is not under the financial aspect that I ask you to ask Gallimard the question about the publication of my book, but under its aspect of intellectual, moral necessity, *which will bring money later*.

Mexico City *is* a city of earthquakes: I mean that it is an earthquake that has not finished its evolution and that has been petrified on the spot. And this in the physical sense of the term. The row of facades are roller coasters, toboggans. The soil of the whole city seems mined, cracked with bombs. *Not a standing* house, not a bell tower. The town contains 50 towers of Pisa. And people tremble like their city: they too seem to fragment, their feelings, their encounters, their business (*asuntos*), all of this is an immense puzzle that is sometimes amazed that it can be recomposed, that it can time again manage to rebuild a unit.

There has been an unlikely mixture of races in Mexico: Indians with Indians, Maya with Aztecs, Aztecs with Zapotecs, Zapotecs with Taraschi, Taraschi with Totonacs, Totonacs with Otomí, Otomí with Huaxtechi, Huaxtechi with Zacatecos, Zacatecos with Kaqchikel,

Kaqchikel with Creoles, Creoles with Creoles mestizos, Creoles mestizos with Yaqui, Yaqui with Kikapu, Kikapu with *Nothing at All*, and it is when it comes to this nothing that the irreducible Seris intervene, the vegetarian Tarahumara, and the Lancandons who are no more than 300 & who die for not witnessing *the domination, itself damned*, of the Whites.

All these breeds boil, I say boil, roll up on themselves, yield, cross and die. There is revolt and abandonment, resignation & rebellion. There are some who go to bed with their mother so as not to go to bed with the white ones, but the mothers who have become sterile have ceased to feed the race, and the race goes to a country *"where the Mother of all takes care that your children always have a peso in their pockets."*

The government policy *is not Indianist*, I mean it is not Indian in spirit. It's not even Pro-Indians, whatever the newspapers say. Mexico does not seek to become Indio or to become Indio again. The government of Mexico simply protects the Indians *as men*; it does not defend them as Indians.

After the Revolution, the Indian ceased to be the pariah of Mexico: but that's all. He has not been given a separate place. I will say more: his rites are not protected. It is enough that their customs be respected. It is not the same thing. And although racial prejudice has officially been fought, there is a more or less conscious *but general* mentality that wants the Indians to still be of an inferior race. However, the Indians continue to be taken for savages. The mass of Indians is considered uncultivated and the movement that dominates in Mexico is "to elevate the uneducated Indians to a Western notion of culture, to the (SINISTER) benefits of civilization."

There are School Masters, whom here are called The Rural, who go before the Indian masses to preach the Gospel of Karl Marx.

But in the face of Marx's Gospel, the so-called uneducated Indian masses are in the spiritual condition of Montezuma in the face of the infantile sermons of Cortés. Throughout 4 centuries, the same eternal White error has not ceased to spread. Reduced in number, sick, crushed, partially degenerated, the Indians keep within them the memory of their ancient, supernatural culture, the fruit of supernatural inspiration. So, far from trying to elevate the Indians to the culture, it is the mestizos of *Creoles* (the Creoles here are the descendants of the Whites) who should rise up to the culture of the Indians. This culture remains, is in tatters, but it remains. The Secrets of healing through plants, which for our white spirits are part of some natural witchcraft, are actually the remains of an ancient occult Science of healing. And the Indians, in their striking atavism, still know how to perceive the origins of this science. They are the heirs of a time when the world still possessed a culture, a culture that was life. Because for them civilization cannot be separated from culture, and culture from the very movement of life. They know it, and they say it, in a language that we no longer come to understand because we are too intelligent. "And the murmuring fire of life," we ended up forgetting what it was.

For the Indians, life is a murmuring fire, that is, a resounding fire, and the resonance of living adopts all the degrees of the tuning fork. There is a noise to make plants die, and it is the noise *according to* which *some plants* die that accompanies the soul of man at the moment of his consumption. This is why the social sermons of Marx's Evangelists make them laugh. Heal life first, they say, this is how the Social State will be reborn with its roaring frameworks, because it is in the crackling of fire that life knots its forces. And it is for this superior & central idea, which lives in the borborygmi of the blood, that very often the School Masters are received with rifle shots.

The Government offers land to the Indians, but at the same time it offers them ballot boxes & the Indians protest that they do not want either ballot boxes or land, but simply Freedom. In practice, on the other hand, the question is not simple. And there we still need to distinguish. It is often out of Christian fanaticism that the Indians, who are all peasants, refuse the ballot boxes and the land, and it is pushed by their Catholic "Priests" who rise up against the envoys of the Government. But it is also out of Pagan fanaticism, to defend their *Jiculi* (God of Peyote), Raïenaï (the Sun), Mecha (the moon), who rush to take up their guns.

Socialist fanaticism responds from the official side to the religious fanaticism of the Tarahumara, the Yaqui, and the Serians. For some Rural Masters, Marx is also a god; and after Marx, I have heard from one of these, we know what History will bring us, and it is by virtue of this eternal & definitive Science of history that we can educate our Children.

It would take forever, my friend, for me to describe the whole state of Mexico to you. One sees how exciting it is and I must say that everywhere there are convinced Men, and in whom honest fanaticism rests on the most indisputable good faith.

Hoping for good news from Paris, I affectionately shake your hands.

ANTONIN ARTAUD

TO JEAN PAULHAN

Mexico City
21 May 1936

Dearest friend,

I have just made an agreement with the main newspapers in Mexico, such as *Excélsior*, *Universal*, and especially the government newspaper *Él Nacional Revolucionario*, which is at the same time the newspaper of the National Revolutionary Party, N.R.P., so that the lectures I sent to you will be published in Spanish. That is why I very much hope, dear friend, that these lectures will be published in their original French, in the N.R.F., before Paris sees them in Spanish, so that we will not be forced to translate them in order to read them. Remember, dear friend, that in February 1932, you published my lecture "Mise en Scène and Metaphysics" which I sent to you on 15 December 1931. That is why I hope so much that in May 1936, these lectures begin to appear. I know well that there are many texts waiting to be published in the N.R.F., but they are purely literary texts: as you may have seen, these lectures touch on extremely current topics, and I must say that, since they were translated into Spanish, by a good translator, they immediately aroused *great emotion*. I will soon send you the note that appeared about me in the *Nacional*

Revolucionario. The same thing happened with the other texts. Fortunately I ran into a Mexican intellectual who had already translated Rimbaud's *A Season in Hell*, and who made wonderful translations of my texts. As soon as the Rector of the University of Mexico City had in hand texts such as "An Affective Athleticism," or the "4 Letters on Language," which are part of my book: *The Theater & Its Double*, he immediately ordered them to be published in the *Revista da Universidade*, which is an important and luxurious organ in Mexico, more or less like *Minotaure*, and they also paid me an exceptional price. Please spare me, dear friend, I beg you, the ridicule of seeing these texts be seen in Paris first in Spanish before they are in their original language.

You will have seen that in these lectures I have made a great effort of concentration, of elucidation. I wanted to create works that serve thought, that fix something in the midst of the chaos in which we live. They touch on vital points of culture, of the sensibility of the world. They must act quickly, because I dare say they act. When having to choose texts, "Surrealism & Revolution" and the "Theater & the Gods" should be chosen, should be the first to be published. I believe that I have not written anything better, up to now, than these two texts and certain pages of "Man Against Fate."

Furthermore 4 months have passed since Gallimard said that *The Theater and Its Double* was far from publication. It seems to me that a new effort could now be made to obtain authorization from Gallimard for this publication to appear. I'm certainly not afraid that the ideas contained there will age, but I would like, dear friend, to personally benefit from their novelty. These ideas, you know, are in the air, others will come to them, write them, manifest them in one way or another, help me break the bad luck that I have had for so long and which gives me the impression that when I speak I am the imitator of myself. That's unjust. A Mexican publisher has just proposed to me to bring together all of my texts on Mexico's autochthonous culture in a book, adding various or diverse texts on theater, including "An Affective Athleticism" and "The Letters on Language." This book will also feature other revolutionary texts, such as an "Open Letter to the Governors of the States of Mexico," "A Message to the Revolutionary Youth of Mexico," and a new anti-Marxist lecture entitled:

"The Universal Revolution & the Indian Problem."

Furthermore, a group of Israelites asked me for a series of lectures on the ancient magickal cultures of Mexico, where I would unite the Kabbalistic culture of the Jews, which modern Jews have betrayed. And I'll tell them. This book will be titled as a whole:

Revolutionary Messages

And it really shouldn't be necessary for Paris to have these *Messages* translated into French in order to know them. And I'll say again that my 3 lectures, sent last February, represent a part of these *Messages*. I really hope, dear friend, to receive a letter from you telling me that my lectures began to appear in June 1936, in the *N.R.F.*, either in full or at least in part, and starting with the first,

Surrealism & Revolution.

Write to me to tell me what you are doing, how Mrs. Paulhan is, & how all of our friends are: René Daumal, Rolland de Renéville, etc. Tell them that I will return soon, in July or October at the latest, & that I hope to bring an important sum of esoteric documents. Here the extraordinary abounds, you just have to bend down and reap the marvels. I hope, when I return, to find my book published, and also, and above all, the lectures. Twice texts like "The Theater and the Plague" & "Mise en scène and Metaphysics" have appeared without so much hesitation, this time it seems to me that these three lectures include even more urgent issues. I count on your friendship, and above all your sympathy for the ideas for which I never stop working.

ANTONIN ARTAUD

Legación de Francia
Lerma 35
Mexico D.F.

P.S. Within a few weeks, the University of Mexico will entrust me with an assignment to study the old Indian races within the country: mountains, deserts, etc.

LETTERS (1935–36)

TO JEAN-LOUIS BARRAULT

Mexico
17 June 1936

My dear Barrault,

No. It is rather me who regrets having been forced to ask you for something more. But it is a trifle. Believe it.

For the last four months I have been struggling with incredible financial difficulties. I have published articles in magazines and newspapers and that is how I fight back. For a month now I have been a regular contributor to *Él Nacional Revolucionario*, a government newspaper. But all this would not be interesting if these articles had not served me to defend a unique point of view and to *disseminate* the ideas that I have come to express here. Few people have really understood the purpose of my trip to Mexico. It was not about changing my life, fleeing France where I found no place. I can't give you any details, but leaving Sonia's house one night I made an allusion to you regarding the true meaning of my trip to Mexico. And I told you that there were caves in Mexico.

The important thing is that certain ideas forge their path, and NOW I'm sure that will happen. What I say and what I write counts; and that is essential. I have come here to find ways to live Securely in France, when I return. And things need to change, at all costs.

So I came to Mexico looking for the strength, and the forces, to push for this change. I don't see why what is extraordinary about a country should continue to be automatically sacrificed.

I struggle then, first to live, and the daily bread is hard; and finally to leave Mexico City and meet with certain indigenous tribes & initiate me into their practices. I am not going by chance, because from Cuba I have a strange thread. I am looking for a precious thing, when I have it in my hands I will automatically be able to carry out the *true* drama that I have to make, with the certainty this time of success.* I have to take revenge against many people and many things. It is not possible that I do not do so. You must understand that I have a lot in my heart and there are some shitty things that I can't forget. I came to Mexico to restore the balance & break the bad luck. Because that's what it's all about. External and internal bad luck, and the external also comes from me.

I hope to return soon, that is to say in 3 or 4 months, toward the end of September or the beginning of October. And I hope to be definitely armed by that time. Regarding the offer you make me, I want to tell you that I live from day to day and without a sou before me. But my situation can change from one day to the next. I work to get a mission, paid for by the government of

---

* This isn't about the theater.

Mexico. Then do what seems right to you. Today a thousand francs would be a goldmine for me. I don't know what the future holds for me. In any case, returning to France will mean for me that I have sufficient means. I will then be able to return what you have advanced me. Make the decision that you think is fair based on what I just told you.

I shake your hands in a friendly way.

ANTONIN ARTAUD

Legación de Francia
Lerma 35
Mexico D.F.
Mexico

TO BALTHUS

Mexico
18 June 1936

My dear Balthus,

I am sending you the text of your article as it appeared in Spanish in *Él Nacional* of México.

What do you think of an exhibition of the New French Painting with works by you, Derain, and other painters that you would select and from which you would send me the list. Perhaps it can be organized with a gallery in Mexico, and it could become a great *artistic & financial success*. It would be worth a shot!!! Speak to Derain.

Warmly,

ANTONIN ARTAUD

TO JEAN-LOUIS BARRAULT

Antonin Artaud
Légation de France
Lerma 35
Mexico

10 July 1936

My old Barrault,

Since my last letter the situation has changed.

A petition signed by the most eminent intellectuals and artists in Mexico has recently been sent to the President of the Republic, signed also by several ministers and ministerial departments, in order to grant me the means to carry out a Mission with the old races of Indians.

This mission is about finding and reviving the vestiges of the ancient Solar culture.

But I have to stay alive until everything is ready; and like Bernard Palissy, I burn the furniture and live ascetically & desperately.

I need my friends in Paris to help me.

I ask you then, without waiting any longer, make an effort to send what you can. Either realize it between friends or send it to me directly. I am no longer ashamed to ask you because my present situation is serious, but the result of this interval can be amazing. It is necessary that there be confidence in me in Paris as there is in official circles here. But they are slow. My effort is desperate. Make a desperate effort and above all act with urgency, great urgency, because I am at the limits of my strength, my resistance, my reserves. I can't take it anymore & I'm counting on you.

ANTONIN ARTAUD

REVOLUTIONARY MESSAGES

THREE LECTURES PRESENTED AT
THE UNIVERSITY OF MEXICO

SURREALISM AND REVOLUTION

I participated in the Surrealist movement from 1924 to 1926, and I was involved in its violence.

I will speak of it with the spirit that I had at that time, and I will attempt to revive for you that spirit which wanted to be blasphemous & sacrilegious and which sometimes succeeded.

But you say that this spirit has died; it belongs to 1926, and if you respond, just respond to 1926.

Surrealism was born out of a despair and a disgust and it was born on school benches.

Far more than a literary movement, it was a moral revolt, the organic cry of man, the kicks of life in us against all coercion.

And from the start the coercion of the Father.

The entire Surrealist movement was a profound and inner insurrection against all forms of the Father, against the pervasive preponderance of the Father in mores and in ideas.

Here, for purely documentary purposes, is the latest Surrealist manifesto, which indicates the new political orientation of this movement:

COUNTER ATTACK
FATHERLAND AND FAMILY

Sunday 5 January 1936, at 9 P.M., at the Grenier des Augustins, 7 Rue des Grands-Augustins (métro Saint-Michel).

ANTONIN ARTAUD

AGAINST ABANDONMENT OF THE REVOLUTIONARY POSITION

PROTEST MEETING

A man who accepts the fatherland, a man who fights for the family, is a man who betrays. What he betrays is what is for us the reason for living and for fighting.

The fatherland stands between man and the riches of the earth. It demands that the products of human sweat be transformed into cannons. It makes a human being a traitor to his fellow man.

The family is the foundation of social constraint. The absence of any fraternity between father and child has served as the model for all social relations based on the authority and the contempt of bosses for their fellows.

Father, fatherland, foreman, *such is the trinity that serves as the foundation of the old patriarchal society and, today, of the fascist shithouse.*

Men lost in anguish, abandoned to a misery and to an extermination of which they cannot fathom the causes, will rise up one day in exasperation. They will then complete the ruin of the old patriarchal trinity: they will establish the fraternal *society of fellow workers, the society of power & of human solidarity.*

We can see from this manifesto that Surrealism upholds against the latest Stalinist orientation the essential objectives of Marxism, that is, all the virulent points through which Marxism touches man and wants to penetrate its secret domains; and we must recognize in this obstinate violence the old Surrealist manner, which can only be lived in exasperation.

But the mystery of Surrealism is that this revolt, from the start, sank into the unconscious.

It has been a concealed mysticism. A new kind of occultism, and like all concealed mysticism, it expressed itself allegorically and through larvae that took on the air of poetry.

All that which had the form of a clear claim, Surrealism dismissed or could not align with.

A terrible boiling of revolt against all forms of material or spiritual oppression agitated us all when Surrealism began: Father, Fatherland, Religion, Family, there was nothing that we did not execrate... that we execrated much less with words than with the soul. In this revolt we engaged our soul, & we engaged it *materially*. Yet this revolt, which attacked everything, was not capable of destroying anything, at least in appearance. Because the secret of Surrealism is that it attacks things in their secrecy.

To reach the secret of things Surrealism had opened a path. Like with the Unknown God of the Mysteries of the Cabires, like with Aïn-Souph, the animated hole of the abysses in the Kabbalah, like with the Nothing, the Void, the Non-Being devourer of the nothingness of the ancient Brahmins and Vedas, we can say of Surrealism what it is not, but to say what it is, one must use approximations and images, and Surrealism is a movement clothed in images. It resuscitates, by a sort of incantation in the void, the spirit of ancient allegories.

There are certain elements in Surrealist poetry that we can speak of and that we find, that we recognize. But other kinds of poetry always lead us into a domain; lead us into a certain country that cannot be confused with others. With Surrealism, on the contrary, begins the path of loss, in such a way that we can never say that its poetry is where we see it.

Surrealism needed to get out.

"To go forth by day, in the first chapter," as *The Egyptian Book of the Dead* says of the Double of Man.

And, as Surrealists, we needed to go forth, always, everywhere in a movement of mortal dissatisfaction; hence, a violence that led to nothing, but manifested something subterraneously: a violence that the mania for clarifying things ended up calling *demoralization*.

Refusal and Violence.

Violence and Refusal.

These two significant poles of an impossible state of mind, of a mysterious electricity, indicate the abnormal character of the poetry of this period which was no longer poetry in the sense in which words mean it, but the magnetic emanation of a breath, a kind of bizarre magick that settled in our midst.

Refusal. A desperate refusal to live, & which nevertheless must accept life.

In Surrealism, despair was the order of the day &, with despair, suicide. But to this question posed in issue 2 of *La Révolution Surréaliste*: Suicide, is it a solution? No, the Surrealists replied with a unanimous movement of the heart, suicide is still a hypothesis because, according to the words of Jouffroy: "In suicide what kills is not identical to what is killed."

All the manifestations of the Surrealists have participated in this suicidal spirit where real suicide never occurs.

Destruction upon destruction. Where poetry attacks words, the unconscious attacks images, but an even more secret spirit strives to fuse the statue back together.

The idea is to shatter reality, to mislead the senses, to demoralize, if possible, appearances, but always with a notion of the concrete. Through its obstinate massacre Surrealism is always striving to extract something.

Because for Surrealism the unconscious is physical, and the Illogical is the secret of an order wherein a secret of life is expressed.

When it broke the puppet, when it injured the landscape, it remade them, but so as to explode with laughter, or to resuscitate the source of terrifying images that swim in the Unconscious.

This means that the Surrealist scorns reason, that the Surrealist withdraws meaning from images, to restore to them their most profound meaning.

This means that the writers of that time sensed a knowledge of the occult depths of Man, lost since before Time.

And Surrealism freed life, it physically decongested life, it allowed a flow of valuable electricity to come to animate stones, inanimate sediments.

Disorganized life reforms itself, in reaction to the chaotic anarchy imposed upon the objects that we see.

The Surrealist world is concrete, *concrete* so that it cannot be confused with anything else.

All that is abstract, all that is not disturbing, tragic, or buffoonish, all that does not manifest an organic state, that is not a kind of physical exudation of the disquiet of the mind, does not come from that movement. Surrealism invented automatic writing; it's an intoxication of the mind. The hand freed from the mind goes where the pen guides it; and, under an astonishing spell, guides the pen so as to bring it to life, but having lost all contact with logic, this hand, thus reconstructed, resumes contact with the unconscious.

It denies by its very miracle the stupid contradiction of the schools between spirit and matter, between matter and spirit.

※

Whenever life is touched, it reacts through dreams *&* through larvæ.

This means that the general Unconscious has been probed by something. It yields that which it conserved.

When a woman has conceived, she dreams without knowing that she has conceived. When a man has been wounded or is going to be sick, or undergoes some agony, he dreams. Alongside the dreams of man, there are dreams of groups and dreams of countries.

I don't know how Surrealist we are to have felt that through our dreams we release a sort of group wound, a life wound.

Alongside the obsession with dreams, faced with the hatred of reality, Surrealism has had an obsession with nobility, a haunting by purity.

The most pure, the most desperate of us, it was commonly said of this or that Surrealist. Because for us only he who was desperate was truly pure.

What does it matter that that pure fire was limited to burning itself? It sincerely wanted to be pure. And it sought that purity on every possible level: love, spirit, sexuality.

※

"The Father," says Saint-Yves d'Alveydre in *Keys of the Orient*, "the Father, it must be said, is destructive."

A spirit desperate for severity and which, to think, places itself on the elevated plane of nature, feels the Father as an enemy. The Myth of Tantalus, that of Mégère, that of Atreus, contain in fabulous terms this secret, this kind of inhuman truth, which all the research of men seeks to come to terms with.

The natural movement of the Father against the Son, against the Family, is hate; this hatred that the philosophy of China cannot separate from love.

And with this general truth, each specific father in his being also seeks to accommodate himself.

Up until 27 I lived with the concealed hatred of the Father, of my own father. Until the day when I saw him die. So this inhuman severity, which I accused him of oppressing me with, gave way. Another being exited his body. And for the first time in my life this father held out his arms to me. And I who am hindered in my body, I understood that all his life he had been hindered by his body and that there is a lie of the being against whom we were born to protest.

※

On 10 December 1926 at 9 o'clock in the evening, at Café du "Prophète" in Paris, the Surrealists gather together.

It is a question of knowing what, in the face of a social revolution that is rumbling, Surrealism is going to do with its own movement.

For me, given what we know about Marxist Communism, to which it was a matter of rallying, the question couldn't even be asked.

Does Artaud give a damn about the revolution? I was asked.

I don't give a damn about yours, nor mine, I replied, leaving Surrealism, since Surrealism had also become a party.

This revolt for knowledge, which the Surrealist revolution wanted to be, had nothing to do with a revolution that already claims to know man, and makes him prisoner in the framework of his coarsest necessities.

The points of view of Surrealism and of Marxism were irreconcilable. And it did not take long to notice that when some of the notorious Surrealists decided to join the party. That is, the Third International French branch of Moscow.

Are you Surrealist or Marxist? André Breton was asked, and if you are Marxist, what need have you to be Surrealist?

In short, it was a question of Surrealism descending to Marxism, but it would have been beautiful to see Marxism attempt to rise to Surrealism.

In 1926, the antagonism could not be resolved because History hadn't advanced. Today, I think that History has advanced & that there is a new fact in France. This fact is the appearance of an historical idea in the consciousness of youth, and this idea that I want to develop I call the reconciliation of *Culture* and of Fate. In the desperate consciousness of youth a new idea of culture is born. And this culture which wants to know man has a high idea of man. It does not accept that we separate the life of man from that of events. It wants us to enter into the inner sensitivity of Man who plays, also, with Events.

The new youth are anti-bourgeois-capitalist and, like Marx himself, they have felt the imbalance of the times when the monstrous personality of Fathers rises based on land and on money. When we accuse Marx of wanting to suppress the family: "The family, but you have destroyed it," he replies, "Where are your ancient virtues? Outside of all virtue, I see nothing but matter, and me, Marx, I organize matter, I organize it technically & coercively." We can say that out of the ancient values of Man, Marx organized what the Bourgeoisie has left.

Before being the exaltation of a superior reality Surrealism was a critique of facts, and of the movement of reason in facts.

Between the real and myself, there is myself, and my personal distortion of the ghosts of reality.

And youth in its current Self consider that Marx started with a fact, but that he remained in that fact without moving out into Nature. In short, he drew a metaphysic from a fact, but he did not rise up to a metaphysic of Nature, and young people first want to rise up to nature before being overwhelmed by the economic part of facts.

But if this youth is for the organization of matter, it is at the same time for the organization of the mind.

It regards Lenin's materialist organization as transitory and punitive, and it thinks that Lenin in Russia applies this materialist and punitive organization with just cruelty. But spirit matter, matter spirit, it affirms the interdependence of these two aspects of its being. Because it eats at the same time as it feels; and it thinks at the same time as it eats. It accuses modern Europe of having invented an antagonism that does not actually exist. And if it condemns Marx, it is as a European, and because this youth loves Man, but the whole Man, it wants to save Europe from Man.

In its new idea of culture there is a counter idea to progress. Modern science teaches us that there never was matter, and it returns after 400 years to the old alchemical idea of the three principles: sulfur, mercury, and salt, which it calls energy, movement, mass. We can certainly say that there was no need to speak of progress.

And all this manifests a superior idea of culture, but for this culture to be good, ideas must be shattered, ideas that are idols, and if we are determined to shatter ancient idols, it is not so as to bring forth new ones under our feet.

This youth no longer wants to be fooled and, when we say that times have changed and that today an intellectual, a poet, can no longer ignore their times, they retort that there is a mistake about intellectuals and about time.

It does not separate intellectuals from their times, & intellectuals do not separate themselves from their times &, as their times, they think that the mind is not an empty thing and that art is only valuable through its necessity. But for them this idea of a necessary action does not mean prostitution of the action.

There is a way of entering into time, without selling oneself to the powers of time, without prostituting one's forces of action to propaganda slogans: "war against war, common front, united front, singular front, war against fascism, anti-imperialist front, contra fascism and war, class struggle, class for class, class against class, etc., etc."

These are the idols of stupefaction which are used in the game of propaganda. Propaganda is the prostitution of action, and, for me & for the young, the intellectuals who write propaganda literature are lost corpses for the strength of their own action.

An intellectual acts on the individual and on the mass and in his unanimous mass action there is a cultural idea about the strengths of the individual. The young want us to give them an idea about the economy of the forces of Man without its action on individuals. There is a technique for triggering the forces of man as there is in Chinese medicine a technique for healing the liver, spleen, marrow, or intestines, touching the extent of the physical body points that are also physical but far from the liver, stomach, marrow, or intestines.

As the world has its geography, inner man has his geography, which is a material thing. But the dialectical materialism of Lenin is afraid of this profound method of knowing geography.

However, a deep culture is not afraid of any geography, even if the search for the unexplored continents of man must lead to this vertigo in which the immateriality of life seethes.

True culture helps to explore life, & the young, who want to reestablish a universal idea of culture, think that there are predestined places to bring forth sources of life and they look both toward Tibet & toward Mexico. The culture of Tibet is valid only for what in the *Egyptian Book of the Dead* one calls the corpses, the Overturned. On the contrary, the ancient culture of Mexico serves to make burst forth the inner senses from their barrier. Ancient culture creates resurrections.

All true culture is based on race and on blood. The Indian blood of Mexico conceals an ancient secret of race, and before the race is lost, I think that we must ask Mexico for the strength of this ancient secret. Where present-day Mexico copies Europe, it is for me the civilization of Europe that must ask Mexico for a secret. The rationalist culture of Europe has gone bankrupt and I have come to the land of Mexico to seek the foundations of a magickal culture that can still burst forth from the forces of Indian soil.

MAN AGAINST FATE

I spoke last night of Surrealism and revolution. I should have said: revolution against Surrealism, Surrealism against revolution.

I tried to define that deep disgust, that vital anguish that never quite found its direction, out of which French Surrealism was born.

For me, to consider it in its essence, Surrealism was an affirmation of life against all its caricatures, and the revolution invented by Marx is a caricature of life.

I felt that that hunger for a pure life that Surrealism was in the beginning had nothing to do with the fragmentary life of Marxism. Fragmentary, but provisionally valid. But responding to a real movement in history. And I said that Marx was one of the first men who lived and felt history. But there is a world of movements in history. And if the Surrealist state of mind is a state of mind overtaken by facts, the historical movement of Marxism is also overtaken by facts.

And here is the latest stage of our thinking on this subject: the thinking of French youth and the thinking of enlightened intellectuals.

Historical and dialectical materialism is an invention of European consciousness. Between the true movement of history and Marxism there is a kind of human dialectic that does not accord with the facts. And we think that for the last 400 years European consciousness has lived on an immense error of fact.

This fact is the rationalistic worldview that in its application to our everyday life in the world results in what I will call *divided consciousness*.

You will understand what I mean in a moment.

You all know that thought cannot be grasped. In order to think, we have images, we have words for those images, we have representations of objects. We separate consciousness into states of consciousness. But this is merely a way of speaking. All this has no real value except insofar as it enables us to think. In order to consider our consciousness, we have to divide it, otherwise the rational faculty that enables us to see our thoughts could never be used. But in reality consciousness is a block, what the philosopher Bergson calls *pure duration*. There is no stopping the motion of thought. What we put before us so that reason can consider it is in reality already past; and what reason holds is merely a form, more or less empty of real thought.

What the reason of the mind looks at can always be said to partake of death. Reason, a European faculty, exalted inordinately by the European mentality, is always a simulacrum of death. History, which records facts, is a simulacrum of dead reason. Marx struggled against the simulacrum of facts; he tried to sense the meaning of history in its particular dynamism. But he too remained fixated on fact: the capitalist fact, the bourgeois fact, the engorgement of the machine, the asphyxiation of the economy of the age due to a monstrous abuse of the use of the machine. From this true fact, a false ideology has *also* emerged *in history*.

The French youth of today, who cannot tolerate dead reason, are no longer content with ideologies. They regard the materialistic explanation of history as an ideology, which risks provoking the end of history. And when they reread Marx's *Communist Manifesto* they realize that what is called Marxism is in turn a false ideology that caricatures the thought of Marx.

Marx started with a fact, but he refused all metaphysics. And the youth consider the materialist explanation of the world to be a false metaphysics. In the face of the false metaphysics stemming from Marx's materialism, the youth demands a total metaphysics that reconciles them with life as it is today.

They deem historical materialism responsible for the birth of a form of idolatry which, like all forms of idolatry, is religious, religious because it introduces a mystical element into the mind. The French youth do not want mysticism, they want people to stop hallucinating the mind; they are hungry for human truth, human without deception.

They sense life, this youth, and they sense life as a single thing, a thing that does not admit of theory. To invoke metaphysics today is not to separate life from a world that surpasses it, it is to reintegrate into the economic notion of the world everything that we sought to remove from the world, and to reintegrate it free of hallucination.

For the youth, it is reason that created contemporary despair, and the material anarchy of the world, through separating the elements of a world that a true culture united.

If we have a false idea of fate, and of how it functions in nature, it is because we no longer know how to see nature, to feel life in its totality.

Antiquity knew not of chance, & fatality is a Greek idea whose opacity was further stressed by a crude Latin rationality. To cure itself of chance the reputed pagan world had knowledge. But when we invoke knowledge, few in the modern world would still be able to say what it is.

There is a secret determinism based on the higher laws of the world; but in the midst of a mechanized science that gets lost among its microscopes, to speak of the higher laws of the world is to arouse the derision of a world wherein life is no more than a museum.

When we speak today of culture, governments think of opening schools, mass producing books, and spilling printer's ink, whereas to let culture mature, we would have to close schools, burn museums, destroy books, and smash printing presses.

To be cultivated is to consume one's fate, to assimilate it through knowledge. It is knowing that books lie when they talk about god, nature, man, death, & fate.

God, nature, man, life, death, and fate are merely forms that life assumes when it is regarded by the thinking process of rationality. Outside of rationality there is no fate; and this is a high idea of culture that Europe has renounced.

Europe has dismembered nature with its separate sciences.

Biology, natural history, chemistry, physics, psychiatry, neurology, physiology, all these monstrous germinations that are the pride of the Universities, just as geomancy, palmistry, physiognomy, psychurgy, and theurgy are the pride of a few separate individuals, are for enlightened minds merely a *loss of consciousness*.

Antiquity had its labyrinths, but it did not know the labyrinth of divided science.

There is in the mind a secret movement that divides knowledge and presents to bewildered reason the images of science as if it were so many realities.

Satan, according to the ancient books of the Magi, is a created image. By dint of invoking Evil, black magicians invent Satan and we can say that they create Satan. Likewise, Divided Reason invents the images of science that are taught in the Universities.

This movement is an idolatrous thing: the mind believes in what it has seen.

And to look at life through a microscope is to look at a landscape through the small end of reality.

French youth are against rationality because they accuse it of estranging them from science. They are against the science that has petrified rationality.

These young people feel that Europe has gone down the wrong road, and they think that it is knowingly, and one can say criminally, that Europe has gone down the wrong road. They attribute the disastrous orientation of Europe to Cartesian materialism.

The Renaissance, which claimed to glorify man, is also seen as culpable of debasing the idea of man through a false interpretation of the Ancients.

They know that history is wrong when it speaks of paganism and that paganism is not what the books have made of it.

It was Europe that invented the idolatry of the pagans, because the form of the European mind is an idolatrous one; and idolatry, as I said earlier, is precisely the separation of idea from form when the mind believes in what it has dreamed of. The Ancients, who believed in their dreams, believed in the meaning of their dreams, they did not believe in the forms they took. Behind their dreams, & at varying levels, the Ancients sensed forces, and they immersed themselves in those forces. They had an overpowering sense of the presence of those forces, and they sought throughout their entire organism, if necessary by means of a real vertigo, for a way of remaining in contact with the release of those forces. The head of a European of today is a cave wherein powerless simulacra move, simulacra that Europe mistakes for its thoughts.

But this is to seek too far afield the critique of a dead thought. What paganism deified, Europe mechanized.

We are against this rationalization of existence that prevents us from believing in ourselves, that is, from feeling ourselves as human, and there exists in our idea of man an idea of the force of thought. And of the dialectical and technical knowledge of the force of thought.

All that science has taken from us, everything that it isolates in its retorts, its microscopes, its scales, its complicated mechanisms, all that it reduces to numbers, we aspire to win back from science, which is stifling our vitality.

Something wants to emerge from us that is not answerable to experiment. And many of us reject the teachings of experiment. We do not believe in the value of experiment or in proof by experiment. First, this is because we do not believe in the illusions of reason and in the forms through which experiment seeks to reach our thought.

All forms of experiment conceal reality.

When Pasteur tells us that there is no spontaneous germination and that life cannot emerge from a void, we think that Pasteur was mistaken about the real nature of the void and that a new experiment will demonstrate that the void of Pasteur is not a void: and this experiment has been conducted.

In our eyes history is a panorama and it is in time that we judge history, for we are educated people. Here people who eat potatoes have the morality of adventurers, but in the same place, five hundred years ago, other people, who also ate potatoes, had the morality of degenerates.

It is not by experiment that we judge reality. For all this does not show us Man. Concern for the external functions of Man distracts from a profound knowledge of Man. And there is a world in thought. The Communist revolution ignores the inner world of thought. But it deals with thought; it approaches it through experiment, that is, from the external world of facts.

It takes madmen and grafts onto them bizarre diseases to see what may result, it injects them with plant viruses, as if it were grafting plants onto them to see what would become of the man in them. If necessary, it would make a caricature of Totemism by researching experimentally the transition between Humanity and beast, between beast and forest.

Yet let us not forget that the materialism of Lenin, which is also called dialectical, claims to have advanced beyond the dialectic of Hegel.

Where Hegel's dialectic finds in three terms the inner force of thought, Lenin's unites the terms, and speaks of the dynamism of thought, which it no longer separates from facts.

There are three forces in life, as shown by an old science known to all antiquity:
the repulsive and dilating force,
the compressive and astringent force,
the rotational force.

The movement that goes from the outside to the inside and which is called centripetal corresponds to the astringent force, whereas the movement that goes from the inside to the outside and which is called centrifugal corresponds to the dilating and repulsive force.

Like life, like nature, thought goes from inside to outside before going from outside to inside. I begin to think in the void and from the void I move toward the plenum; and when I have reached the plenum I can fall back into the void. I go from the abstract to the concrete and not from the concrete to the abstract.

To arrest thought from the outside and to study it for what it can do is to misunderstand the internal and dynamic nature of thought. It is refusing to perceive thought in the movement of its internal fate, which no experiment can capture.

I call poetry today knowledge of this internal and dynamic fate of thought.

To rediscover its profound nature, to feel itself alive in its thought, life rejects the analytical spirit in which Europe has strayed.

Poetic knowledge is internal, poetic quality is internal. There is a movement today to identify the poetry of poets with that internal magickal force that provides a path to life and enables it possible to act upon life.

Whether or not thought is a secretion of matter, I will not dwell on this fact. But I will simply say that Lenin's materialism appears in fact to ignore this poetics of thought.

There are plants for illnesses and illnesses have the color of these plants. Between the color of the illnesses and the color of the plant, Paracelsus who, even as he cures men, thinks of finding a way for man in the road of diseases (and we can say that he cures life), in order to cure life, Paracelsus establishes through the imagination a relationship between the disease & the plant, and he cures the disease.

This is the origin of spagyric medicine from which homeopathy originated.

There are cries for the passions, and within the cries of each passion there are degrees of the vibration of the passions; and at other times the world has known a harmonics of the passions. But every illness also has its cry and the form of its groan: there is the cry of the plague victim when he runs through the street with the mind drunk with images, and the peculiar death rattle of the plague victim when in agony. And the earthquake has its own sound. But the air vibrates in a particular way when we say that an epidemic is passing. And between an illness and a passion, between a passion & an earthquake, one can establish resemblances and strange harmonies of sound.

But the determinism of facts is not separate from a living appearance. There is no event in history that is not associated with a color or a sound.

Epochs of genius have thought, through using the relation of color or noise in relation to the rhythm of death rattles and the tremor of epidemics, to the sound made by a plant that resembles a disease, with a combination of expressions, with the modulations of a sob in which all the torture of humanity torn to pieces by fate is painted, epochs of genius have thought by these means to rediscover the movement of history, to trace anew the flow of fate.

The ancient games were based on this knowledge that tames fate through action. The entire ancient theater was a war against fate.

But to tame fate one must know nature as a whole, and in man one must know consciousness as a whole, consciousness subject to the rhythm of events.

We have the idea of a unitary culture and we call this culture unitary in order to rediscover an idea of unity in all the manifestations of nature that man punctuates with his thought.

The 380 points of Chinese medicine that govern all human functions treat man as a unified whole, just as the universal cure of Paracelsus elevates human consciousness to the plane of divine thought.

Anyone who claims today that there are several cultures in Mexico: the culture of the Maya, of the Toltecs, the Aztecs, the Chichimecs, the Zapotecs, the Totonacs, the Tarascans, the Otomies, etc., does not know what culture is and confuses the multiplicity of forms with the synthesis of a single idea.

There is Muslim esotericism and Brahmanic esotericism; there is Occult Genesis, the Jewish esotericism of the *Zohar* and of the *Sefer-Yetzirah*, and here in Mexico there is the *Chilam Balam* and the *Popul-Vuh*.

Who does not see that all these esotericisms are the same, and mean spiritually the same thing. They indicate the same geometric, numerical, organic, harmonious, occult idea that reconciles man with nature & with life. The signs of these esotericisms are identical. They have profound analogies between their words, their gestures, and their cries.

Of all the esotericisms that exist, Mexican esotericism is the last to be based on blood and the magnificence of an earth whose magick only certain fanatical imitators of Europe can still be ignorant of.

I am for drawing out the occult magick from an earth that bears no resemblance to the egoistical world that persists in walking on its surface & does not see the shadow that falls on it.

THE THEATER AND THE GODS

I did not come here to deliver a Surrealist message; I came to say that Surrealism had become passé in France: and many things have become passé in France which may still continue to be imitated outside of France as if they represented the thought of that country.

The Surrealist attitude was a negative one, and I came to speak of what an entire youth, hungry for positive solutions and who want to regain a taste for life, thinks in my country. And what they think is what they are going to do.

The new aspirations of the youth in France are not something that we can speak of in books, or in newspapers, since we describe a strange disease, a curious epidemic that has nothing to do with life.

In the body of French youth an epidemic of the spirit is burgeoning, which should not be taken for a disease, but which is a terrible demand. It is a characteristic of this time that ideas are no longer ideas, but a Will that will pass into action.

Behind everything that is being done in France currently exists a Will that is ready to take action.

When the young painter Balthus composes a portrait of a woman, he manifests his desire to really transform the woman, to make her conform to what he thought. He manifests through his painting a terrible, demanding notion of love and of women; and he knows he is not speaking in a void, because his painting possesses a secret of action.

He paints like someone who knows the secret of lightning.

Until the secret of lightning has been applied, the world thinks it is science, and leaves that to the scientists; but one day someone applies this secret of lightning, and he applies it to the destruction of the world; it is then that the world begins to consider this secret.

Young people want the secrets of things to be connected to their multiple concerns.

This is also an idea of culture that is not taught in Schools; because behind this idea of culture there is an idea of life that can only hinder the Schools because it destroys their teachings.

This idea of life is magickal, it supposes the presence of fire in all manifestations of human thought; and this image of thought catching fire, it seems to all of us today that it is contained in the theater; and we believe that the theater is only made to manifest it. But today most people think that the theater has nothing to do with reality. When we speak of something that caricatures reality everyone thinks it is theater; while many of us in France believe that only real theater can show us reality.

Europe is in a state of advanced civilization: I mean it is very sick. The spirit of the youth in France wants to react against this state of advanced civilization.

It did not need Keyserling or Spengler to sense the universal decay of a world that lives on the misconceptions of life that the Renaissance left to it. Life seems to us to be in a state of violent loss; we have nothing to do with a new philosophy.

Things are at the point where we can say that, as in other times, the young ran after love, had dreams of ambition, material success, glory, today it has a dream of life; and it is after life that it runs, but this life it pursues, so to speak, *in its essence*: it wants to know why life is sick, and what has spoiled the idea of life.

To find out, it examines the entire universe. It wants to understand nature and Man above the market. Not Man in his singularity, but Man as immense as nature.

When we speak to the youth of Nature, they ask what Nature we want to speak of today. Because they know that, as there are three Internationals, it also has three natures, three staggered Natures.

This too is science.

"There are three suns," said the Emperor Julian, "of which only the first is visible." And Julian the Apostate is not suspected of contributing to Christian spirituality, he who is one of the last representatives of the SCIENCE of the Ancients.

French youth introduce Man into Nature; as it sees the rungs in Nature from the outside in, it also sees the many-tiered Man.

And young people know that theater can convey this lofty idea of man & of nature.

The youth don't believe in betraying life with such a grand idea of the theater, but, contrarily, they think that the theater can help them to cure life.

There are ten thousand ways of dealing with life and belonging to your time. We are against intellectuals indulging in pure speculation in a disorganized world. And we no longer know what the ivory tower is. We are in favor of intellectuals also being part of their time; but we do not think that they can be part of it other than through making war on it.

War for peace.

A great ignorance is responsible for the present spiritual disaster of minds; and there is a very strong current to cauterize that ignorance; I mean to cauterize it scientifically.

For us, life is neither a lazaretto, nor a sanatorium, nor even a laboratory, and we on the other hand do not believe that a culture can be learned with words or with ideas. It is not from outside of its mores that a civilization communicates. Before having pity on the people, we are in favor of reviving the forgotten virtues of a people who could thus, on its own, become civilized.

I say therefore that the youth, not uneasy, but worried, worried about what appears and does not resemble what they think, blames the ignorance of the time.

The youth notices the ignorance of the time as it waits for itself to speak out against it.

When they learn that Chinese medicine, arch-millennium medicine, knew how to cure cholera by arch-millennium means, whereas against cholera European medicine still only knows the barbaric means of flight or cremation, it is not enough for the youth to introduce this medicine into Europe, but they think of the vices of the spirit of Europe & seek to cure this spirit.

They understand that it was not through a trick, but through a deep understanding that China may have known about the nature of cholera.

Culture is this understanding. And there are cultural secrets that texts cannot apprehend.

Before the culture of Europe that is contained in written texts and which believes that culture is lost if texts are destroyed, I say that there is another culture on which other times have lived & that lost culture is based on a materialistic idea of the spirit.

Before the European who knows only his body and who has never been able to dream of organizing nature since he does not see beyond the body, the Chinese, for example, acquire a knowledge of nature through a science of the spirit.

They know the degrees of emptiness & of fullness that describe the ponderable states of the soul; and through the 380 points of the physiological functioning of the soul, the Chinese know how to discover nature and its diseases and it can be said that they were able to discover the nature of diseases.

Jacob Boehme, who believes only in spirits, also knows how to say when spirits are sick, and he describes in all of nature the states that manifest the Wrath of the Spirit.

Those luminaries and others give us a new idea of man. And we are in favor of being taught again what Man is, since other ages have known of him.

We are beginning to detect the Taboos that a frightened and petty science has placed before the vestiges of a culture that knew how to explain life.

The whole man, the man with his cry which can ascend the path of a storm, for Europe it is poetry, but for us, who have a synthetic idea of culture, to get in touch with the cry of a storm is to find a secret of life.

There is a current around the world today that is a claim of culture, the claim for an organic and profound idea of culture, which can explain the life of the spirit.

I call organic culture a culture based on the spirit in relation to the organs, and the spirit bathing in all the organs, and responding at the same time.

There is a sense of space in this culture, and I say that true culture can only be learned in space, and that it is culture oriented, just as is theater.

Culture in space means the culture of a spirit that never ceases to breathe and to feel itself living in space, and which calls to itself the bodies of space as the very objects of its thought, but which as long as the spirit is in *the middle* of space, that is to say at its dead point.

It is perhaps a metaphysical idea, this idea of the dead center of space through which the spirit must pass.

But without metaphysics there is no culture. And what about this notion of space suddenly thrown into culture, if not the assertion that culture is inseparable from life.

"Thirty spokes end at the hub," says the *Tao Te Ching* of Lao-Tse,

"but it is the void that is in the middle which allows the use of the wheel."

When there is agreement in the thoughts of men, where can we say that this agreement is made, if not in the dead void of space.

Culture is a movement of the spirit from emptiness to form, and forms enter into the void, into the void as well as into death. To be cultivated is to burn forms, to burn forms in order to acquire life. It is learning to stand up straight in the incessant movement of forms that are successively destroyed.

The ancient Mexicans knew of no other attitude than this coming and going from death to life.

That terrible inner station, that movement of breathing, that is what culture is, and it moves both in nature and in the spirit.

"But this is metaphysics, but you cannot live in metaphysics."

Now I say precisely that life must live again in metaphysics, & this difficult attitude, which sends people into a panic today, is the attitude of all the pure races who have always *felt both* in death & in life.

This is why culture is not written, and why, as Plato says: "Thought was lost from the day a word was written."

To write is to prevent the spirit from moving in the midst of forms like a vast breath. Since writing fixes the spirit & crystallizes it in a form, and, from form, idolatry is born.

Real theater like culture has never been written.

Theater is an art of space and it is by weighing on the four points of space that it risks affecting life. It is in the space haunted by the theater that things find their figures, and under figures the sound of life.

There is a movement today to separate the theater from all that is not space, and to send the language of the text back to the books it shouldn't have emerged from. And this language of space in turn acts on the nerve sensitivity; it ripens the landscape unfolding below it.

I don't have to repeat here this theory of theater in space, which acts simultaneously through gesture, movement, and noise.

Occupying space, it stalks life & forces it out of its lairs.

It is like the cross with six branches that spreads an occult geometry on the walls of certain temples in Mexico. The Mexican Cross is always surrounded, it is in the center of a wall, it comes from a magickal idea.

To make the cross, the ancient Mexican puts himself in the center of a kind of void, and the cross grows around him.

It is not a cross to encrypt space as scientists today think; it is a cross to reveal how life enters space, and how to find the bottom of life from outside space.

Always the void, always the point, around which matter thickens.

The Mexican Cross indicates the rebirth of life.

I looked for a long time at the Gods of Mexico in the Codex, and it appeared to me that those Gods were above all Gods in space and that the Mythology of the Codex hid a science of space with its Gods like shadow holes, and its shadows where life roars.

That is, without literature, those Gods were not born of chance, but they are in life as in a theater, and they occupy the four corners of the consciousness of Man where nestles sound, gesture, the word, and the breath that spits out life.

Who still thinks of feeling the Gods and searching for the place of the Gods. To search for their place is to seek their strength and to give oneself the strength of a God. The White World calls those Gods idols, but the Indian spirit knows how to vibrate the strength of the Gods, by locating their musics of strength; and the theater, by a musical distribution of forces, calls to itself the power of the Gods. Each has its place in the vibrant space of images. The Gods come out toward us through a cry or through a face, and the color of the face has its cry; and the cry is worth its weight of images in the Space where Life ripens.

For me, these rotating Gods, who take up lines, lines to probe space, as if they were afraid of not feeling space well enough, give us a concrete means of understanding the formation of life. This fear of empty space that haunts Mexican artists, and makes them throw line after line, is not only an invention of lines, of shapes that flatter the eye, it indicates a need to *ripen* the void. To populate space to cover the void is to find the way to the void. It is to start from a blooming line and then to fall dizzily into the void.

And the Gods of Mexico that revolve around the void provide a sort of quantified means of regaining the forces of a void without which there is no reality.

And I think that finally the Gods of Mexico are the Gods of Life in the grip of a loss of strength, of a vertigo of thought; and that the lines which rise above their heads give a melodious and rhythmic means of raising thought above thought.

They invite the spirit not to petrify itself, but on the contrary, so to speak, *to walk*.

"I go to war," the God seems to say, holding a war machine in its fist, and holding it out before him; "And on top of that advance I think," says a sort of flashing line that zigzags above his head. — And this line, at some point in space, multiplies again.

"And if I think, I probe my strength," says the line behind him. "I call the force out of which I emerged."

This is how, in their inhuman form, those Gods, who are not content with their mere human stature, show how Man could emerge from them. — Because I also think that there is a harmony in such lines, a kind of essential geometry that corresponds to the image of a noise.

For the theater a line is a noise, a movement is a music, and the gesture that emerges from a noise is like a clear word in a sentence.

The Gods of Mexico have open lines, they indicate everything that has emerged, but at the same time they offer the means of entering into something.

The Mythology of Mexico is an open Mythology. And Mexico, that of yesterday and that of today, is in turn holding open forces. You don't have to push very far in a Mexican landscape to feel everything that comes out of it. It is the only place on earth that offers us occult life, and *offers it on the surface of life*.

MEXICO

THE POST-WAR THEATER IN PARIS

In the post-war theater movement in France I will try to discern a movement that is both that of the theater and that of the French spirit.

For this, it would not be sufficient to have attended all the shows which, from 1920 to 1936, left their mark on Paris, but, I can say that I was involved in the intimate life of the theater, in its troubles, in its failures, its hopes, its difficulties, & sometimes also its triumphs.

I have worked as an actor or director in no less than ten theaters: the Œuvre, the Atelier, the Vieux-Colombier, the Comédie des Champs-Élysées, the Studio des Champs-Élysées, the Théâtre de Grenelle, the Théâtre Pigalle, the Théâtre de l'Avenue, & the Théâtre Folies-Wagram.

I personally knew intimately, and I have worked with all the prominent individuals of the theater: Lugné-Poe, Sylvain, Charles Dullin, Jacques Copeau, Louis Jouvet, Georges & Ludmilla Pitoëff, Suzanne Desprès, Gaston Baty, Valentine Tessier, Génica Athanasiou, Roger Karl, Falconetti.

I attended the period of maturity of the Théâtre de l'Œuvre, before the departure of Lugné-Poe, and daily lived the first adventures of the nascent Atelier, which persisted perilously for three years, always at the edge of disaster until one day it could finally stand firm.

It is not a mere list of actors, an inert record of achievements, that I want to give here, but the life and the animating spirit of the theater in France that, just a few months ago, gave birth to a mysterious phenomenon.

In Paris, in 1920, as the Vieux-Colombier reopened its doors, a few great actors roamed the stage of the Comédie-Française: Sylvain, De Max, Paul Mounet, etc.

In avant-garde theaters, we had fun making people laugh while counteracting the tics of the great actors: we imitated the throaty, sonorous voice of Paul Mounet, that big, heavy voice of Cerberus and of earthquakes, and his passive and mechanical style.

We mocked the expression of De Max's mouth and other peculiarities, such as his particular way of turning and standing up with studied attitudes; and we would say: "This is exactly what one must not do."

But, in my opinion, despite their quirks, these tragedians were the last to uphold the heroic tradition of the theater. And with them now dead, it must be stated, no tragedy has really been performed in Paris.

Sylvain had an amusing way of wrapping his arms together, at the height of the solar plexus; he also used to stress certain syllables with a slap of his chest.

De Max, without knowing the meaning of his gesture, pricked his solar eye with the tip of his index finger — he sought, with that finger, to find the survival of the third eye and the place of what, in the Metaphysics of India, is called the pineal gland.

In all such exaggerated gestures one must see the instinctive survival of a magick whose meaning is no longer known to those who practice it, and those who laugh at it laugh without knowing why. And I would even say that if, at that moment, they could know what in them was laughing, they would be afraid of themselves.

This is where we can find the reason for the movement of religious terror that seized the crowds at the Colonial Exhibition in Paris in 1931 when they could see the actor from the Balinese Theater advancing toward them and, after stomping three or four times and executing a curious upward movement of the hips, touching on his head the third eye.

When De Max touched his head, we had to translate:
I think with my dark head. I search in my tormented head for the lost place of thought.

But when the actor of the Balinese Theater taps his head, we should translate:

I am aware of a lost pain; I point to the lost place with one eye in the head of criminal humanity. I appeal to this science that men lost in the early days of the Dark Age. That is, 60 centuries ago. Because, as we know, the Dark Age, for the Hindus, began 3120 years before Christ.

This is indeed, when we penetrate into it, what true theater manages to suggest to us.

In Germany, a staging is being invented; in Russia, the staging of the masses; but in France, one of the rare countries in the world where from nothingness even they manage to extract something, in France they have been able, almost without means, to find the secret life of the theater just as Arthur Rimbaud knew how to discover anew the secret life of poetry...

But I come back to the alchemy of theater in France, to its new beginnings in the post-war years, that moment when life in Paris was emerging.

It was Lugné-Poe who presented Jarry, Strindberg, and Ibsen to the French, brought to the stage *The Creditors*, *Hedda Gabler*, *Ghosts*, *The Dollhouse*, etc., in the small private room of the Cité Moncey, at number 55 rue de Clichy, in Paris.

L'Œuvre is a "closed" theater where only subscribers have access. One day, I go there to attend a performance, without having previously paid for a subscription, I meet Lugné-Poe, who invites me to come in without paying and proposes that I work in his theater. That same year, I started out as an administrator, handyman, prompter, actor, and extra.

Backstage, I witnessed Jean Sarment's acting debut in *Ghosts*, *Hedda Gabler*, *The Dollhouse*, etc., and, on stage itself, the following year, Lugné-Poe's astonishing creation in *The Magnificent Cuckold*, by Crommelynck.

In this role Lugné-Poe created an unforgettable type of intellectual buffoon, introducing on the French stage a composition in the style of Brueghel, with a sort of voice that seemed to growl from the shadows, and cascades of laughter followed cascades of expressions that rolled from his head to his feet.

As an actor, Lugné-Poe was often uneven; the dramatic performance bored him. He acts with contempt for the public. But if he does step into his role, the entire room laughs loudly. He is, from head to toe, a complete actor. His surprising changes of voice, his fingers that become pointed, his fiery gazes at times remind one of a now lost tradition of the theater. It looks like we are in the presence of an actor from the *Mysteries of the Middle Ages in France*.

Yet it is on a completely different side of the theater, without gestures, with only her voice, an Argentinian voice that sobs, that in D'Annunzio's moving work Suzanne Desprès weeps over her severed hands.

Around the same year, 1920, Durec, who died shortly after, had performed in an Icelandic play, *Desire*, by Sigurdjöhnson, the role of a magician trapped in his evil spells when he believed himself to be the possessor of the secret. I do not remember ever having heard such a voice of the possessed in any theater until one day in *The Dybbuk* I heard Marguerite Jamois literally screaming after her soul.

1920 was again the year in which Jacques Copeau, at the Vieux-Colombier, brought to the stage the Unanimiste School, which is also a school of naturalism and simplicity. Unanimism is populism avant la lettre, but a populism that deliberately exalts the forces of reality.

To this school belong Charles Vildrac, Luc Durtain, Georges Chennevière, Georges Duhamel, Jules Romains and, in a way, Jean Schlumberger.

It was above all the decor that made Charles Vildrac's *Paquebot Tenacity* successful. Before a glass door opening on to a verdigris light, Copeau evokes all the misty nostalgia for a port in a Nordic country.

The Vieux-Colombier was the first French stage to be equipped with modern lighting, and also the first to adopt stylized decor. It was the first attempt in France of what has been called "constructive decoration." Walls and stage levels, from the perspective of the decor, are like an immense set of cubes with the help of which we create a palace, an underground passage, an alley, a cave, a mountain, an immensity.

I will never forget, in André Gide's *Saul*, staged in 1922, this vault open to light, a ghostly green light in which Saul-Copeau was engulfed.

In addition to the stylization of the decor, Copeau's staging brings into play the stylization of costumes such as that of the attitudes in the *Night of the Kings*, *Princess Turandot*, *The Brothers Karamazov*, *The Death of Sparta*. He composes vast frescoes in which the connoisseur of museums, the lover of painting with refined taste, and the talented literary man prove themselves.

With Copeau the spirit of the theater consists in subjugating the staging to the text, in bringing out the staging of the text by means of an intelligent twist of this very text. Because, for Copeau, it is the text, the word, which he embraces above all, he therefore has a Shakespearean conception of gesture, movement, attitudes, and decor. In short, it is the submission of the theater to the language of written literature. Only, here it is: subsequently, the French theater continued his approach.

In October 1921, Charles Dullin, defector of Vieux-Colombier, founded the Théâtre de l'Atelier.

Dullin had already emerged as an actor before the war with what one might call his dark creation of Smerdiakov in Dostoyevsky's *The Brothers Karamazov* in 1913 at the Théâtre des Arts.

Dullin is one of the last actors in France to possess real, overwhelming intensity in action, and his acting sometimes conjures up the image of a perforating machine breaking through the toughest walls.

To found the Théâtre de l'Atelier, Dullin had not only left the Vieux-Colombier, he had also left the Comédie Montaigne directed by Gémier, where, in 1920, the revelation of Marguerite Jamois had taken place in *les Amants puérils*, by Crommelynck.

A new interpretation of Paul Claudel's work, *The Announcement of Mary*, was given on that same stage, which was a triumph for Eve Francis. In the scene from "The Mystical Birth," this actress was particularly moving. It was also at the Comédie Montaigne that Lenormand's *Simoun* was premiered, this play where the desert wind blows above men.

The beginnings of the Atelier were epic. Dullin wanted to resuscitate the spirit of the ancient companions of the Middle Ages, of those traveling troupes where the actor was at the same time craftsman, poet, author, beggar, and adventurer.

In his troop everyone worked, with their hands as well as with their heads. The actors turned into masons, painters, machinists, administrators, improvisers, tailors. It was the intoxication of work. Work above all. Food was for after. And this heroic love of the theater very often made us forget to eat.

L'Atelier held out for three years in total uncertainty of tomorrow, each day on the verge of falling into the precipice to which its creditors called it. Such heroism finally found its reward in the triumph of *Volpone*, by Ben Johnson, a work in which a blood-red decoration vibrated, like a flag fluttering in the sun.

From 1921 to 1936, L'Atelier achieved its most brilliant success with *The Occasion*, by Prosper Mérimée, *The Miser*, by Molière, *Life is a Dream*, by Calderon, *Antigone*, by Jean Cocteau, *Volpone*, by Ben Johnson, *The Birds* and *Peace*, by Aristophanes.

I have some personal memories of Cocteau's *Antigone*. In this "reduced tragedy" I played the role of the soothsayer Tiresias, Dullin played that of Creon, and Génica Athanasiou was Antigone.

If in this play there was a truly human triumph, it was the tragedian Athanasiou who returned for her interpretation of Antigone.

I will never forget the golden, quivering, mysterious voice of Athanasiou-Antigone bidding farewell to the sun.

Her plaint came from beyond time, and as if carried by the foam of a wave on the Mediterranean Sea, on a sun-drenched day; it sounded like flesh music spreading through icy darkness. It was truly the voice of archaic Greece, with the virginal flesh, when from the depths of the labyrinth Minos suddenly saw the Minotaur crystallize.

In 1925, the Vieux-Colombier finished in style. Copeau, disappointed by the relative failure of his work, *The Native House*, left the stage.

Copeau cultivated the graceful, fantastic, enchanting genre; he never cared about tragedy. But the Vieux-Colombier left some of its greatest players as a bequest to present-day France: Louis Jouvet, Charles Dullin, Roger Karl, Valentine Tessier, Bacqué, Bouquet, and Auguste Boverio.

The cycle of the Vieux-Colombier, which began with *Les Fourberies de Scapin* where the actor launched himself into the text like a runner, ended with *The Native House*. The Compagnie des Quinze led by Michel Saint-Denis takes the plastic principles of Copeau to their limits with regard to staging.

It was in 1923 that Jacques Hébertot launched Rolf de Maré's Ballets Suédois at the Théâtre des Champs-Elysées. Under his direction, this auditorium was transformed into a sort of large theater factory where various trends met.

Cocteau recounted this anecdote in a book: the mysterious way in which Picasso, in the twilight of a December evening in 1922, invented the set for *Antigone*. I was privileged to witness this strange flowering myself.

Here and there, behind a few blue cloth rocks, lamps had been placed. A wall, also of blue canvas, rising to the height of an arch, and in the center a panoply of revolving masks. Below the panoply hung a wide strip of cardboard, about two meters wide by three meters high. The material of this was grainy and reddish, the color of the volcanic stones that in Mexico were used to build colonial palaces. The red of burnt blood; but it would have taken just one drop of water to turn that ruddy blood into faded pink.

Picasso, having rolled up his sleeves, walked forward as if he had been both a tamer, wrestler, surveyor, prestidigitator... and then we could see his stocky black back moving. Lines rose on the pink surface. Picasso threw himself backward, reflected, oriented himself, and the lines around him began to spring out like a living geometry.

Even more than he drew, he felt. The lines sprang out, one might say fatally. And those lines made up a geometry that was going to support who knows what, something which, in the middle of the wall, would quickly set ablaze who knows what thing... His hand went back and forth — like the hand of a seer — and suddenly, in front of us, as if drawn by an authentic magick, we could contemplate a brilliant column. A Doric style colonnade. In truth, Picasso did the work with all the vigor of a man.

In 1923, Gaston Baty, who had cut his teeth as a director with Gémier at the Comédie Montaigne, had the Baraque de la Chimère built, near Saint-Germain-des-Prés.

The Chimera managed to present a number of minor authors; and it was from their works that critics deduced the "theory of the theater of silence"; a theory which, in fact, the authors themselves rejected.

The star of the Baty shows was Ms. Jamois. She plays with her eyes and, if I may put it this way, reluctantly. Beneath her eyes in which the tides overflow, her mouth is like a recumbent blade that throbs to leap, to live.

For me, it was in the *Dybbuk* that Jamois made her great creation. We know the argument of this play. A young theology student is forced to separate from the woman he loves and who was, *theologically*, fated for him. The student dies the instant he goes to reveal his big secret and the way it all unfolds can make him think he's already dead when he reveals his secret. At the moment of death, his spirit begins to prowl about and comes to be incarnated in this woman; and, in an extraordinary scene, Marguerite Jamois speaks with the very voice of the man who claims what was intended for her, that is to say the woman, that is to say herself.

I saw Jamois in almost all of these creations. I saw her acting, her eyes closed & her mouth closed, closed beings. In this work, she embodied a being enclosed within herself, but who spoke from the depths of herself; & the voice with which this being claimed her property is one of the most terrible things that I have heard.

Baty has a theory of the theater. For him, the text, in contrast to Copeau's conceptions, is no more than one element of the stage, and the light plays its part in the whole. But when one attends the shows brought to the stage by Baty, it does not appear that he has succeeded in fully realizing his ideas.

If in the theater the text is not everything, if light is also a language, this means that the theater retains the notion of another language that uses text, light, gesture, movement, noise. It is the speech, the secret speech that no language can translate. It is in a way the language lost since the fall of Babel. This language, this lost tongue, this sort of ancient madness, this vertiginous utopia, in France some men believed they had found it in the theater.

Baty obtained with *Maya* and *Dybbuk*, and, most recently, with *Crime and Punishment*, some of the greatest public successes of post-war theater in Paris.

In 1923, Jacques Hébertot brought together in his city of theater, Avenue Montaigne, in Paris, four avant-garde directors: Louis Jouvet, Gaston Baty, Georges Pitoëff, & Komisarjevsky. At the same time, he gave asylum to the Ballets Russes, the Ballets Suédois, and *The Brides of the Eiffel Tower*, by Cocteau; to music as well as avant-garde painting of the years 1920–1926. We could see sets by

Picasso, Braque, Othon Friesz, Derain, de Chirico, and even Surrealists like Max Ernst & Joan Miró. The Surrealist group rose up against what they called a betrayal of Surrealist painting, and there was a memorable scandal in which Ernst and Miró were taken to task. Multicolored butterflies were seen tumbling down from the galleries, accusing them of betraying pure poets. Aragon was seen, shrieking breathlessly, running like a madman, at the risk of falling, on the parapets of the loges on the third floor. And like a shroud, a huge black flag fell over the bare shoulders of the worldly ladies.

At the same time, on the third floor of the theater, Georges Pitoëff directed *Liliom*, by Ferenc Molnar, and *He Who Receives Slaps*, by Andréiev. And Komisarjevsky introduced *R.U.R., Robot*, by Čapek.

Pitoëff first gained fame in Paris in 1919 with Lenormand's *Les Ratés* and an Irish play, *The Playboy of the Western World*.

In directing, Pitoëff's discoveries were in lighting and atmosphere. Thanks to him, for the first time, Russian plays, *The Power of Darkness*, by Tolstoy, and *Uncle Vanya*, by Chekov, were shown to the French public in a truly Russian atmosphere. For the first time on a French stage we therefore had, with Pitoëff, the feeling that an actor was playing with his own life and was ready to give his life. But the great revelation of Pitoëff's theater was undoubtedly Ludmilla Pitoëff. Who has not seen her cry before Liliom's corpse does not know what it is to cry, not only on stage, but in life, for Ludmilla is a soul in whom one feels life pulsate.

Louis Jouvet, who was an actor with Copeau and who, among other things, knew how to cultivate the authentic violence of an actor, presented with Hébertot a theater of stage technique; and there is no one like Jouvet to know the stage both as an actor, a director, an architect, and lighting designer.

Later, Jouvet was able to found his own theater, and the style of decor and lighting in the style of Jouvet is known today in Paris and around the world.

Jouvet's great theatrical discovery was Jean Giraudoux, who from a sophisticated and stylized writer turned into a stylized and sophisticated playwright. And all those who have a taste for gymnastics and the cabrioles of thought will take pleasure in the plays of Giraudoux.

In 1925, a year which seems to have been fateful for the theater and from which a whole world will emerge, a mysterious man appeared who lived in rooms without furniture and who was later called "the dervish" because he claimed to have spent several years of his life among the dervishes of the Caucasus.

At the revival of *Pelléas et Mélisande*, by Maeterlinck, in a scenic arrangement by Copeau, I was surprised by an extraordinary lighting system; now the light truly lived, smelled, gave off an odor, had become a kind of new personage. And bringing light to his sets and his actors seemed to be the last of the "dervish's concerns."

A light that does not illuminate and from which seems to emanate a strong smell, there is in it, I thought, a rare spirit.

And one evening, in a cafe, a hundred yards from the theater, I found myself before an irascible character, with a large mustache, his face twisted like a vine branch, who answered with insults every question that was put to him.

And in the midst of these insults, at times, a strange idea of nature and life seemed to emerge.

"It was Salzmann," I am told, "the author of the lighting style that made such an impression on you."

"Would you believe," he replied, "that those fools could not see that that light was sensitivity, that there is no light without sensitivity?"

And for over three hours, walking from Place de l'Alma to Gare Saint-Lazare, we spent a terrible February night together talking…

There were only idiots for him. Life, in the minds of present-day humanity, was no more than an obscure notion. And the men of the theater were the dumbest of all. "These dark lights that have moved you," he said to me, "they find them too dark. It is because they have not yet reached a notion superior to that of the five senses: smell, taste, touch, sight, hearing. As if the theater was not made to transgress the world of the senses. The life of the senses, we live it daily. If the theater does not help us to surpass ourselves, what will it be used for!…"

And then I spoke to him about a lost language that could be found in the theater. His response was that poetry, true poetry, & not the poetry of poets, keeps this language secret, and that some sacred dances come closer to the secret of this poetry than any other language.

Salzmann was an engineer, architect, and inventor. He had built on the stage of the Théâtre des Champs-Elysées a sort of luminous arc that carried no less than sixty thousand lights.

Salzmann died last year in Switzerland from a cancerous throat tumor.

But since then we have been able to see on stage lighting in the style of Salzmann where a certain way of handling the light, as if we were playing a color organ, and which we find in the lighting of Jouvet, comes directly from his ideas.

In June 1927, the Théâtre Alfred Jarry was founded. At the now demolished Théâtre de Grenelle it presented two performances of a Surrealist play, *Les Mystères de l'Amour,* by Roger Vitrac.

Athanasiou obtained in the role of Léa the second triumph of her career; it is a work in which she must multiply and transform from butcher into tamer, seductress, passionate esthete in the style of Burne-Jones. The play owed its success to the way it was staged. For the first time on stage real objects could be seen: a bed, a cupboard, a stove, a coffin, all of this subject to a Surrealist order, which is disorder for ordinary reality, responding to the deep logic of dreams on the point of suddenly being realized in life. Multicolored lights that responded to the same strange logic, to an identical concern for balance and musicality, spread profusely over things, coming from multiple sources.

From 1927 to 1930 the Théâtre Alfred Jarry ran: *The Mysteries of Love, Partage de Midi, The Dream, Victor or the Children in Power.*

The extraordinary performances of the Théâtre Balinais at the Colonial Exhibition in July 1931, which were a brilliant success, are, for me, part of the theatrical movement in France; there is indeed a strange resemblance in spirit between the shows at the Théâtre Alfred Jarry and those at the Théâtre Balinais. Both, one would say, were nourished by their own magickal sources of the same primitive unconscious, this unconscious into which the bitter impulse of its research plunges the Théâtre Alfred Jarry and of which the Théâtre Balinais seems to know by tradition the secret sources.

In reality, all French theater, since the war, has felt driven by a confused desire to return to a certain tradition.

It is not about any particular tradition, more or less linked to a certain social conservatism. French theater has also been bitten by a general anxiety and is participating in this immense revision of values that characterizes the world today.

If the Freudian "unconscious" made its appearance with Lenormand and Pirandello, that does not mean that this appearance had a great success.

On all sides we are returning to the sources: that of the fatherland, that of the family, that of love, that of paternity. All the great problems of humanity are evoked, considered, reactivated. During the year 1932 one could see manifesting itself in several plays a real obsession with incest, & in works such as *The Criminals* and *The Evil Youth*, by Bruckner, one returns to the very sources of morality and of the despair of life.

All of this should be seen as a sign of disorder and of research where research prevails over disorder.

What results from this gathering, from this shattering of values, is a depreciation, an abandonment, a loss of the feeling attached to human individuality. One runs away from disjointed feelings. One no longer sees two beings face to face striving out of love to unite their unique individualities, but two beings attempting one above the other to attain an idea of humanity.

It is not a mere coincidence that in avant-garde French theater the main attempts at research have focused on directing. This is because it was urgent, thanks to the development of external scenic possibilities, to rediscover this physical language that French theater had entirely forgotten for four centuries; and, by developing such possibilities, it is not for the French theater to seek to discover a decorative effect; no, what it claims to find under the decorative effect is the universal language that unites it to the entire space.

French theater seeks space to multiply its expression in space; it wants, like Mexican art, to make space flourish because it believes that the theater had until now forgotten to make it speak.

And making space speak is to give a voice to surfaces and masses; and that is why we despise individualities today. It can be said that for too long, "the ménage à trois" which for the foreigners represented the theater in France, has no longer been part of the French theater. Only a few Anglo-Saxon tourists now come to study a boulevard stage for the remnants of this outdated theatricality.

Jean-Louis Barrault is the representative in Paris of this search for a spatial theater, with a hidden internal life. This is not a social theater, although it does not stop being; it is a theater of masses; it is, more than a social theater, a theater of human anguish in reaction against fate. It is a theater of the human revolt that does not accept the law of fate; it is a theater filled with cries that are not cries of fear but cries of rage, and even more than of rage, of the feeling of the value of life.

It is a theater which knows how to cry, but which has an enormous awareness of laughter, and which knows that there is in laughter a pure idea, a beneficent and pure idea of the eternal forces of life.

OPEN LETTER
TO THE GOVERNORS
OF THE STATES OF MEXICO

Gentlemen, Governors,

I came to Mexico on a mission from the French National Education Secretariat.

The purpose of this mission is to study all manifestations of Mexican theatrical art; but it is in life that I want to do it, not on the boards.

And it is the indigenous art of Mexico that interests me here above all.

For me, the culture of Europe has failed and I believe that in the unbridled development of its machines Europe has betrayed true culture; and myself, in turn, I want to be a traitor to the European conception of progress.

The sacred Indian rites and dances are the most beautiful possible form of theater and the only one that can really justify itself.

So far these rites have interested only archæologists & artists.

Archaeologists have spoken of them as scholars, that is to say very badly; artists have spoken of them as artists, which is to say even more badly. They did not know how to extract both the secret science and the deep meaning these rites conceal.

There are predestined places on earth, made to preserve the culture of the world. And in France, the enlightened, but also worried, anxious youth, and I would say even desperate, are now turning their gaze with all their soul to these predestined places.

Present-day Tibet and Mexico are the nuclei of the culture of the world. But the culture of Tibet is made for the dead; this is where we can still learn, to detach ourselves from life, the technical means of dying well.

The eternal culture of Mexico was always made for the living. In the Maya hieroglyphs, in the vestiges of Toltec culture, one can still discover the means of living well; to drive sleep from the organs, to keep the nerves in a state of perpetual exaltation, that is, completely open to immediate light, water, earth, and wind.

Yes, I believe in a force sleeping in the land of Mexico. And it is for me the only place in the world where sleep the natural forces that can be useful to the living. I believe in the magickal reality of these forces as one believes in the salutary and curative power of certain waters.

I believe that Indian rites are the direct manifestations of these forces. I do not want to study them either as an archeologist or as an artist, I will study them as a scientist, in the true sense of the term; and I will try to let myself be consciously penetrated by their soul healing virtues. When human magnetism is exhausted, one must return to the earth to regain one's strength.

The primitive rites of the Indians are in communication with the earth, and their dances, their animated hieroglyphics, their occult movements, unconsciously translate its laws.

Between the earth and man, the spirit of man periodically interposes, disturbing the pure forces of the earth by extracting from them the mire of divine superstitions.

But just as periodically the natural forces of the earth reappear and put an end to the false spirits of the gods.

I want to thank the Government of Mexico here for allowing me to get in touch with the true culture of Mexico; and I want to thank the Governors of the States in advance for their help, hoping that they will enable me to travel to any place where the red soil of Mexico continues to truly speak its language.

UNIVERSAL FOUNDATIONS OF CULTURE

Today, in Europe, culture, like instruction, like education, is a luxury that can be bought. It's the best proof that the meaning of words is being lost and there is nothing like confusion in words to reveal a state of decadence that has now become widespread in Europe. This is why, before discussing culture, I must clarify the meaning of this word. I will first say what everyone means by that or believe they hear, then I will say what it really means. We speak of cultivated man and we speak of cultivated land, and in this way we express an action, an almost material transformation of man and of the earth. One can be educated without being really cultured. Education is a garment. The word instruction signifies that a person has clothed himself with knowledge. It is a veneer whose presence does not necessarily imply the fact of having assimilated this knowledge. The word culture, on the other hand, means that the earth, the deep humus of man, has been cleared. Education is generally confused with culture, and in Europe, where words no longer mean anything, in everyday speech the words education and culture are used to express one and the same thing, when in reality it is about two things that are profoundly different. And even if we do not, strictly speaking, confuse education and culture, we place them on the same level; we consider them as going hand in hand, when everything we see around us proves to us that the scattered, contradictory culture of Europe no longer has anything to do with the absolutely uniform state of its civilization.

When I arrived in Mexico and spoke of its ancient culture, people from all sides more or less replied: "but there are a hundred cultures in Mexico!" — proof that Mexicans today have forgotten even the meaning of the word culture and confuse uniform culture with a multiplicity of forms of civilization. As distinct as its civilizations were, ancient Mexico had in reality only one culture, that is, a unique idea of man, of nature, of death, of life; on the contrary, modern Europe, which has known how to standardize its civilization, has infinitely multiplied its conception of culture and, relative to the very idea of culture, it is, one can say, in complete anarchy.

If Europe conceives of culture as a veneer, it is because it has forgotten what culture was during the epochs when it truly existed; words have in fact a rigorous meaning, and it is not possible to extract from the word culture its profound meaning, its meaning of integral modification, even magickal one might say, not of man but of being in man, because the truly cultivated man carries his spirit in his body and it is his body that he works through culture, which is equivalent to saying that he works his spirit at the same time.

Europe imagined that culture was contained in books, and every European nation has its books, that is, its philosophy. A multitude of systems have been born in recent years, each of which corresponds to the appearance of a new book, and not only each nation, but each political party has its own system too. And contrary to what happened in the great eras when philosophers ruled life & gave birth to politics, each new political system creates philosophers who try to justify its demagoguery.

Marxism, a political system based on a certain number of elementary verifications in matters of economy, produced a whole materialist conception of the world. Italy is so spiritually impoverished that it could not even generate a single philosopher, yet Hitlerian Fascism has its philosophers whose system is a monstrous hodgepodge of Nietzsche, Kant, Herder, Fichte, and Schelling. In Europe, alongside the prophets of the new West, we find the prophets of the decline of the West, and alongside serious men, such as Spengler, Scheller, and Heidegger, we find the little masters of the decline who, like Keyserling, are nothing other than traveling salesmen, amateurs of a shoddy Hinduism and, beyond measure, cat burglars of the theme of the unconscious, from the Freudian form to the American one, this unconscious of which they imagine they do spectroscopy. For me, nothing could be more odious than the philosophical snobbery of a Keyserling, especially when this snobbery, beliefs on which the primitive & occult life of humanity nourished itself, barely knows how to make a fashionable object.

There is no sacred philosophy or great culture that Keyserling has not touched in order to odiously popularize its doctrines whereas, for their manifestation, the ancient Brahmins of India sometimes went so far as to sacrifice their lives. Keyserling's case is aggravated by the fact that he deduced a system, I mean a personal dogma, from traditions that represented the collective and anonymous wisdom of immense countries and epochs, when the men who were the vehicles of those traditions and those doctrines were always careful not to appropriate them individually. In this, Keyserling obeys the individualistic, anarchic spirit of a Europe that currently has as many philosophies as philosophers and as many cultures as philosophies.

For two or three years we have been talking in a grotesque way of the United States of Europe. It would have been more profitable to speak of the total imbalance of European culture because the lamentable state of this dust of cultures that today represents Europe would have been for everyone the very proof that the United States of Europe was already nothing more than an antiquated buffoonery.

FIRST CONTACT WITH THE MEXICAN REVOLUTION

The current global crisis has reached France after the other countries, but, although this is not so evident, it has affected France more seriously. Unlike what is happening elsewhere, today's France is suffering more acutely from the crisis in its consciousness than from the one affecting its capital and its wealth, & French youth are particularly sensitive to the effects of this crisis. Anyone who knew Paris three years ago and returned there now would not recognize it. In appearance the city has changed little, but the life of Paris, its vibrancy, its youth, its activity, its zest, its pleasurableness, that is what has changed terribly. It is above all the youth who suffer, and there is nothing that so profoundly affects the life of a country as much as the illness of its youth.

I would not say that French youth have lost hope; I would say that they are touched in the very springs of hope because they are on the verge of losing confidence in the resources of life. The government is concerned with keeping prices up on essential items so that they are not sold at a loss, thus allowing French peasants to maintain their old standard of living, but it is not at all concerned, as here, with the lives of the youth. And the French youth, left to themselves — I am speaking above all of young painters, sculptors, actors, filmmakers, etc., — are close to despair.

It is therefore unnecessary to describe my emotion when, upon arrival here, I saw what care the revolutionary government of Mexico takes in the works of its youth; I spoke with artists, painters, revolutionary intellectuals, and also with musicians; the Department of Fine Arts, headed by Prof. Muñoz Cota, did me the honor of inviting me to its Children's Theater Conference as a delegate of the French Republic; and I was able to realize that the Mexican revolution has a soul, a living soul, an exacting soul that not even the Mexicans can say how far it can take them. This is what is so moving about the revolutionary movement in Mexico. Young Mexico is forging on, determined to remake a world, and in reconstructing this world, it withdraws from no transformation. Question the young revolutionaries of Mexico, none will give you the same answer; this chaos of opinions is the best proof of the dynamism of the revolution. The youth all agree that the life of Mexico must be socialist, of course, but opinions differ as to the means to be employed to achieve this socialism of Mexico totally and quickly.

These very differences have their own force of exaltation. The consciousness of present-day Mexico is a chaos where the new forces of a world are at boiling point. And if the youth of France despair, the youth of Mexico are certainly not close to despair, as I was able to realize on the occasion of this conference on Children's

Theater at which I was asked to give a speech on the dynamism of puppet shows.

It must be said that French youth, currently in full effervescence, stirs up the most daring ideas, sometimes without being aware of it. Thus, as regards the theater more specifically, a new concept has emerged in recent years. Abandoning the research of Jacques Copeau, for example, purely plastic research where the staging only embellishes the text & is strictly conditioned by it, we seek to rediscover, to invent a pure language that is the very language of the theater. That is to say that literature, the written word, dialogue, cease to hold the first place in a theater thus conceived. The staging is no longer conditioned by the text, but we tend to remake the text, as in the Mystery Plays of the Middle Ages, as the servant, the slave of an order come from far off, from the very sources of the language in the mythical ages when language, the primitive idiom uttered by man, merged with the organic power of breath. Little by little, modern French theater is en route to rediscovering the very necessity, the central and moving necessity of expression. This means that the theater is abandoning literature, is abandoning books to find the space of the stage, to be deployed in the entire perspective of space, because theater is an art in space and it was necessary at all costs to recover consciousness of the spatial value of expression. Sound, movement, light, gesture, voice, and even the shape of the voice are part of this new language of theater. It is primarily because of the way in which it is pronounced and the place where it is pronounced that speech lives, and what is most alive is the rhythmic beat of the breath, which is solar and lunar, male and female, active and passive. There is a whole technique of breathing that a young actor, Jean-Louis Barrault, fresh out of Charles Dullin's Théâtre de l'Atelier, has begun to study in detail.

I presented this technique in my talk on the dynamism of puppets. I had already described it in the "Manifesto of the Theater of Cruelty" which appeared in the October 1932 issue of *La Nouvelle Revue Française*, and in an article on the ternary numbers of the Cabala and their application to the art of theater, an article which will appear in the next issue of *Revista de la Universidad* under the title "An Affective Athleticism."

All this seemingly arid and surly technique actually expresses is an elementary and very simple thing. But it is essential. Whether we admit it or not, there is a profound idea of culture here, and it is this essential idea of culture that forms all the hopes of young French intellectuals today.

French youth are suffering today, are enduring the pangs of a real childbirth, and they have a revolutionary idea of culture. What I came to seek in the land of Mexico is precisely an echo, or rather a source, a real physical source of this revolutionary force. And with the French youth I count on the support of the Mexican youth to help us to release this force & this idea.

The effort that I ask of the youth of Mexico, which I also ask of the Mexican revolution, will be great, and it must be terribly effective.

In short, we expect from Mexico a new concept of Revolution, and also a new concept of Man, which will serve to nourish, to feed with its magickal life this ultimate form of humanism, being born in France, with a spirit diametrically opposed to the spirit of the XVIth century.

As you may be aware, on the subject of the Mexican revolution, Europe is currently in a state of complete phantasmagoria, in the grip of a kind of collective hallucination. It is close to seeing the Mexicans of today, dressed in the costumes of their ancestors, actually sacrificing to the sun on the steps of the pyramid of Teotihuacán. I assure you that I am hardly joking. In any case, one has heard of grand theatrical reconstructions that took place on this same pyramid, and one believes in good faith that there was in Mexico a well-defined anti-European movement, just as one believes that modern Mexico wanted to found its revolution on the basis of a return to the pre-Cortézian tradition. A fancy of this kind circulates in the most advanced intellectual circles in Paris. In short, people believe that the Mexican revolution is a revolution of the indigenous soul, a revolution to conquer anew the *indigenous soul* as it existed before Cortés.

This was to have been the subject of the investigation that I was asked to undertake here.

However, it does not seem to me that the revolutionary youth of Mexico care much for the indigenous soul. And this is where the drama arises. When I came to Mexico, I dreamed of an alliance between French youth and Mexican youth with a view to fostering a unique cultural effort, but this alliance does not seem possible to me as long as Mexican youth remain solely Marxist. Marxism claims to be scientific, it speaks of a mass mentality, but it does not destroy the notion of individual consciousness, and thus, leaving it intact, it is gratuitously, and with a romantic spirit, that it addresses itself to mass consciousness. However, the destruction of individual consciousness represents a high idea of culture; it is a profound idea of culture that gives birth to a whole new form of civilization. Not to feel that you are living as an individual is to escape that deadly form of capitalism that I call the capitalism of consciousness since the soul belongs to everyone.

It is in this sense that in France young people believe in a renaissance of pre-Cortésian civilization. They do not want to fall back into the North American error of a civilization developing on the fringes of culture, they want first of all to arrive at that profound and central idea of culture upon which any revolution must depend.

To impose the forms of white civilization on the Indians would be to risk the destruction of everything that they might have preserved of their ancient culture, for culture & civilization are connected.

Ultimately, the problem is as follows:

There is in Europe an anti-European movement, I am afraid that there may be an anti-Indian movement in Mexico. Caring for the body and not for the mind is at the same time risking the loss of the body. I know perfectly well that the problem of consciousness does not exist for the Marxist youth of Mexico or, if you prefer, that it is conditioned by external elements.

But for the revolutionary youth of France, Marxism, by preserving a sense of individual conscience, prevents the Revolution from returning to its sources, which means that it impedes the Revolution.

A *MEDEA* DEVOID OF FIRE

Seneca's *Medea* is a mythical world; Margarita Xirgu lacks fire and misses this world. We must not attenuate the myths, otherwise we resign ourselves to being simply human, and that is a miserable anthropomorphism. This is how we discover ourselves as human, and we discover ourselves in man, small in stature, feeble in noise, naked in the end.

In this tragedy it was necessary for monsters to startle, it was necessary to show that we were among monsters, the monsters of the primitive imagination seen through the primitive mind. Monsters don't approach others that easily. Jason and Medea are unapproachable to each other: each has their own circle, each one stands within their own realm. To manage, Jason must make his way between the gods; and Medea, too. A god before another god. At all times the atmosphere of the drama is brought to its highest point.

The ancients had all the tragic material available for this: cothurnes, marionettes, masks; the symbolism of masks, lines, & costumes. Not so as to enable us to see them from afar, but in order to surpass, to subdue the stature of man.

"I invoke you with a sinister voice," said Medea, "a voice that calls for crimes, that is the invention and imagination of crimes." The particularity of modern theater is that it systematically loses the opportunity to represent a tragedy, that is, to really tear attention to pieces through crime. It is a theater which tricks because it is afraid to deal with the powers which are, which exist, those powers which it is not possible to pretend to evade.

There is a technique of tragedy.

A material and decorative technique.

A physiological technique.

Finally, a psychological technique.

Its aim is to truly deceive the senses; that is why there is in the first place a need not to awaken them. The theater is the world of true illusion. The imagination of the spectator wants to believe in what it sees, & to present the spectator with sets that move and which on top of that are painted in trompe l'œil, it is not only to deceive the eye, it is to despair and disgust the eye that would laugh at it if it could.

In the *Medea* of Xirgu, the three dusty, moth-eaten pieces of fabric were hung to evoke the Cyclopean mountains. And, to complete it all, these mountains were stylized. I cannot swallow this filthy dust rag stylization. It was Gordon Craig who invented the system, but in Europe we have been literally satiated with stylizations in the manner of Craig. Of an even more filthy color are the sacks with which the servants are covered, who almost sprawl out head first upon entering.

I especially recommend the chorus, this chorus of warriors with rose-colored arms that look like they've come out of a hospital for sick children. They are all dressed in green cloth, to convey that, in order to dress them, one trashed a hundred pool tables.

Creon's costume is the most implausible of all. He carries a banner, a string of acanthus leaves, each as wide as the thigh of an elephant. If this garland of barbarian leaves claims to signify his royalty, it succeeds much more in showing that we take kings for vagabond drunkards. And if, indeed, many kings have the habits of drunkenness and the degenerate souls of vagabonds, the mythical kings must offer us on all occasions a superior image of royalty. The directors of modern theater no longer have a sense of what true royal power is, any more than they have a sense of tragedy.

It is not by displaying modern music hall lighting on the dusty fabric that I described earlier that one will be able to convey an idea of the supernatural atmosphere of dread that overflows from a truly magickal text by Seneca, who was an authentic initiate when modern tragedians are nothing but puppets and saltimbanques.

On stage, objects must be taken for what they are; this is, in my opinion, the only way to create the scenic illusion. One should not take a dust rag and try to make us believe it is a mountain, but take a mountain and use it like a rag. Certainly, you cannot transport a mountain on stage, but it is possible to bring a mirror there and reflect a mountain in it. The technique consists in not trying to represent what cannot be represented.

All authentic theatrical traditions have always despised reality, but they have never substituted a rickety artifice in its place. Wherever it is, it is with objects from life: tables, chairs, cupboards, ladders, that the actor acts, to them he is limited; the rest he makes live through his gestures. The scenery is in his arms, in his body, in his feet, in his hands, in his eye, and above all in his face as changeable as a landscape where clouds playfully hide the sun. But that does not prevent natural objects from undergoing a real psychological demonetization: changing the decor, they change value; and they change the decor because their psychological situation is new, strange, surprising and unexpected. The light embroidering everything as if by magick adds to the illusion or disillusion. Because light has moral value; it doesn't just illuminate objects. On stage, objects become monsters to which the words, gestures, and movements of the actors lend a supernatural soul.

Tragedy is born of myth. All tragedy is the representation of a great myth. The language of myths is symbol, allegory. Allegory is manifested through signs. There is a sign language that is part of the plastic technique and of the stage design of tragedy.

The representation of Xirgu lacks allegorical signs: it hardly has more than two or three invariable gestures, such as the hand on the head and crossed arms.

From the point of view of the stage design, the tragedy also has symbolic signs from which came, for example, the fasces of the lictors, the cross, the caduceus of Mercury, the Roman Armies marched behind a forest of signs. Where were the symbolic emblems of the *Medea* of the Palais des Beaux-Arts?

As for the physiological technique that proposes to transform the human voice thanks to the knowledge of the breath and its muscular support points, I must say that it was absent from this *Medea*. Xirgu cries out evenly, without nuance, without an inflection of voice that makes us tremble in the guts and have the soul recoil inside the body. It does not occur to her, it seems, that one could adjust the pitch of the human voice to the point of making it sing like a real organ. There are ways to make your voice lunge, to make it quiver like a landscape. There is a whole scale of the voice.

Finally, it is in psychological technique that the poetic gift must intervene; it is poetry that allows Jason to arrive trailing monsters when he enters with the grace of a god. We can bring gods onto the stage, we can, around unapproachable characters of a truly figurative myth, draw magick circles, but, I repeat, this gift is necessary. The principle is to introduce on stage the irrational and monstrous logic of dreams, this logic which in a hand shows a face & which, through a sigh exhaled very close to the ear, suggests the passage of a hurricane. It is this technique of images that is, in everyday language, at the origin of metaphor. With bifold gestures, the tragic actor walks in an environment of metaphors wherein he constantly creates through voice, gestures, and movements.

YOUNG FRENCH PAINTING AND TRADITION

In current French painting, there is a marked reaction against Surrealism, represented above all by the young painter Balthus who, weary of a painting of larvæ, seeks to organize his world, a world of his own, where he nevertheless takes advantage of the in-depth probings which authentic Surrealist thought has carried out in the domain of the unconscious.

Surrealist painting was a negation of reality, a sort of fundamental disrepute hurled at appearances. If it does not deny objects, the Surrealist world disorders them, in its conception of things it installs in the first place a divorce between the limitless & reason. There is no difference between the world of dreams and that of applied reason.

The forms of Surrealist culture live in a hallucinatory light. Struggling against this divorce & this destruction, Balthus takes over the world *beginning with appearances*: he accepts the data of the senses, he accepts the data of reason; he accepts them, but he reforms them; I would say even better that he recasts them. In a word, Balthus starts from the *known*; there are universally recognizable elements and aspects in his painting; but the recognizable in turn has a meaning that not everyone can reach nor recognize. Balthus's painting is a revolution unmistakably directed against Surrealism, but also against academicism in all its forms. Beyond the Surrealist revolution, beyond the forms of classical academicism, Balthus's revolutionary painting joins a kind of mysterious tradition.

Contrary to what is taught in textbooks and in schools, a tradition of painting was lost during the Renaissance. Painters like da Vinci, Titian, Michelangelo, Veronese, Giorgione, Correggio, etc. ..., broke with a universal sacred tradition of painting; they have betrayed this tradition. Between the plastic secrets of a life whose appearances painting translates and manifests, and the appearances that one could call epidermal, the whole of European painting has, since the Renaissance, decided in favor of the appearances of life, that is, for the natural. It is since then that we have been able to see the faces of women and men in the attitudes of laughter or tears, the sun, the wind, the passions, the bad weather. Painting has fallen under the anecdotal domination of nature and psychology. It ceased to be a means of revelation to become an art of simple descriptive representation. It has lost that universal and secret reason for being which made it, in the proper sense of the word, magick.

In pre-Renaissance painting, faces have perhaps something a bit dead for psychology, but it is that reputedly primitive art has always been the supernatural manifestation of a science; and beyond human psychology, which they despise, the faces in primitive painting transmit to us the vibration of the soul, the deep efforts of the universe.

Between the hieratic and sacred primitivism of a Cimabue, of a Giotto, of a Fra Angelico, and the painting that adores the material for the material of a Michelangelo, a Titian, a Veronese, and even of a Tintoretto and a Rubens, painters like Piero della Francesca, Simone Martini, Piero di Cosimo, Tura, Antonello de Messina and Mantegna reconcile the demands of the sun, time, darkness, human psychology, in a word, topicality, with those of that old sacred art that was based on the knowledge of what I will call the Energetics of the Universe.

Where Cimabue seeks to manifest essences hierarchically, Paolo Uccello paints form with science; and the form is still fiery because it is close to the essence that gave birth to it. It is to this esoteric and magickal tradition that a painter like Balthus returns. Surrealism helped him to clarify the forms and, under the fixed convention of such forms, it allowed him to discover in the unconscious of man the rustling life of the naked forces of the universe.

Pre-Renaissance painting had a form and it had a number. In their lines, in their plans, those called the primitives manifested the Pythagorean tradition of numbers. There is in their representations a kind of esotericism, a manner of enchantment, and through its lines the human figure becomes the fixed sign and the transparent filter of a certain magick.

This is how Balthus proceeds, he who will reject anarchic carelessness and the more or less inspired disorder of a painting which calls itself modern, and give us landscapes, portraits, groups which have their own code and whose symbolism is not immediately apparent. Balthus painted mysterious groups, a street where dream automata parade; he made concentrated portraits wherein, as on an astrological atlas of the heavens, a color, a flower, a metal, fire, earth, wood or water allows the person represented to recover his identity.

Palmistry knows the hand of metal, that of wood, water, earth or fire.

Similarly, in a Balthus portrait, the figure evokes the element it most resembles in its life, character, or spirit.

Balthus has an ascetic soul and there is a true "asceticism" in the way he uses color. He practices this "asceticism" when he paints. He restrains his secret sensuality as he repels the temptation to indulge in the artificial and facile intoxication of color. He thus achieves a darker intoxication that makes objects sing in their own light. He manages to bring objects to life in a light that he has made his own. One might say that there is a Balthus color, a Balthus light, a Balthus luminosity. And the characteristic of this luminosity is above all to be invisible. Objects, bodies, faces are phosphorescent without our being able to discern from where the light comes. In this realm, Balthus is infinitely more skillful than Goya, Rembrandt, or Zurbarán, than all the great agonists of that painting which rises out of the darkness plane by plane to clarity.

Combined with his science of color, Balthus possesses a science of space. He immediately knows where exactly to place in a canvas the vibrating point, following in this the great tradition of painting for which the painted canvas is a geometric space to be filled. But in that painted space, which vibrates, in that illuminated invisible space, it is the personality of Balthus that calls colors and forms to him and imposes his dark stamp upon them. He curdles them as we say an acid ferment curdles milk.

Balthus does not play with ochres, reddish browns, earthy greens, bitumen, or the blackness of lacquers, but it is a fact that the world he sees stays in this minor scale.

The bitter color of Balthus above all means that the life of this time is bitter. In his agile and at the same time concentrated forms, Balthus proclaims the bitterness & despair of living.

A drawing by Balthus oozes the science of living when life seizes us by the throat. It is this mixture of geometry and tenderness that is the bed of a dying man, but who by miracle has succeeded in triumphing over his death throes.

All his painting, to the rhythm of a human breath, is impregnated with a vast respiratory harmony that ranges from the precipitous breath of anger to the slow and great breath of agony.

There is in a portrait by Balthus this principle of synthesis that makes it similar to ancient Chinese calligraphy and to certain primitive paintings.

The portrait painted by Balthus joins its historical model through his art of portraiture. And all of this is not obtained by distention, but by what one might call a laying bare. The head stands apart from time, in a luminous atmosphere, in an exposure to light that immediately gives its raison d'être and the key to its fate.

With his angular and strangled drawing, his earthquake color, Balthus, who has always painted hydrocephali with gaunt legs and long feet — proof that he himself bears his head poorly, — Balthus, when he is finished digesting his skills, will assert himself as the Paolo Uccello or the Piero della Francesca of that time or, better still, as a Greco who would have lost himself there.

FRENCH THEATER SEARCHES FOR A MYTH

Tired of the plastic research of Copeau, Dullin, and Baty, the young French theater is searching for a myth that it is on the verge of discovering. For it, the famous "respect for the text," this invention of Copeau's, has only led to the resuscitation of old texts, and the theater, today, does not seek texts, but a "language"; and the language of the theater is not located in the choruses, but in space itself.

In order for this myth of modern theater to emerge, it must first be given a "language." The communist group October, under the leadership of Jacques Prévert, and the group led by Jean-Louis Barrault, are inventing this "language," each in their own way. In the October group, they represent farces that are bloody critiques of bourgeois mores and spirit. Prévert participated in the Surrealist movement. This is visible in the technique of his buffooneries where suddenly the life of dreams bursts into the midst of dreaded caricatures of a world that, before dying, hurls its poison. In the farces of Prévert, the homey & lewd spirit of the modern French bourgeois is cruelly castigated and, as a consequence of this absurd spirit, *the demon of the absurd* of Edgar Poe and Baudelaire has free rein. The lust that seeks refuge in the double-bottomed bed of old French adultery is driven out by its own phantasms. It frightens itself to contemplate itself. The ménage à trois becomes a ménage of six, eighteen, twelve, twenty-four, thirty-six, and there are maddening races of multiples of three that end up blushing on their own; then arrives a proletarian stagehand who throws all this pretty theater into the basket.

Prévert's buffoonery is both psychological and objective. I mean *lust, the demon of the absurd, the multiples of threes* take shape and as the play unfolds take on the proportions of a nightmare. For the young modern French theater there is no difference between myth and nightmare: their characteristic is that they avenge us. They avenge us for the dreams of our vicious life. Likewise, if we seek to create a myth in the theater, it is to charge this myth with all the horrors of a century that makes us believe in our failure in life.

The highest form of theater is tragedy. And the latest living creations of modern French theater participate in this form, which does not mean that they are in five acts and in verse. This division into acts is an invention of French psychological tragedy, which has forgotten the penetrating and morbid soul which finds, like ancient myths, tragic inspiration in the darkness of an ambient nightmare.

With its ferocious humor, Prévert's theater is a theater of darkness; that of Barrault too.

The theater is born of darkness like light of chaos, and as it emerges to overcome the darkness of chaos.

The theatrical performances of the Orphic Mysteries showed forms that expanded to conquer darkness; these forms had the face of the night and took on the aspect of "invading evil."

Every great myth has one foot on "evil," that is to say on the disaster that threatens all of us, we men, periodically, and if a leap is necessary to annihilate the disaster, it is up to the theater to realize through its images and its forms the poetic and magickal sign of this leap.

Prévert's humor signals that the life of the time is sick; Barrault's theatrical film seeks to find the secret hieroglyphics and the signs of a magickal life that the stage must resuscitate.

Through these signs and these revealed hieroglyphs, the true language of the theatrical will finally manifest itself.

Because the error of a Copeau is to count on the author to revolutionize the theater, whereas the resurrection of the theater must be the work of a sort of "Proteus man" who responds as well to hieroglyphics animated by the staging only of the actor's work, the spoken parts of the speech now being linked to the rest to compose a single voice, a single being, a single movement.

WHAT I CAME TO MEXICO TO DO

I came to Mexico in search of politicians, not artists.

And here's why:

Until now I have been an artist, which means that I have been a yoked man. For there is no doubt that from a social point of view artists are slaves.

Indeed, I say, me, that this must change.

There was a time when the artist was a sage, that is, a cultivated man who also doubled as a thaumaturge, a magus, a therapist, and even a gymnasiarch; what is called in the language of fairs the "one-man-band" or "Protean man." The artist united in himself all the faculties and all the sciences. Then came the age of specialization, also that of decadence. It cannot be denied. A society that turns science into the dust of sciences is a society that degenerates.

There is a disease of the polar regions that consists of an essential alteration of the tissues: this disease is called scurvy. For want of an essential vital principle, the cells of the organism dry out. And just as there are diseases particular to individuals, there are diseases particular to the masses. The proliferation of the industrial harvests gave birth in the organism of Europe to a collective form of scurvy.

This is the ransom that progress has had to pay.

The Mexico of today, which is aware of the flaws of European civilization, must react against this superstition about progress.

And since politicians have replaced artists in the management of public affairs, this task falls to them, not to artists.

We can say that present-day Mexico is faced with a grandiose problem; and if I came to Mexico it was to study *in situ* the solutions in existence there.

It is a question of nothing less, in fact, than to break with the spirit of an entire world and to substitute one civilization for another.

Doctor Alexis Carrel, who also recognizes the defects of the mechanized civilization of Europe, does not fail, in his book entitled *Man, the Unknown*, to advocate the need for a revolution, and he even suggests means for carrying it out.

Mexico, which has had two or three revolutions in a century, need not fear another; and the next, if it occurs, will undoubtedly be exceptionally serious, because this time around it will have to solve some fundamental problems.

Only, this future revolution in Mexico — and this will be its originality — will not be a fratricidal revolution because, as regards the fate of civilization, a unanimous thought animates present-day Mexico. This moving unanimity is what I wanted to witness.

The question in essence is:

The current civilization of Europe is bankrupt. Dualist Europe has nothing more to offer the world than the improbable dust of cultures. Extracting a new unity out of this crop dust is a necessity.

As for the Orient, it is entirely decadent. India falls asleep in the dream of a liberation that is only valid after death.

China is at war. The Japanese of today seem to be the fascists of the Far East. China, for Japan, is a vast Ethiopia.

The United States has done nothing other than multiply ad infinitum the decadence and vices of Europe.

There remains Mexico and its subtle political structure which, basically, has not changed since the time of Montezuma.

Mexico, that precipitate of innumerable races, appears as the melting pot of history. From this very precipitation and from this mixture of races, it must extract a unique residue, from which the Mexican soul will emerge.

But to form a unique soul you need a unique culture and this is where the problem becomes impassioning.

On one side there is culture, on the other, civilization, and civilization and culture both risk moving in diametrically opposite directions. Although there may be a hundred cultures in Europe, contrarily, there is only one civilization. A civilization that has its own laws. Whoever is devoid of machines, guns, planes, bombs, and asphyxiating gases necessarily falls prey to the better-armed neighbor or enemy: see the case of Ethiopia.

Modern Mexico could escape neither this necessity nor this law, but, beyond that, Mexico has a cultural secret that the ancient Mexicans bequeathed to it. Unlike the modern culture of Europe, which has arrived at an insane pulverization of forms and aspects, the eternal culture of Mexico has a unique feature. Here is what I wanted to come to: any culture of synthesis has a secret. With time, and under the external influence of the civilization of Europe, Mexico gave up the knowledge and use of this secret, but — and this is the sensational event of the time — there has been a movement in Mexico to reclaim this secret.

When Mexico will have actually reconquered and resuscitated its true culture, neither guns nor planes will be able to do anything against it.

Listen to what I am going to say; these are not the sentences of a Sunday drama. Behind this puerile guise, this assertion contains a fundamental truth.

Every important cultural transformation begins with a renewed idea of man; it coincides with a new surge of humanism. We suddenly begin cultivating man exactly as one would cultivate a fertile garden.

I came to Mexico looking for a new idea of man.

Man in the face of inventions, sciences, discoveries, but as only Mexico can still give it to us, I mean with this open framework, but carrying deep within it the ancient animal relationships of man with nature that were established by the old Toltecs, the ancient Maya and, in short, all the races that from century to century have created the greatness of the Mexican soil.

Mexico cannot, under pain of death, renounce the current conquests of science, but it holds in reserve an ancient science infinitely superior to those of laboratories and of scientists.

Mexico has its own science and its own culture. Developing this science and this culture is a duty for modern Mexico, and such a duty is precisely the impassioning originality of this country.

Between the now degenerated remains of the ancient Red Culture, such as we can find in the last pure indigenous races, and the no less degenerate and fragmentary culture of modern Europe, Mexico can find an original form of culture that will constitute its contribution to the civilization of this time.

The task to be accomplished in this sense is enormous, and if I am in Mexico today it is because I felt that this enormous task, this task of epic dimensions — let's not be afraid of grand words — is being realized by modern Mexico.

Under the contributions of modern science, which day after day discovers new forces, there are other unknown forces, other subtle forces that do not yet belong to the domain of science but which may belong to it some day. These forces are part of what in pagan times was known as the soul realm of nature. The superstitious spirit of men gave a religious form to this profound knowledge that made of man, if we can risk the expression, "the catalyst of the universe."

Yet, the conquest of modern Mexico and this contribution of capital importance which Mexico can bring us today consist precisely in the discovery of those *analogical forces* thanks to which the organism of man functions in harmony with the organism of nature and governs it. And insofar as science and poetry are a single and identical thing, it is as much the business of poets and artists as that of scientists, as was clear at the time of the *Popol-Vuh*.

But, this time, the rediscovery will be free of all superstition, of all religious meaning, however slight.

In short, it is a question of resuscitating the old sacred idea, the great idea of pagan pantheism, in a form that will no longer be religious, but scientific. True pantheism is not a philosophical system; it is merely a means of a *dynamic investigation* of the universe.

This is the lesson that modern Mexico can teach us. Mexico is appropriating the forms of the mechanistic civilization of Europe and adapts them to its own spirit. What does it matter if this spirit is precisely the destroyer of these forms!

If it destroys them, it will be in time, when it has already armed itself with its own strength, that is, when the spirit of the ancient synthetic culture of the Toltecs and the Maya has regained sufficient force to allow Mexico to abandon European civilization without danger. Once again, this is not a utopia, but a scientific reality that cannot be denied. If we are to accept the idea that man is the catalyst of the universe, we must deduce that the moral forces of man vibrate in unison with the forces of the universe, those forces which, according to the teachings of the high monist philosophy, are neither physical nor moral, but take on a moral or physical aspect according to the sense in which one wishes to use them.

The Cross of Palenque perfectly embodies the synthetic image of this bifold action.

There is there, inscribed in stone, the hieroglyphic representation of a single energy which, through the cross of space, that is, through the four cardinal points, moves from man to animal and to plants.

THE ETERNAL CULTURE OF MEXICO

I came to Mexico to make contact with the Red Earth. It is the separated soul, the original soul of Mexico that interests me above all else, but before confronting it and to be sure of touching its depths, I want to study real life in Mexico in all its aspects.

I arrived here with a blank mind, which does not mean without preconceived ideas. Yet, preconceived ideas are of the realm of the imagination; and that's why I distrust them.

Not that I lack ideas about what the real culture of Mexico once was, but I see a fundamental difference between civilization and culture. The external forms of art can distinguish between them a multitude of civilizations, their variety leaves intact the deep spirit of a culture; and in Mexico, under multiple external aspects that art alone differentiates, a unique cultural aspiration is concealed: the copper culture of the sun.

I know almost everything that history teaches about the various races of Mexico and I admit that I have allowed myself to dream like a poet about what it does not teach.

Between the known historical facts & the real life of the Mexican soul there is an immense margin where the imagination — & I even dare say personal intuition — can be given free rein.

I have therefore my idea about Maya culture, about Toltec culture, about Zapotec culture; and what interests me now is to find in present-day Mexico the lost soul of these cultures and their survival both in the way of life of the peoples and of those who govern them.

Mexico is on the road to the sun, and on this road we have to chase the secret of that force of light that made the pyramids turn upon their bases until they were placed on the line of the magnetic attraction of the sun. Yet this is not the secret of a charlatan.

In my way of seeing things, nothing resembles the poetic and sterile nostalgia for a dead past, but the regret for a lost science, for a profound attitude of the human spirit which I estimate, me, to be of a vital importance to recover.

If it is certain that I have an idea of the eternal culture of Mexico, it is also certain that I have no judgment to formulate, nor opinion to express on the current politics of Mexico. Such a subject is not my responsibility and it does not concern me. I am here as a spectator and I would even say as a disciple. I came to Mexico to learn something and I want to bring lessons back to Europe. This is why my research can only relate to the part of the Mexican soul that has remained free from all influence of the European spirit. It is not the culture of Europe that I came here to seek, but the original Mexican culture and civilization; it is of this originality that I proclaim myself a disciple, and it is from it that I want to draw lessons.

We are speaking of the Latin spirit of Mexico. And the first question I asked myself was to know to what extent the European spirit in its Latin form still permeates the Mexican soul today.

The Latin spirit is rational culture, the supremacy of reason. It is against this frenzy of inventions that it is currently important to react, against this frenzy that has moreover produced the chemical industry of crops, laboratory medicine, mechanization in all its forms, etc. Mechanization renders all effort sterile & it leads, in short, to disparaging human effort, to discouraging emulation between men and to rendering all research aimed at quality useless and intrusive. As for laboratory medicine, which is incapable of perceiving the subtle & fleeting soul of diseases, it treats living man as if he were a corpse.

Moreover, it is to the Latin spirit that we owe the democratic ideas of Europe, nationalism, not natural nationalism, but a certain form of egotistical nationalism from which present-day Mexico does not suffer.

For there is a form of cultural nationalism wherein the specific quality of a nation and of the works of that nation are affirmed & which distinguish them; this nationalism is irreproachable; and there is the nationalism that we can call civic and which, in its egoistic form, resolves into chauvinism and results in customs struggles and economic wars when it is not total war.

As for what concerns laboratory medicine, for example, we should know that there is in France a reaction against this medicine that is based almost exclusively on experience and experiments and which draws its conclusions from the information procured by the microscope, the dissection of dead matter, etc....

I must point out a return to empiricism which in its primary and transcendent form provides healers and bonesetters with the basis of a formula as grandiose as homeopathy.

Homeopathy, with its principle of similitude, is closely linked to plant medicine. I will therefore seek in Mexico the survival of an ancient plant medicine comparable to what in Europe is called spagyric medicine, the most remarkable theoretician of which was Paracelsus, at the end of the Middle Ages.

I have no conclusion to draw from this for the moment, but I seem to discern two currents in Mexico: one which aspires to assimilate European culture & civilization, giving them a Mexican form, and the other which, extending the secular tradition, remains stubbornly rebellious to all progress. However thin this last current is, it is in it that all the strength of Mexico is to be found, it is there that I will encounter what survived of the empirical medicine of the Maya and the Toltecs, the true Mexican poetics which cannot be reduced solely to writing poems, but affirms the relations of poetic rhythm to the breath of man and, through the intermediary of the breath, to the pure movements of space, water, air, light, wind.

The deep culture of Mexico comes from far away. It carries within it the tradition of the races that once dominated civilization.

Faced with the obvious collapse of the current civilization of Europe, I came to realize how Mexico intends to strengthen its traditional culture & if, without trying to resuscitate wasted forms of its life, it aspires to prove the permanence in it of a spirit which, from my point of view as a poet, I would call magick; a spirit which, considered from a strictly scientific point of view, can become the manifestation of a true psychological energy.

Thanks to this energy diffused to infinity in Nature, the man of antiquity came, so to speak, into possession of events. We know that for the Maya, for example, fate did not exist. Nature has power over us only because of our ignorance and our secular blindness.

But when we speak again and almost everywhere of humanism, the opportunity presents itself to assert the true powers, the high dominating power of man which makes him the master of events.

A culture for which the Universe is a whole knows that each part acts automatically on the whole. You just need to know the laws.

To know fate is, in short, to dominate it, since in the present as in the future the external world falls under the domination of intelligence.

By means of very precise astrological data, drawn from a transcendent algebra, we can predict events and act on them. The ancient Maya brought such data and the mastery of this science to a rare degree of perfection.

That being established, I conclude that at the bottom of true solar culture there is a secret meaning that I will try to define.

The sun, to use the ancient language of symbols, appears as the maintainer of life. It is not only the fertilizing element, the sovereign provocateur of germination; it is all that, it makes everything that exists ripen, but that is, so to speak, the least of its faculties. It burns, it calcines, it eliminates, but it does not destroy everything it eliminates. Under the accumulation of destroyed things, and thanks to this destruction itself, it maintains the eternity of the forces by which life is preserved.

In a word — and in this lies the real secret — the sun is a principle of death and not a principle of life. The very basis of the ancient solar culture is to have shown the supremacy of death.

In India there are worshipers of Shiva the Destroyer, and worshipers of Vishnu the Conserver. But destruction is transformative. Life maintains its continuity through the transformation of the appearances of being.

Now, the worshipers of Shiva have as their emblem the spirit of fire, the great current devouring forms, this kind of impulsive force which changed the copper men of ancient Mexico into determined maintainers of death. And this is not a verbal paradox.

Realizing the supremacy of death is not the same as not exercising the present life. It is to put the present life in its place; to have it overlap several planes at the same time; to experience the stability of the planes that make the living world a great force in balance; it is, finally, to restore a great harmony.

I came to modern Mexico to seek the survival of these notions or to await their resurrection.

THE FALSE SUPERIORITY OF THE ELITES

Rather than crushing the elites, we must understand them first, & to understand them we must define them.

The modern world, in the midst of spiritual rout, & all the more so because it justly hates the spiritual as a whole, must, if it wants to recover peace, restore the balance between the two fundamental movements through which they become manifest, and so that head & hands are equal, an activity and an identical dynamism whose equalization composes the complete man.

And just as there is in the present world a formidable misunderstanding between the opposing faculties of spirit and matter, so there is emulation, or rather rivalry, between the work of the hands and that of the head. The elites, it cannot be denied, enjoy no credit in today's society. The great mass of mankind is not interested in the labors of the mind and it would not be an exaggeration to assert that we are preparing to reduce to famine those who, with a disinterestedness that was in other times better recognized, profess to devote themselves to the pure work of thought.

But before reducing intellectuals to starvation, before fissioning the elites that make the glory of a society, & above all make it last, society should at least make an effort to get closer to these elites, that is, to understand them.

An eminent man to whom I complained about the sad situation in which artists have fallen in France replied: "What do you want? In our world, artists are made to die on a pile of straw, when it is not the straw of a dungeon."

I replied that there were times when artists were given their rightful place, that is to say the first, and when society was eager to provide them, & even beyond what is necessary, the means of subsistence.

That money has become what it is today — a sort of force majeure and, one might say, a touchstone of life — well, but that is a fact, not a law of evidence. And just because things are like that doesn't mean you have to accept them as they are. There are many reasons, & very elevated ones, to initiate a transformation.

What then are revolutions for if not to restore social balance and inject a bit of justice into the injustice of life? At the bottom of this rivalry, this struggle between the antagonistic forces of spirit and matter, we find an error of conception that belongs to the modern world: I mean that other centuries have ignored it.

If in the modern capitalist world, which puts money above all else, there is, it cannot be denied, a characteristic contempt for the elites that in turn masks the hatred that all true superiority inspires, it is precisely because of that that the modern world gives the elites a reality, an existence they do not have.

Those who work with their hands have forgotten that they have a head, and those who work with the head are generally despondent, believing themselves to be diminished, when it is necessary to work with their hands.

It is these conditions that explain the contempt that the communist masses feel for gratuitous activities of the mind. It is because they despise the works of the mind that the modern world is in complete ruin; we can even say that it has lost its spirit; and the spirit, from being at odds with life, has in turn become useless. That the elites cease to believe in their superiority, that they acquire a salutary humility, that they restore to the spirit its former function of organ, that they show the works of the intelligence under an advantageously material aspect, and as if by enchantment will end this idiotic war between the sumptuous refinements of the spirit and the work of the hands, which is worthless if it is not governed by the logic of the head.

Whether we like it or not, the elites are this ballast, this sovereign counterweight that keeps life upright.

Intellectuals will occupy their rightful place in society when this society has sufficient discernment to understand that there is an absolute identity between the forces of the body and those of the intelligence, and that the spirit is the sieve of life. I am not claiming that the spirit is as useful as the body, I am claiming that there is no body and no spirit, but modalities of unique strength and action. And the question of the rivalry between these two modalities does not even have to arise.

It is up to intellectuals to apply their spiritual strength to useful tasks that are like the very salt of life, and not to speculations of the mind, of those which are said to be disinterested and gratuitous, but which are in reality so selfless and so gratuitous that they are of no use to anyone or anything. This does not mean that intellectuals must indulge in the activity of workers, but that they must finally understand the functional utility of the spirit.

If the body and the spirit are a single movement, it is on the side where the spirit touches the rhythms of sick life that the intellectuals must direct their efforts and, as in the times when the great unitary culture reigned from which all civilizations emerged, they must again become the leaders, healers, therapists of the high functions of life in man since it is in the disordered organism of man today that the disordered organism of the universe is reflected.

Male, female. The ancient societies consecrated in famous terms the eternal antagonism between the forces of the spirit, which are masculine, and the forces of the body or of matter whose passive gravity is precisely feminine.

It would require something like a magick trick to resuscitate these old notions today without which life is incomprehensible.

Indeed, for that, we have at hand a magick organ, a weapon that allows us to imagine life.

This weapon of exceptional power and of inexhaustible fruitfulness is theater. But modern society has forgotten the therapeutic virtues of the theater, and we would make it laugh if we told it that in ancient times the theater had been considered an exceptional means of restoring the lost balance of forces and that the ancient theater apparatus features healing music & dances.

We have forgotten that the theater is a sacred act that engages both the viewer & the performer, and that the fundamental psychological idea of the theater is this: a gesture that we see and that the spirit reconstructed in images has as much value as a gesture that one makes.

This is why there is no better instrument of revolution than the theater; and it is through the theater, through this dissolving and formidable weapon, that any shrewd revolutionary government directs & ensures its revolution.

There is no revolution possible without the integration of the elites into the masses, which thereby reach a high spiritual level.

With its autochthonous indigenous races in which there is an abundance of music and healing dances, Mexico is even in the position to understand the meaning of a similar revolution; and the best of this healing indigenous music awaits the moment to reclaim its place among the mass of workers.

P. S. — There is indeed no reason not to incorporate Indian folk art into the elite. To put the life of folklore and the research of the great Mexican writers on an identical cultural level seems to me to be a refined way of putting an end to the antagonisms that exist between the elite and the masses, popular art and bourgeois art, intellectual life and instinctive life, the effusions of pure thought and the harmonies, also intellectual, of the organic life of the Indians.

P. S. — I'm looking for Doctor José Miguel Gómez Mendoza, well versed in the ancient occult medicine of the Toltecs. If he reads these lines, I ask him to write to me giving me his address and indicating where & when I can meet him.

ETERNAL SECRETS OF CULTURE

Every authentic culture has its secrets.

Before speaking of the universal foundations of culture, we should speak of the eternal secrets of culture, secrets that no one has ever fathomed.

Culture is a refined effusion of life into the awakening human organism. And life, no one has ever been able to say what it is. Therefore, to affirm the flowering in man of an eternal spirit of culture amounts to affirming man's ignorance before the sources of his true life.

This humility is the very basis of science. Even more than science, ignorance is a stimulant because above all it encourages us to be careful not to make mistakes.

Ignorance, but enlightened & conscious ignorance, is the mortar of truth.

With his conscience as a barrier, a man who wishes to build on firm ground immediately knows *where he must not set foot*.

Undoubtedly, the origin of all that exists is obscure, and the clairvoyant man — in the beginnings of his science — opens a pathway, a margin, a place where universal darkness manifests itself.

Because the strange thing is that, not knowing where he comes from, man can use his ignorance, this kind of *original* ignorance, to figure out exactly where he must go.

And this is where empiricism serves him; empiricism, that is, the spirit of hypothesis; that is, the beneficent and fruitful use of his indefatigable imagination.

To help himself, he turns his gaze to the *past*, he uses the fruits of this age-old tentative march of men who, by dint of imagination and hypotheses, have wrested from *nature* its secrets.

Yet the real secret will not be revealed because it is part of the ineffable. At the bottom of any true culture there are necessarily ineffable secrets since they proceed from this margin of emptiness where our eternal ignorance forces us to locate the origins of truth.

There is no civilization or culture more *rational* than the civilization and culture of China and China has pushed the domination of *nature* to the extreme, but for the sole purpose of extinguishing its obscurity. No traces of occultism nor even of mysticism in the rational conceptions of China; everything is real there and the real is concrete. But, according to Lao Tzu's *Tao Te Ching*, at the center of everything, of the universal *whole*, is the void. This means that there is a void that science will never fill; however, poetry, if it is conceived as a useful and rational means of divination, can help us to establish the foundations that will enable us to advance.

Ancient Mexico contributed a great deal to the constitution of this secret treasure where eternal humanity is nourished.

We owe it first-rate psychological discoveries, those same discoveries that the European Middle Ages imagined in the allegory of the Macrocosm and the Microcosm that placed man, like a universe in reduction, at the point of the convergence of all cosmic forces.

Thus, to be considered a miniature universe, man *could not despair.* Thus, that despair — which has also been called *"world-weariness"* and which, in France, made a new and formidable appearance, signaled by several resounding suicides, at the time of Surrealism — that despair was therefore automatically reabsorbed since all the forces of the world contributed to its absorption.

Man, then, stood in equilibrium over the world; he breathed with the life of the world, and had known of means to heal psychic life *through the world*.

Awakening the obscure life of the world and searching for accomplices therein was a way of combatting certain crimes, combatting a certain category of inexplicable crimes.

Unlike today, education was not a simple *mnemonic technique*; it was a material convocation of forces and, if I dared to express myself thus, I would say that through education we *rubbed* the human organism so that forces would surge within it.

This is what the theater was used for, what the great sacred festivals served with their fulgurant calls for sounds, their rhythmic repetitions of images that charged into the human *unconscious*.

Totemism was moreover not a crude magick, a superstition hailing from the early ages of humanity; it was the obvious application of a science. For what then are we made of? Does man believe that he is alone, without correspondence to the life of other species — flowers, plants, fruits — or that of a city, a river, a landscape, a forest?

The spirit of matter is the same everywhere. The religious rites of today then appear, thanks to the theater, as stripped of their superstitious apparatus. The theater was a social force that knew how, through making use of scientific ritual means, to act outside the conscience of the people that Religion had fanaticized.

We participate in all possible forms of life. A thousand-year-old atavism weighs on our human *unconscious*. And it is absurd to limit life. A bit of what we have been and above all what *we must be* lies stubbornly hidden in stones, plants, animals, landscapes, & woods.

Particles of our past or future *self* roam in nature where very precise universal laws work to bring them together. And it is right that we are looking for replicas, active, nervous, even fluid replicas, in all such disintegrating elements.

To be aware of everything that, materially, unites us to general life, is a scientific attitude that today's science cannot deny since, through its recent discoveries in physics, it reduces the world to being one energy,

& through its latest psychological discoveries, it shows us that humanity is not an immobilized entity, but that, through the subterranean regions of its consciousness, it participates in the future as well as in the past.

To a greater or lesser degree, and according to the strength of its own genius, the *unconscious* of each human being possesses a treasure of archaic images that the ancient races of Mexico had obscured with a cloak of impenetrable allegories. Along with the *indispensable* social & economic revolution, we are all waiting for a revolution of consciousness that will allow us to heal life.

It is up to modern Mexico to undertake this revolution.

THE OCCULT FORCES OF MEXICO

I have already spoken of the kind of hallucination that reigns in France in intellectual circles relative to the Indianist policy of contemporary Mexico.

But I must clarify.

For France, the revolution of modern Mexico is a revolution of man. I mean that it has as its goal not only the constitution of society but the internal constitution of man.

It is a Revolution against progress, against the ideas of the modern world, against the scientific civilization of today.

We have spoken of an Indianism of Mexico, of an Indianist politics of the current Mexican government, we have spoken of an awakening of the Indian spirit. And the French youth, animated by an immense desire for universality, thrilled at the idea that a people were returning to their cultural origins, returning to the sources of the primitive spirit.

However, these are clearly false rumors. To tell the truth, there is no such awakening of the Indian spirit of Mexico, and the Revolution, on Mexican soil, is not as one imagines it in France.

But if these rumors are false, if they did not come from Mexico, I still think that it would be of the utmost importance to know from where they hail.

Because if the Revolution of Mexico is not Indianist in this exclusive sense in which the young intellectuals of France understand it, nonetheless, it tries to resuscitate the principles, the forms of pre-Cortésian culture; the thought of French youth, and in this it is indeed a universal thought, wants us to return to the sources, it is completely impregnated with the dreams of the primitive unconscious and wants to change these dreams into reality. This is why it sees in the buried traditions of Mexico a means of saving life.

There is a German book that is currently enjoying great success in the circles of intellectual youth in France: *The Sources of the Magical Inspiration of the Spirit of Primitive Peoples*.

French youth want to understand life and the original powers of life; they want to penetrate in its totality the fundamental quivering of life.

It imagines, this youth, that Mexican intellectuals have put themselves at the head of a similar movement to revive the inspired soul, the magickal soul of the ancient Mexican peoples.

And, I insist on this, it is not a moral chimera. There are forces of life buried in the earth, and if the modern era is in the midst of a catastrophe it is because it has lost the meaning of universal life. And there are material means of grasping the synthetic forces of life.

In France, young intellectuals have imagined that Mexico, without renouncing the conquests of the modern world, wants new blood, and this new blood, paradoxical as it may seem, is none other than the vehement blood of the old races whose eternal strength, under a renewed guise, can be revived.

French youth have observed a sort of essential exhaustion in the spirit of the modern world, a world that lost its vigor when man turned in on himself and renounced locating his strength in the diffuse life of the universe.

It is in reality nothing other than the magickal sources of the primitive spirit, at the bottom of which an uninterrupted exchange of forces takes place between man and the universal.

In awakening, & in contact with all that surrounds him, man draws powers from everything that surrounds him, that is to say from the universal life that completely submerges him.

Yet, whereas the culture of Europe has hardly ever been aware of this taking possession by man of natural forces, ancient Mexico has. This is why the French youth are turning their eyes toward Mexico as toward a land of resurrection. And it believes that the Mexican Revolution, in seeking a vigorous idea of man, seeks to make old cultural principles reappear.

It is the unilateral development of progress that has made men lose an essential idea. In Europe, man is bored and he cannot explain this loss of the taste for life. He does not understand that by dint of considering life only in its material aspect, he has come to confuse life with mere dead appearances.

Yet, we can say that a simple glance is enough for the world of dead appearances to decompose.

Spain is on fire; the fire in Ethiopia has only just died down. On the soil of immense China, war threatens to break out anew; Germany and Italy are the prey of a singular order that is only the legalized organization of a disorder. And this order in turn threatens the order and peace of its neighbors, that is, the order and peace of the whole of Europe. As for France, we can say that it is virtually in a state of revolution.

We are on the eve of a new confusion of languages. Modern man no longer understands himself. Humanity needs a rejuvenation. Virgin sources of life must be found. And it is the eternal culture of Mexico that has these sources of life which nothing can alter.

The Mexican soul has never really lost contact with the earth, with the telluric forces of the ground.

However small my contribution may be, I only ask that I be allowed to contribute to this search for living sources, a search that will one day turn into a resurrection.

In all points of the Mexican ground where these sources of culture emerge, I ask that I be allowed to discover them, to make them spring up. I did not come to Mexico as a curious person, but as a worker. The marvelous meaning of the current Mexican Revolution,

I think I understand. This Revolution, which is made for Mexicans, ignites the need for the ideal of all French youth. However, the French government cannot take an official interest in it. This is precisely why I allow myself to ask the Mexican government for the means of action that my own government cannot give me.

No one has hitherto thought of making manifest the hidden forces of the Mexican soul, of *enumerating* them, of methodically bringing them together. I know the names of these psychological forces and I want to write a book about them, but I lack elements that can only be obtained on the ground itself: the rites, the beliefs, the festivals, the customs of the authentic indigenous tribes. I will write a book based on this research and this book will be used for Mexican propaganda.

I ask the Mexican government to let me undertake this work because it would be very sad for me, very sad for young French intellectuals, if the Mexican Revolution did not meet our hopes. I have no other ambition than to contribute to the glory of the land whose guest I am today.

THE SOCIAL ANARCHY OF ART

The social duty of art is to give way to the anxieties of its time. The artist who has not auscultated the heart of his time, the artist who is unaware that he is a *scapegoat*, that his duty is to magnetize, to attract, to make fall on his shoulders the wandering anger of the time to relieve it of its psychological discomfort, that one is not an artist.

Just like men, epochs have an unconscious. And these *dark parts of the shadow* of which Shakespeare speaks also have a life of their own, a life of their own that *must be extinguished*.

That is what works of art are for.

The materialism of today is in reality a spiritualist attitude because, the better to destroy them, materialism prevents us from reaching in their substance those values that escape the senses. Materialism calls such values "spiritual" and disdains them: they then poison the unconscious of the epoch. But nothing that reason or intelligence can achieve is spiritual.

We have the means to fight, but our epoch is dying by forgetting to use them.

In its beginnings, the Russian Revolution caused a real carnage of artists, and everywhere people rose up against this contempt for spiritual values that the executions of the Russian Revolution seemed to signify.

But, on closer inspection, what was the spiritual value of the artists that the Russian Revolution had shot? How did their works, written or painted, testify to the catastrophic spirit of the times?

Artists, and today more than ever, are responsible for the social disorder of the time, and the Russian Revolution would not have shot them if they had had a real sense of their epoch.

It is because in all authentic human feeling there is a rare force that commands respect from all.

During the first French Revolution, the crime of guillotining André Chénier was committed. But in an epoch of shootings, of hunger, of death, of despair, of blood, when nothing less than the equilibrium of the world was at stake, Chénier, lost in a useless and reactionary dream, was able to disappear without pity neither for poetry nor for his time.

And the universal, eternal feelings of Chénier, if he experienced them, were neither so universal nor so eternal that they could justify his existence at a time when the eternal was effaced behind a particular with innumerable concerns. Art, precisely, must take hold of particular concerns and raise them to the level of an emotion capable of dominating time.

Yet not every artist is capable of achieving the sort of magickal identification of their own feelings with the collective furies of man.

And not every epoch is capable of appreciating the social importance of the artist and the safeguarding function that he exercises for the benefit of the collective good.

Contempt for intellectual values is at the root of the modern world. In reality, this contempt conceals a deep ignorance of the nature of such values. But we cannot lose our strength in making this understood during a time which, among intellectuals and artists, produced a large proportion of traitors, and, among the people, engendered a collectivity, a mass which did not want to know that the spirit, that is to say the intelligence, must guide the course of time.

The capitalist liberalism of modern times has relegated the values of intelligence to the background, and modern man, faced with these few elementary truths that I have just stated, acts like a beast or like the terrified man of primitive times. To worry about it, he waits for these truths to become deeds, for them to be manifested in earthquakes, epidemics, famines, wars, that is to say in the roar of cannons.

I CAME TO MEXICO TO ESCAPE EUROPEAN CIVILIZATION …

I came to Mexico to escape European civilization, born of seven or eight centuries of bourgeois culture, and out of hatred for this civilization & this culture. I hoped to find here a vital form of culture and I have found only the corpse of the culture of Europe, which Europe is already beginning to rid itself of.

There are conscious people in Europe; in France there are also some. These people are the revolutionaries and I am a revolutionary like them. But, we want to pose the problem of revolution in a total way, and, in order to bring an idea of total revolution to fruition, we think that Marxism is not sufficient.

The revolution of Marx posed the problem of social revolution in a technical way. We think that the social revolution is only a separate aspect of the total revolution and that to consider the revolution exclusively from the social aspect is to prevent it from being brought to a successful end.

The problem does not appear to us as the substitution of one class by another class to ultimately arrive at the suppression of the classes; but it is to seek in man's ways of living the reasons for an eternal perversion.

When someone talks to me about eating right away, I answer that we must immediately look for ways so that everyone can eat right away. But when I am told:

Let's feed everyone immediately and, afterwards, the arts, sciences, and thought will be able to develop, I answer no, because that is where the problem has not been well posed.

For me, there is no revolution without a revolution in culture, that is to say, in our universal way, our way, for all of human beings, of understanding life and of posing the problem of life.

To dispossess those who own property is good, but it seems to me better to deprive every man of the taste for property.

Culture is eating; it is also knowing how to eat; and for me when I think, I eat, I devour and I assimilate thoughts. I receive the impressions of nature from outside and I expel them outward in thoughts. It is the same vital act, it is the same function of life that makes me think and eat. Separating the activity of the body from that of the intelligence is to pose the problem of life badly. The materialist concept of the world actually separates the two functions. Marxists believe in nourishing the body to allow the mind to function freely. This is for me a lazy attitude, a false notion of human happiness.

All creation is an act of war: war against hunger, against nature, against disease, against death, against life, against fate.

I am not for the sybaritism of individual peace. I am not for the arts of peace. Creating in peace is a bourgeois attitude, and if I am against all bourgeois attitudes, it is because I have a real notion of the spirit of property. Hunger, cold, love, sickness, and lack of sleep are not things from which one can derive artistic enjoyment. I am not in favor of artists procuring artistic pleasures at the cost of cold, hunger, sleep. I do not accept that artists individually possess their own satisfactions, because I am against the spirit of property, against the spirit of possession, on all possible levels.

There is a war between Marxism and myself, and this war rests on a distinct notion of individual consciousness. Marxism claims that it is impossible to reach consciousness directly because consciousness is something that we have no knowledge of. We want to force individuals to behave socially in an equitable manner by forcing them to do so through the determinism of facts. There is in this attitude a contempt for human consciousness which I share, and I think with Marxism that every individual is rotten.

I am in favor of the enslavement of human consciousness by matter, but I do not believe that the economic analysis of the world, that the reduction of all of the problems of the world to the simple economic factor, is the best means of achieving this goal.

To feed everyone is not to cure the world, but alongside a satisfied stomach there are the vices of the conscience, the passions, the idiosyncrasies of individuals, the spirit of madness and of crime, and also the betrayals of individuals. Every revolution has its traitors, and when, in a proletarian government, a proletarian betrays and passes over to reaction, is it because he ate too much or because he did not eat enough? I am asking you to answer me and, in doing so, please do not believe that I am oversimplifying the question.

Like you, I have a material notion of life and of being. But it is not enough for me to feed man; I want to understand how the life of man is perverted. Just as there are diseases of human organs, so there are alterations in human consciousness that to me are diseases. Stealing, betraying, deceiving are diseases that must be controlled. Hoarding is also a disease. I try to get a clear idea of human biology, and I want to attack human biology to prevent my ignorance from ever allowing it to enact vengeance.

Marxism has posed the problem of human biology badly. It denies the world of consciousness, and I want us to enter the world of consciousness with iron in hand, and for the revolution to take place, first, in that world. We know that the Marxist position is to succeed one day in mechanically explaining consciousness, but before we can do that I don't know what new madness will have time to crush the revolution.

Marxism cannot explain consciousness and refuses to recognize the world of consciousness because it believes that this would be to recognize the absolute reality of the spirit. And me, I say that because of this it adopts a spiritualist attitude. Its fear of studying consciousness as a world in itself means that, in speaking of the phenomena of consciousness, it continues to apply the old spiritualistic language that still draws a distinction between matter and spirit. Before the spirit, the materialist finds himself disarmed. I want one to enter into armed combat with the realm of consciousness because I have a material idea in mind, although I have an anti-materialist philosophy of life. I believe that life exists. I don't believe that life is born of matter, but I believe that matter is born of life.

There is a mysticism in Russia. Materialism is a mysticism, anti-imperialism is a mysticism, the struggle against fascism is a mysticism, the destruction of the family is a mysticism. I mean that there is a collection of ideas here which, by the mere fact of being formulated, provoke a direct action on the mind. The human mind, which moves fast, corrects its outward attitude and behavior in life according to its ideas. There is in this an immediate alchemy of consciousness. Those who betray their ideas are shot in the name of the value of those ideas and of the human and material attitude they entail. This supposes that we admit a particular life of consciousness, of consciousness that forms and deforms reality.

I say that if materialism did not believe in the life of ideas, it would renounce speech. It is therefore obliged, first of all, to admit a life of ideas and to judge ideas according to unverifiable laws. It takes this attitude because it cannot have another, and because the materialist explication of the world has stopped without explaining a whole set of facts that ceaselessly transform the life of the world.

Shooting traitors is fine, but it's a bit of a simplistic attitude. Who would venture to say that we have thus extirpated the spirit of betrayal? I claim that the spirit of betrayal is a curable and material thing, which it is possible to achieve materially.

Revolutionary biology has abandoned within consciousness a whole collection of notions that also belong to the counterrevolutionary consciousness, that is, to a bourgeois idea of man, nature, and life.

This is why I say: there is no revolution without a revolution in culture, that is, without a revolution of modern consciousness in the face of man, nature, and life.

It is for me a bourgeois idea to separate the problem of life from the problem of culture, the problem of life in man from the problem of life in nature, the problem of the body from the problem of the mind, and the problems of physiological diseases from the problems of mental diseases.

This analytical concept of the world is a lie of European culture, that is, a lie of the white spirit. So I add: there is no revolution without a revolution against the culture of Europe, against all forms of the white spirit, and I do not separate the white spirit from the forms of white civilization.

The white spirit is materialistic, but if life arose out of matter, it would take 50,000 years of experience to extract the laws of life from the experience of matter. If, contrarily, I believe that life governs matter, I can immediately organize matter through a knowledge of life.

The bourgeois world has never known life, but it has always known matter. It is on an exclusive idea of matter that the European world has lived. To know life solely through experience is to think that each experience in itself has a particular life value and from there it follows that each art form has a particular life value, that works of art are valid in their form and by their form and books by their written content.

There is an idea of the capitalization of forms as there is a capitalist form of life. You think like me that culture is not in books, but that it is a way of being in life. Eating, drinking, sleeping, loving, thinking, dreaming, that's culture, but you still have an experimental idea of life, and I ask you to tell me how you reconcile this contradiction.

If you admit that culture is a vital thing, you cannot recognize an existence in itself in written, painted, or sculpted forms of life, since you think that what lives is not the forms but the life that is found below them. Therefore, you must be ready like me to burn all forms that only imitate life. Alongside the capitalization of forms there is an idea of the petrification and conservation of forms, and that too is bourgeois.

It is because I have a unitary idea of culture that I say that thinking, sleeping, dreaming, eating, it's all the same thing. All of this is life. But I say that this same spirit of the collector who accumulates paintings and books and amasses stones in museums is also the spirit that hoards provisions, that asphyxiates the production of the world, and that diverts for the benefit of a few individuals a whole ensemble of material wealth whose enjoyment belongs to all.

If I say that true culture is not the one that is written, it is because I have a sense of life as that which moves, and culture is linked to a principle of life as that which moves. Capitalist Europe believes in the culture of books because in its conservative soul it has an idea of life that is not dynamic.

I don't believe in the culture of books, I don't believe in the culture of written things because I consider life as a free man; free, that is to say, that which has never been able to be concatenated.

However, I ask what happens to the materialistic idea when science, in its last stage, teaches us that there is no matter, that all life is energy, and that matter, in its multiple forms, is only one expression of this energy.

We examine atoms to understand matter, but each atom disappears in the sieve of science and transforms into a particular version of the dynamism of energy. Human thought is also an energy that takes on forms. And what prevents us from considering this energy in its particular form and from capturing this intense source of energy?

At the same time as matter, science destroys spaces. It is said that the notion of space is no more than a form that allows the human mind to distribute, each in its place, the various forces of energy. All great cultures deny this notion of space. China, for seven or eight thousand years, has been talking about emptiness and says that it is emptiness that is found at the origin of life. The Mexican Cross emerges from the void; it represents an idea of space that unfolds from the void. The six branches of the complete cross intersect at the same point, and this central point represents the void.

The cross of Christ symbolizes a human idea; it represents the death of Christ. It is an anthropomorphic idea. The Mexican Cross emerging from the void shows us how life enters space. It indicates how the emptiness of space can give an outlet to life.

**FRANZ HALS
— ORTIZ MONASTERIO —
MARIA IZQUIERDO**

FRANZ HALS

Franz Hals was born in 1580, either in Malines or in Antwerp. Historians disagree on this point. He spent his entire life in Harlem — a city of images — & died in poverty in 1666.

In any case, he is one of the most authentic representatives of specifically Flemish painting which, like all the great schools of painting, contains both myth and reality. The reality of Flemish painting is represented by the Brueghel brothers, Peter de Hooch, Van der Meulen and, finally, Franz Hals. The myth of Flemish painting is a myth of strength, of fullness, of solar joy. Each of the painters I have just mentioned participates more or less in this myth, but Hals expresses its social strength more particularly. His technique is similar to that of Rubens, with something less luminous, less radiant, less sunny, less smoky. Smoldering. The painting of Hals plunges into the smoke of a hundred pipes, into the sulfurous residues of a large firework on a Carnival day. Brueghel the Elder manifests the obsessions & larval anxieties, so to speak, of the Flemish soul that pursue the infernal terrors of his old racial unconscious. Hals embodies the joy of the surface, the laughter, the noise. The painting of Hals is a painting that laughs in a range of ash blue, salmon, acid green, sometimes noisy pink and dark garnet always similar to coagulated clouds of smoke. A painting that laughs less than that of Jordaens — that is really a burst of laughter — but that gives powerful pictures of the life of peasants, kings, nobles, bourgeois, with, here and there, a vague tinge of crepuscular melancholy. Rubens is the jubilation of the flesh, a feast of voluptuousness in the radiations of a great solar magick. Jordaens is the artificial and disguised gaiety, he is the theater transported into family life. Hals is the nostalgia for latent pleasure, the desolation of the inner life in the midst of dynamic scenes of pathic outer life. In the painting of Hals, the shadows of an early dusk rise to the heart of the sun of life.

The painting that is reproduced here has this particular feature: where painters usually conceal their technique, Hals openly shows his, but every visible stroke of the brush carries in itself the tormented thrill of his life.

A TECHNICIAN WHO WORKS IN STONE: ORTIZ MONASTERIO

May the Mexican artists please excuse me: there is no Mexican art in Mexico. Nowhere have I found that dazzling stroke, that unmistakable outburst which distinguishes the works of a race, which marks the spirit of a continent where it is finally time for Mexicans to begin to find their personality, after four hundred years of influence — I should say of *fascinating domination* — of Europe.

If the 1910 revolution has a meaning, it is not only because it freed the oppressed classes from capitalist influence — an influence that, moreover, still persists —, it is because it gave rise to the forgotten unconscious of the race, but how many modern Mexicans have understood this necessary liberation of their unconscious?

In his cut stones, the young sculptor Ortiz Monasterio shows that he suffered the intellectual oppression of Mexico and, of course, one feels that something is gestating in his stone, although *the form* is still contaminated by the fashionable plastic speculations of Parisian sculpture.

Yet the Paris school knows, better than any other, that the strength of the white world is dried up and it is in the arts of the past that it seeks new sources.

Monasterio's technique is powerful. He blasts the stone with great blows, revealing a rounded life under the stone, disangular bodies in which I don't know what pure force shines circularly. I have already seen, in Parisian sculpture, this generous and broad technique, more voluntary than spontaneous. Modern French sculpture has exasperated the influence of Black sculpture to the point of slavish imitation, and especially of certain Hittite or Assyrian bas-reliefs.

Imitating that stylization, Monasterio imitates the forms of the Assyrian stylization through Parisian sculpture: it is a stylization of the second degree. And all the painting, all the modern Mexican sculpture, bear the imprint of this stylization to the second degree.

But it must be said that they have the providential fortune of possessing the primary sources of every stylization on their own soil. It is with the same spirit of generous mortification of forms that the Toltec, Maya, and Totonac sculptors worked in other times; imitating the stylization of Paris, which is arbitrary, Monasterio rediscovers through his old racial unconscious the revived *necessity* of this same stylization, from which it follows that Monasterio's stylizations, which at first sight seem the result of a technical artifice, live, when you examine them more closely, with the strength of an atavistic inspiration that, in a certain sense, justifies them.

There is, without a doubt, a technician emeritus in Monasterio, a man who does not ignore the difficulty of cutting the stone in any way, and whose works manifest in a moving way the sense of this surmounted difficulty: one feels the human *sigh!* in his works, the panting breath of man who by force of labor and torments has come to dominate nature, but who, by dominating it, wanted to erase all traces of his torture to offer us an agile, light, balanced, and round work. The sculpture opens like the wings of a very ancient triptych and presents us with flattened and rough forms, the forms of a compact and opulent humanity that strives to unfold itself in the sense of amplitude. The bodies are heavy and powerful, and as if barely detached and distinct from the mass of a nature that lends them all its strength, but thanks to forms that could be called inhuman, since they lack muscles and nerves: they are like the petrified sketches of a form *on its way* toward the human, and as if preparing to support the soul; but it is precisely the confused, material soul of these bodies that shows that the skilled technician is still looking for inspiration.

Yes, for the moment one can see in him *only a refined craftsman* of the stone, and I still await the poet that is in him.

When Monasterio shows us a man undressed and lying under the pipes of a factory that oppresses him, I am amazed by the fact that the undressed man reminds me, with his forms, of that almost divine humanity that swarms in the lines, in the bas-reliefs & on the facades of certain ancient Maya temples, in the vestiges of Toltec or Totonac architecture. It is this racial influence that invincibly imposes itself on the artists of Mexico, and if I have any reproach to them, it is not to persecute, relentlessly, even violently, with an obstinacy that should always be tireless, the originality of this inspiration.

But, apart from the stylization, the piping of the factory remains, which represents the sectarian symbol, the ideology of the *political party* that has nothing to do with the sculpture itself: it is enough that the prone man is a proletarian and that he has chains at his feet to secure them.

Yet, in my view, the problem that arises is not that the proletarian has chains on his feet — chains that must be broken, — but that modern man has come to be the victim of a civilization that he himself has invented.

Another sculpture by Monasterio shows us a Venus transformed into a machine. The tragedy is that he has eluded the problem of love that has become a machine. It is on this problem that he should have rested and insisted. Monasterio has carved a body largely supplanted by pipes and, from a pure human point of view, it is a horrible torture; but this torture, he forgot to represent it *on a higher plane*.

Monasterio defines it as a Surrealist sculpture, forgetting that Surrealism has never exalted the machine. Surrealism has mixed the appearance of the machine with all the outward appearances of a world that, for it, does not deserve to exist. Surrealism seeks a higher reality and, in order to reach it, it destroys forms, transitory forms, in search of what in the language of the ancient Vedas is called the *Non-Manifested*.

The Venus of Monasterio has the air of adapting perfectly to machines, but, it should be remembered, the art that enhances the conquest of the machine, speed, the modern world and all its easiness, is Futurism, whose frantic, useless, bubbling and misguided kaleidoscope Surrealism later came to overthrow.

There is no thought in Futurism; there are only frenetic representations of forms, while Surrealism takes possession of *manifested* forms to extract from them the *Non-Manifested*.

The imbeciles have called the Surrealist movement a destroyer. Undoubtedly it is the destroyer of every transitory and imperfect form, but farther than forms it seeks the occult and magickal presence of a fascinating irreality.

It is precisely that absolute reality which is lacking in the intermediate art of Monasterio, but Monasterio — who has a perfect technique — deserves that his intermediate art, his art in full gestation, becomes a fixed, inspired, and firm art, as well as the art of Mexico, today still in a larval and impersonal state, deserves to rediscover the ancient solar inspiration of the great artists of the past.

P. S. — I know well that when I speak of the impersonality of art in Mexico, one can answer: Diego Rivera. Yes, there is an embryo of personality in Rivera's frescoes. Excuse me, but this embryo is still weak. On the other hand, Rivera worked in Paris, and this does not fail to be seen. We are far from the mighty solar fulguration of original Mexican art.

Furthermore, Rivera is a materialist, and this too shows. When you do not have the sense of a transcendent force — in the art of painting as in any art — this is noticed by a kind of *block* of inspiration, by an *inner opacity* of the forms.

However closed they are, Monasterio's forms are not opaque. One feels in them the hope, the appeal, the echo of a higher light, which has nothing to do, moreover, with the light that emanates from the unfathomable mysteries of nature, those mysteries that the ancient artists of Mexico seem to have scrutinized.

THE PAINTING OF MARIA IZQUIERDO

I came to Mexico to look for indigenous art and not an imitation of European art. Indeed, if imitations of European art in all its forms abound, there is no strictly Mexican art.

Only the painting of Maria Izquierdo testifies to a truly Indian inspiration. That is to say that, among the hybrid manifestations of current Mexican painting, Izquierdo's sincere, spontaneous, primitive, disturbing painting was a sort of revelation for me.

In any case, a clarification is required: this painting is spontaneous, but it is not entirely pure; here and there, in some works, a direct influence of modern European art can be seen. Here then is the danger: as it develops, Izquierdo's pictorial activity is increasingly influenced by modern European techniques and, in some canvases, even by its spirit. And this is even more regrettable.

The Indian spirit is lost, and I am really afraid of having come to Mexico to witness the end of an old world, while I thought I was witnessing its resurrection.

My emotion was all the greater when I saw, in the gouaches of Izquierdo, indigenous characters shivering naked among ruins. There they perform a kind of ghost dance: the ghosts of the life that has been lost.

And it is not only the European technique that so often transpires in the art of Izquierdo, it is also the mechanistic civilization of Europe; but the use that she makes of European machines and planes is the strangest. We know the hieroglyphic procedure of the Indians, which consists in placing the imaginary sign of the voice, of speech, in front of the mouth of an orator or a cantor. It looks like an inverted snail, a circular tangle of lines. Now, in an oil painting by Izquierdo, a naked Indian sings before an open window; and the smoke from a nearby factory, which rises in spirals in the air, seems to form like circles before the mouth of the Indian. These spirals, in this canvas, are the breath itself, the animated breath of the singer. But the canvas carries within it the germ of a double idea: Izquierdo uses the smoke of Europe as if she wanted to cancel it. She does not clearly distinguish all this, but the spirit of the Indian race speaks so loudly in her that, even unconsciously, it repeats its voice.

For my part, I will say that I infinitely prefer the canvases in which there is no trace of the European spirit.

Countless subdivisions can be established in Izquierdo's painting, corresponding to all the influences that painting has undergone in the course of her work, already very important.

There are hybrid canvases, like the one I just mentioned, in which the spirit of the race defends itself.

There are also those in which the technique of modern European art is directly perceived, and in which the tics of Derain, of Picasso, of Kisling, of [Otakar] Kubín, of Kremegne are expressed from below.

I have before my eyes a beautiful nude sitting on a chair. There are reminiscences of the arbitrary deformations typical of Paris painting, especially on one side of the back and in the right arm. But where the Parisian deformations are only arbitrary and do not correspond to reality at all, Izquierdo finds the "necessity" of the deformation. A little of the tortured, restless, and I would even dare to say metaphysically restless spirit of the Tarasca race has passed over this deformation. I would not like to use grandiloquent terms, but these arms and this back that seem to move, whose pieces seem to vibrate to build a real man's arm and back, lead us by the hand to an essential geometric problem. We think irresistibly of the architecture of man. And this is precisely the purpose of painting, of art seen from the inside of painting, of art considered in its purity: to bring us each time before a vital problem, and lead us there *inevitably*, that is, *dynamically*.

What is very beautiful, so precious in this canvas, is the hand. A hand without deformation, with a particular structure, and which looks like a tongue of fire. Green, like the dark part of a flame, and which carries within itself all the agitations of life. A hand to caress and make graceful gestures. And that lives as a clear thing in the red shadow of the canvas. Because the whole canvas has the hue of the colonial stones of Mexico, a dark color of fire. All of Izquierdo's painting develops within this color of cold lava, in this penumbra of a volcano.

That is what gives it its disturbing character, unique in all Mexican painting; brings the reflection of a world in the making, of a world still in fusion. Her ruins do not evoke a world in ruins, they evoke a world about to be remade.

    Undoubtedly, Izquierdo does not escape the reproach of aestheticism; in her, here and there, there are a lot of undressed virgins who lament before a crucifix. Here is the amalgamated part of the current civilization of Mexico: a kind of pagan Catholicism that, behind the Latin cross of Christ, strives to find the cross with the same arms of the old geometric palaces of Uxmal, of Mitla, of Palenque, or of Copan.

    Izquierdo, as long as she takes the trouble to appreciate her own strength, is able to revive, before a caravan of naked, red-faced Indians, the natural cross, the scientific cross of the ancient solar culture that bears its gods as banners.

P. S. — The Indian spirit has its synthetic laws. Its allegorical force is so powerful that, wherever and from wherever it speaks, it unconsciously leaves behind it a whole system of the world and its life.

    Undoubtedly, Izquierdo is in communication with the true forces of the Indian soul. She carries its drama within herself, and this drama misunderstands its sources. To safeguard her personality, she must make a considerable effort for purity, and this effort will soon find its reward. Because a horse by Izquierdo immediately evokes all the horses that, at the time of the conquest, impressed the spirit of the old Mexicans. There is totemism in Izquierdo's painting. Her wild horses can be confused with the evil spirits of the earth. And this totemism produces a kind of millenary animism: thus, I find it in another of the canvases I know, of which I remember at this moment: animals that gallop and pass from one side of the canvas to the other, and in the center a moon shines like a bull's-eye on a wall. Now, after about ten thousand years, the religion of the bull's-eye on the wall is practiced by a sect of thirty thousand people on the borders of Eastern Siberia, between Russia and Mongolia. Without knowing it, Izquierdo found, in these canvases, the very soul of an ancient human concept.

THREE NOTES ON MARIA IZQUIERDO

Maria Izquierdo's painting proves that the red spirit is not dead: that her sap boils with an intensity increased by the same long work of waiting, of incubation, of maceration.

※

The red soul is concrete, and it speaks. It can even be said without exaggeration that it *roars*. Among contemporary Mexican painters, Maria Izquierdo is the only one to have felt this vehement, whirling side, transported by the original Mexican soul, which without difficulty and as if playing with it, it tames lions. Izquierdo's painting returns us to the fabalistic times when, within the walls of a holy city, lions ran, more alive, more intelligent, more lucid than humans.

※

Inspiration, this powerful atavism of the race, abounds in Izquierdo's art. The forms and colors born under her brush with a kind of interior vivacity which is a mark of her predestination. The characters arrive in the form in which they have previously lived; the colors are united with the vibration of a solar specter of the kind that they correspond in a harmony that is more than strange: a red and a blue perform this miracle by mutually returning to their mystery, the mystery born of color.

MEXICO AND THE PRIMITIVE MIND:
MARIA IZQUIERDO

If it is with objects that we know the Sensate, it is with the dream that we know objects. In the waking state, everything that exists is dead; and objects do not reveal their code. One has to sleep for them to start talking. If there was a time when things spoke without being solicited, you need to be a man of the present age to believe that this time belongs to the past.

It is said that the primitive mind is that which cannot see what it is, because nothing really exists, but which, through the brush or the pen, reproduces what it supposes; and what it supposes is always a measure of its limitless imagination. Yet imagination is linked to knowledge, & knowledge to Unity. The great imaginations are not those which make the Sensate flow under the multiplicity of its aspects, but those which, in the midst of the Sensate, move with that kind of alchemical virtue which belongs to the state of sleep.

For those who know how to use its codes and its strange operations, sleep takes us back to the time when things had to speak, because the waking consciousness of man was like a muzzled animal.

The primitive, not feeling distinct from what it is, cannot believe that something lives outside of itself, and does not have the feeling of ownership; and in turn, the things that are cannot have properties that really belong to them, since they partake of all that which is; this is how the feeling of the eternal altruism of things leads us back through a sort of alchemical transmutation to a feeling of unity.

But whoever says unity says knowledge, since "knowing" is "resurrecting with"; and in sleep, the figures of moving objects have, together with their singular properties, the properties of all other objects. Because objects do not form the real, but they are traveling in the real; and in the dream they are the properties of objects that travel; and passing their strengths on to each other, they teach us reality in its entirety.

Thus, it is with the loss of their singular qualities that objects teach us reality; and consciousness, by showing us what it is, only kills the things that speak; because an object must always cease to be itself in order for us to learn *in reality* what it is. The absurd words of the dream are the words of reality on the move, that is, words that have just begun to speak.

To sacrifice oneself is to enter into murmuring reality; it means allowing all objects of the Sensate to truly use their properties. Giving up a single property is the means to truly enter all the others. And primitive altruism, which resides in an unlimited abandonment of self, provides a richness of which the narrow consciousness of modern man does not even suspect the properties.

What does the dream do if not take away from the ear which speaks the property of receiving something which the noises of the world give it to become in turn capable of emitting concerted sounds.

A color that causes the mind to hallucinate a marching army, if it explains how the mind works in dreams, also explains how the extreme particularity of things can, by their very being particular, bring us closer to the unity of that which is.

This is how the Primitive broke down the barriers that currently separate us from the knowledge of objects.

If all is in all, only the primitive mind allowed human consciousness to enter the variety of objects through the metamorphosis of an object.

And the dream, through time, brings us back to that time when, under the shock of human spontaneity, the whole of Nature became bewitched.

We now understand by what mechanism of natural sorcery that what is called the primitive or sacred mind was able to breathe into everything it touched a world of infinite & contradictory qualities; and how nothing that it offers us seems in reality what it is.

"This lion believes that it is a man," Rimbaud says in essence, "but I teach him that he is nothing but a pug."

By contrast, the lions of Izquierdo are like the figure of the volcanic crater on which they were born.

There is in Mexico a plant-principle that makes you journey into reality. It is through it that an infinitely stretched color spreads out to the music from which it came; and this music brings beasts howling with the sonority of hammered metal.

One understands the adoration of certain tribes of Mexican Indians for Peyote, which does not make the eyes marvel as the European vocabulary teaches us, but which possess the strange alchemical virtue of transmuting reality, of plunging us to the point where everything is abandoned to be sure to start over. Through it we leap over time, which takes millennia to transform a color into an object, to reduce forms to their music, to return the mind to its sources, and unite what was believed to be separate.

The gouaches of Izquierdo seemed to me, at least to a certain extent, to participate in this spirit; and that's why I brought them back. Certainly, this spirit is not pure, and if there remain strange foci of sacred spirit, in Mexico, it is not in the cities that you need to go and look for them, because this old spirit is Indian and today's mestizo Mexico does the impossible to make it disappear. Because if the mestizos of the cities, who have to fight between two types of blood, cannot kill their red blood, they are determined to ruin in themselves everything that can exist of red spirit. And this in the morbid fear of not being of their time.

Although a pure Tarascan, Izquierdo lives in Mexico City. And we know that for Mexicans everything that is autochthonous culture, this whole system of concrete exchanges between the man with overwhelmed senses & the world injected with forces that cross it from all sides, everything that, for some of us, participates in an effective magick capable of regenerating us, it appears to the mestizos of the cities as something equally outdated as the myths of ancient Greece, or as the magick tricks of an old Babylonian priest.

And this struggle of influences is visible in the art of Izquierdo.

With Derain, Masson, Salvador Dalí, Chirico, Matisse, modern painting bursts into Mexico City; and although Indian, Izquierdo is concerned with what she can bring the city.

You can see in her gouaches lost architectures, statues on dead lands, stones that, in a cave light, take on the air of human organs.

But here and there her inspired race is the strongest. She knows what hazardous spells modern painting is made of, and that these spells evoke disease, not health. Why do the painters I have just mentioned do anything other than blindly bring back the forms that rise from their troubled Unconscious?

Of course, we all feel confusedly here in Europe that the external world is over, and that it is time to return to something else. What we no longer find in the waking world, we look for in the dream. And it is by drawing on the life of dreams, where everyone's psychology disappears, that today's artists bring back these figures, these form-signs, which have such strange kinship with primitive productions.

They have rediscovered the old spirit that wants reality to obey the forms of an invented intelligence. And it is man that magically invents them. And the world is what he makes it. They have given up on unnecessary art. But what they find, they themselves are the first to claim that they don't understand it.

This is because today's art-inspiration is an art that has lost science. When the ancient artist painted, he painted as one exorcises; and he traditionally knew the gestures that allow us to dissociate what is. Art was an open hunt whose journey we followed anxiously. Because each time an artist worked, we felt very well that the world did not remain inert; and it was something of collective life that was reworked each time.

Now, although life has changed, it seems that we have returned to these same regions of consciousness where the mind directly invented forms to refresh reality. But with the past forms the painters had probably come to command everything that moves, while today those same forms, which the collective Unconscious has resurrected, may exorcise us, but it is because they command us, and we no longer know how to command them.

If, even in Mexico, the primitive mind is in decline, it is very evident that an Indian artist can only be herself when she is truly inspired by it, rather than, as Izquierdo sometimes does, to reproduce images of Europe that are only the reminiscence of the pure forms which revolve in her own unconscious.

The Indian mind, when it remains, obstinately continues to produce those symbols, those forms-signs that instigate our wonder.

I have seen in magic dances women with their child in their arms making the gesture of embracing the sun; and they atavistically know the code that makes this intertwining effective.

Ancient rites and ancient virtues rest in Mexico in the mountains; and man systematically burns the trees there in the form of signs; and these signs, which are exactly those of every traditional magick, Nature, as if to respond to the increasingly desperate appeal of men, carves them, with an obstinate and mathematical rigor, in the shapes of its rocks.

We can therefore see that Mexico, when it remains faithful to itself, has nothing to receive from anyone, but on the contrary that it has everything to give.

The Indian soul does not know what to do with these lost sections of a reality in which today's spirit is hopelessly seeking the trace of something else; because it knows the meaning of secret alloys. It is by tapping into her racial unconscious that Izquierdo brings back to us her lions, which deserve to be adored by the human spirit because they participate in all the Kingdoms where Nature has examined itself.

A man, a horse, a color, a crater, with the kind of colored vibration in which their unusual figures sink, in painting them, Izquierdo explains to us why these objects are made to go together. And it is by their very particularity that the properties of objects attract each other; and they are only artificially separated.

If the last Mexican Indians no longer know how to consider what they possess with the spirit of property, if they do not know the love of duality, if they no longer see what they are divided from, it is that they have never lost this unique spirit which reduces the world in a single movement; it is that they always have this spirit of death which made the life of Ancient Mexico; and which, detached from all accidents, from all the fleeting aspects of the Sensate, the Indian, who knows how to kill that which passes, joins life in its totality.

THE TARAHUMARA

TEXTS PUBLISHED IN
ÉL NACIONAL AND *VOILÀ*

THE LAND OF THE MAGI

Where have I already heard that it was not in Italy but in Mexico that pre-Renaissance painters took the blue of their landscapes, and the immense tapering of the backgrounds with which they decorated their Nativity scenes.

In the land of the Tarahumara the most incredible legends provide proof of their reality. — When one enters this country and one sees gods on top of the mountains, gods with a shortened arm on the left side, and an emptiness on the right side, and who lean on the right side; and that, stooping, one hears rising at his feet the crash of a waterfall, and, above the waterfall, the wind that runs from summit to summit; and climb until you discover an immense circle of summits around you, you can no longer doubt that you have reached one of those neuralgic points of the earth where life has shown its first effects.

The Italian painters before the Renaissance were initiated into a secret science that modern science has not yet fully discovered, and in this Science the art of the Higher Eras also participated.

The blue of the remote depths of the high Mexican mountains calls for precise shapes and ideas, it imposes on the mind like the memory of a Science to which the Intervention of the Three Wise Men is linked!!!!

It is not out of a religious spirit that Piero Della Francesca, Lucas de Leiden, Fra Angelico, Piero di Cosimo, and Mantegna painted so many Nativity scenes. It is by a traditional preoccupation with the Essential, by a search for the secrets of life, and because of this natural obsession of the Great Spirits with the How & the Why of the principles & the primitive explosions of Nature that the *Pagan Christmas Legend* has manifested.

If Religion then seized these principles and if the peoples had the weakness to turn away from the Principles to adore the religion, so much the worse for the stupefied and fantasized peoples, but it is not so much the worse for the Principles. In the Tarahumara mountain everything speaks only of the Essential, that is to say of the principles according to which Nature was formed; and everything lives only for these principles: men, storms, wind, silence, sun.

We are far from the warlike and civilized actuality of the modern world, and not warlike although civilized, but warlike *because civilized*: this is how the Tarahumara think. And their legends, or better *their Traditions* tell (because here there are no legends, that is to say no illusory fables, but perhaps incredible Traditions, the reality of which is gradually demonstrated by scholarly excavations), they relate, these traditions, the passage in the tribes of the Tarahumara of a race of Men who bring fire, and who had three Masters or three Kings, and walked toward the Polar Star.

Now, if Science has its Great Men: like Newton, Darwin, Kepler, Lavoisier, etc., Civilizations also have them from a moral & Social point of view: Odin, Rama, Fo-Hi, Lao-Tse, Zoroaster, Confucius; and it seems that the legend of the Three Wise Men hides, in the geographical line, the passage of the great Solar Tradition, wherever the *Scientific* Cult of the Sun has erected pyramids and mathematically oriented altars, of three Civilizers initiated into a transcendent astronomy whose laws were parallel to those of Maya astronomy.

When it is known that the astronomical cult of the sun has been universally expressed by means of signs and that these signs are the same and belong to an ancient and very complete Science, which the absurd language of Europe has called Universal Esotericism, and when these same signs: the handle cross, the swastika, the Double Cross, the great circle with a point in the middle, two opposite triangles, three points, four triangles in the four cardinal points, the twelve signs of the zodiac, abound in the East as in Mexico on temples and in manuscripts, which I have never seen *in Nature* as in the heart of the Tarahumara Mountain; — when you know all this and suddenly enter a country literally haunted with signs of this kind and when you find it in the gestures and rites of a race, and when the men, women, & children of this race wear them embroidered on their cloaks, the spirit feels troubled as if they had reached the source of a mystery.

But if we also think that the Sierra Tarahumara is the country where the first skeletons of giant men have been found, and at the precise moment that I write this they are still being found; if you think about all this, the legends lose their quality as legends, becoming realities. The Renaissance of the 16th century has broken with a reality that had its laws, perhaps extra-human, but natural; and the Humanism of the Renaissance could not magnify but diminish man, since man has stopped raising himself to nature to lower it to his size, and the exclusive consideration of the human has spoiled the Natural.

It is then that the astronomical science of nature, whose life revolves around the Sun, has become secret; but in this magickal naturalism, everywhere the same, whose tradition advances without stopping from the East to the West, the primitives of Florence, Assisi, Como, etc., had been initiates.

In their paintings of the Nativities and the Magi, these painters have expressed a mystery of life as children of a time when art was, above all, the Servant of science. For this reason, the paintings of these painters, if it were possible to read them with the affective fibers of the soul, could also be read with the high rational Science of the spirit. If a color enchants the heart, it is because it corresponds to an exact and scientific vibration in which the Primary Numbers can be found.

Having said this, it seems more than strange to me that the country where the tradition of the Maya bearers of fire lives on the face of the rocks, in the costumes *&* in the sacred rhythm of men, is also the country of colored noise; the grandiose vibration of Nature recalls with the most obsessive intensity an entire era of painting, whose Great Men were also obsessed by the same signs, the same shapes, the same lights, *&* the same secrets.

NOTE

Nature has produced dancers in their circle as she produces corn in its circle & signs in the forests.

A PRINCIPLE RACE

With the Tarahumara one enters a terribly anachronistic world that is a challenge to our time. I would dare to say that this is so much worse for our time than it is for the Tarahumara. It is thus that, to use a term now in complete disrepute, the Tarahumara say, feel, believe, they are a Principle Race, and which they prove in every case. In our time no one knows what a Principle Race is, and if I had not seen the Tarahumara I would believe that this expression concealed a Myth. But in that Sierra Tarahumara many Great Ancient Myths are relevant.

The Tarahumara do not believe in God and the word "God" does not even exist in their language; they only worship a transcendent principle of Nature, which is Male and Female, *as it should be*. And they carry that principle on their head like the Initiated Pharaohs. Yes, this sort of two-pointed headband that they use to surround their hair indicates that they still have in their blood the consciousness of a high natural selection; that they feel, and are, a race related to the originally Male and Female forces with which Nature worked.

So, too, the Chinese initiated in the true traditions of their fathers, wear two braids on their backs. Moses is represented by statues of him with two horns that rise out of his forehead; one for the male on the right, one for the female on the left; and some Tarahumara also carry their hair thrown back in the shape of horns.

This is reminiscent, as the statues of Moses, of certain Maya or Totonac masks that have two holes marked on the forehead, vertically, as if in memory of a petrified ocular system.

Many Tarahumara Indians, either because they do not want to say anything, or because they have forgotten what this means, claim that the headdress described is the effect of chance and that the band serves only to hold their hair, but I have seen that they tie it in such a way that the ends are hanging; and above all I have seen the Peyote priests at the moment of executing this rite, by nature male and female, throw down their European hat and put on the two-cornered headband again, as if they wanted to show by means of this gesture that they were entering into the circle of the magnetized poles of Nature.

There is an indisputable initiation in this race: he who is close to the forces of Nature participates in its secrets. But this initiation has two very marked aspects, because if the Tarahumara are physically strong like Nature, it is not because they live materially close to it, but because they are made of its very fabric, its same texture, and like all the authentic manifestations of Nature, they have been born from a primary mixture.

It could be said that it is the natural Unconscious that restores in them not only the usury of fatigue but also the natural perversions of a great principle by which they explain the existence of all infirmities. In part, they demonstrate their initiation in the signs that they engrave with obsessive abundance on the trees and rocks, and in part they reveal them in their bodily virtues, by their admirable resistance to fatigue, and by their disdain for physical pain, evil, and diseases.

It is false to say that the Tarahumara have no civilization when their concept is reduced to simple physical freedoms or material comforts that they have always despised.

For, if the Tarahumara do not know how to work metals, they are still in the age of spears and arrows, if they work the land with carved tree trunks & if they sleep on the ground fully clothed, on the other hand they have the highest idea of the forces that intervene in the philosophical movement of Nature. They have grasped the secrets of those forces in their idea of Number-Principles just as exactly as Pythagoras himself did. The truth is that the Tarahumara despise the life of their bodies and live only for their ideas: I mean, in constant and almost magickal communication with the superior life of those ideas.

Each Tarahumara village is presided over by a cross, surrounded by crosses oriented toward the four cardinal points of the mountain. It is not the cross of christ, the Catholic cross; it is the cross of Man dismembered in space, of the invisible Man who has open arms and who is nailed to the four cardinal points. Through this figure, the Tarahumara manifest an active geometric idea of the world to which the very form of Man is linked.

This means: here the geometric space is alive and has produced what is best in it, that is, Man.

The stone that each Tarahumara must put, on pain of death, at the foot of the cross, in passing, is not a superstition, but an awareness.

This also means: Mark the point. Realize it. Become aware of the opposing life forces, because without this awareness you are dead.

But the Tarahumara do not fear physical death: the body, they say, is made for its disappearance; it is spiritual death that they fear, yet not in a catholic sense, although the Jesuits have passed through here.

These Indians have a tradition of metempsychosis; and it is the further fall of their Double that they fear above all else. Not being aware of what it is, of what it can become, is exposing yourself to losing your Double. It is to risk, suffering beyond physical space, a kind of abstract fall, a wandering through the high planetary regions of the disembodied human principle.

Evil, for them, does not consist in sin. For the Tarahumara, sin does not exist: evil is the loss of consciousness. Because higher philosophical problems count more for them than the precepts of our Western morality.

The Tarahumara are obsessed with philosophy; are even obsessed with a kind of physiological spell; there is no lost gesture between them, a gesture that does not have a direct philosophical meaning. The Tarahumara become philosophers just as a little child grows up and makes itself a man; they are born philosophers.

And the band with two points on the back signifies that they belong to a race originally Male and Female; but this band also has another signification: an obvious historical signification. The *Puranas* bear the memory of a war that the Male and the Female of Nature waged on each other, and men of old took part in this war in which the forces of the two opposing principles fought against each other. The supporters of the natural Male sported the color white: those of the Female the color red, that same esoteric and sacred red from which the Phœnicians, who were of the Female race, took the idea of purple, which they then industrialized.

Yet, if the Tarahumara race wears a band that is sometimes white and sometimes red, it is not to affirm the duality of the two opposing forces, it is to mark that *within* the Tarahumara race, the Male & the Female of Nature exist simultaneously, and that the Tarahumara benefit from their joined forces. They carry, in short, their philosophy on their head, and this philosophy unites the action of two opposing forces in an almost divine balance.

THE RITE OF THE KINGS OF ATLANTIS

On 16 September, Mexico's Independence Day, I saw in Norogachi, deep in the Sierra Tarahumara, the rite of the kings of Atlantis as Plato describes it in the pages of the *Critias*. Plato speaks of a strange rite to which, in desperate circumstances for their race, the kings of Atlantis abandoned themselves.

However mythical the existence of Atlantis, Plato describes the Atlanteans as a race of magickal origin. The Tarahumara, whom I consider direct descendants of the Atlanteans, continue to devote themselves to the cult of magickal rites.

Let those who do not believe me go to the Sierra Tarahumara: they will see that in this country where the rock offers the appearance and structure of fable, legend becomes reality and that there can be no reality outside of this fable. I know that the existence of the Indians is not to the liking of the world today; yet, in the presence of a race like that, by comparison, it can be concluded that it is modern life that is lagging behind in relation to something, and not that the Tarahumara Indians are backward compared to the present world.

They know that every step forward, every ease acquired in the domain of a purely physical civilization, also implies a loss, a regression.

Consequently, it can be said that the question of progress does not arise in the face of every authentic tradition. True traditions do not progress, since they represent the advanced point of every possible truth. And the only achievable progress consists in preserving the form and the strength of these traditions. Over the centuries, the Tarahumara have learned how to retain their virility.

So then, returning to Plato and to the true esoteric traditions that manifest his written works, I saw in the Tarahumara Sierra the rite of those chimerical & desperate kings.

Plato tells us that, at sunset, the kings of Atlantis gathered before a sacrificed bull. And while the servants dismembered the bull, others picked up the pieces, pouring the blood into cups. The kings drank this blood & got drunk singing a kind of mournful melody until there was nothing left in the sky but the head of the dying sun, and on the ground nothing but the head of the sacrificed bull. Then the kings covered their heads with ashes. And their funeral melody changed pitch as they tightened the circle they formed. Everything that was an invocation to the Sun became a kind of bitter reproach, acquiring the form of a public contrition, a remorse that the kings expressed in mutual agreement until the moment when night had completely fallen.

Such is the sense of the rite described by Plato. Now, a little before the sun set in Norogachi, the Indians led an ox to the village square and, after tying its legs, they began to tear its heart to pieces. Fresh blood was collected in large jars. I will not easily forget the ox's rictus of pain, while the knife of the Indian tore its bowels to pieces. The *matachines* dancers rushed to gather before the bull, and as soon as it died, they began their flower dances.

Because the Indians dance dances of flowers, dragonflies, birds, and other things before this carnage, and it was truly a strange spectacle what two Indians offered, perched on the dead bull, while they made the blood gush and separated the pieces with ax blows, while the other Indians, dressed as kings and with a crown of mirrors on their heads, performed their dances of dragonflies, of birds, of wind, of things, of flowers.

The dances lasted well into the night.

An entire village can participate in the dance of the *matachines*; however, for each stage of the dance there is one king. And the kings of the *matachines* take turns. Each dances according to his temperament.

That day there was only one musician, sitting on the ground, playing the violin. However, the complete orchestra consists of a guitar, a small drum, bells, and iron batons. The small drum is a musical instrument of war; its noise reverberates from peak to peak.

The kings of the dance wear a crown of mirrors, the Masonic apron in the shape of a triangle and a large rectangular cloak on their shoulders. In addition, they wear special pants, which end in a triangular shape, a little lower than the knees.

The *matachines* are not a sacred rite, but a popular, profane dance that was brought to Mexico by the Spaniards. However, the Tarahumara gave it an Indian form, marking it with their spirit. Although, in principle, these dances imitate the movements of external nature: the wind, the trees, an anthill, a troubled river acquire a highly cosmogonic sense among the Tarahumara, and I had the impression of contemplating before me the agitation of the cosmic ants to the rhythm of celestial music.

They dance to the sound of childish & refined music, which no European ear can recognize; it seems to always hear the same sound, the same rhythm; however, over time, these always identical sounds & this rhythm, suggest in us the memory of a great Myth; they evoke the feeling of a mysterious & complicated story.

The director of the dance writhed in time with the rhythm, imitating with his dance the step of a tiny staggering ant; the dancer broke, bent over with the ataxic movements of an excessively swollen frog; his right hand skillfully held a calabash full of hardened orugo rings that had taken on the consistency of glass, while his left hand played with a fan of flowers.

The music of the Tarahumara is divided into a very small number of bars that are repeated indefinitely. And with each new beat the director of the dance leaves his place, abandons the space where he was contorting and, afterward, goes around the other dancers.

These dancers are divided into two groups, and each, subsequently, presents his face to the director. He presents him as a knight in arms with the splendor of the ancient warrior covered in his armor, then turning in the opposite direction. When the director has turned around each dancer, he returns to take his place by stamping his feet. And one phase of the dance is completed. But others come later, and the frenzy that lasts one night begins again, until the sun is close to dawn, without the dancers ever getting tired.

In a row, standing, leaning obliquely against the wall, that is, not with their backs against the wall, but now presenting the left side, now the right side, some young people occasionally let out a cold cry, like a hunting trumpet in the forest, and their voice evokes the painful cry of a hyena, of a sick dog, or of a strangled rooster. This cry is not uttered jointly, but in succession; it passes from mouth to mouth, like a human spectrum that takes on the value of a call in the shadows.

They danced in this way until the sun set, and while they danced, other Indians collected, piece by piece, the body of the bull, leaving only its head on the ground, at the same time as the head of the sun fell into the sky. It was then that the dance directors stopped, while the dancers circled around them. And they all started again some kind of mournful melody. A melody of remorse, of religious contrition, a secret invocation of I don't know what dark forces, of what presences from *beyond*.

Afterwards, they all went to sit before a great fire placed much lower than the previous place, in a site, covered & closed like the night itself, because the second part of the rite was to show what was hidden. It was at this point that they were given the living blood served in cups. And the dance began again, all night long.

The pieces of the ox had been collected in four jars, and above them the women formed a large cross. They all drank the hot blood & began to shake a thousand & one thousand times like frogs. Sometimes, everyone slept. Then, the violin granted its music and the dance started again. And the men, joining from time to time, uttered the cry of a strangled jackal.

Think what you will of the comparison that I present. In any case, since Plato never went to Mexico and the Tarahumara Indians never saw him, it must be admitted that the idea of this sacred rite came to them from the same fabulous & prehistoric source. And this is what I have wanted to suggest here.

THE RACE OF LOST MEN

There is, in Northern Mexico, forty-eight hours from Mexico City, a race of pure red Indians, the Tarahumara. Forty thousand men live there, in a state like before the flood. They are a challenge to this world where one does not talk so much about progress, because without a doubt one loses hope of progress.

This race, which should be physically decayed, has resisted for four hundred years everything that has come to attack it: civilization, miscegenation, war, winter, animals, storms, and the forest. It lives naked, in the winter, in the snow-clogged mountains, defying all medical theories. Communism exists as a spontaneous feeling of solidarity.

As incredible as it may seem, the Tarahumara Indians live as if they were already dead... They do not see reality & draw magickal forces from the contempt they have for civilization.

They sometimes come to cities, driven by a desire to travel, to see, they say, *what men who are deceived are like*. For them, to live in the cities, is to be deceived.

They come with their wives and children, through impossible twists & turns that any animal would not dare to follow.

Seeing them walking straight along the road, crossing streams, landslides, thick forests, rock steps, perpendicular walls, I cannot help but think that they knew how to conserve the natural gravitational force of the first men.

※

At first glance, the Tarahumara country is inaccessible. Just a few vague traces that, every twenty meters, disappear underground. Come night, it is necessary to stop if one is not a red man. Well then, only a red man sees where to put his feet.

When the Tarahumara go down to the cities, they beg. It's startling. They stop in front of the doors of the houses and stand in profile with an attitude of absolute contempt. They seem to say: "Because you are rich, you are a dog, I am worth more than you, I spit on you."

Whether you give to them or not, they always withdraw after the same period of time. If you give them something, they don't say thank you. Because giving to those who have nothing for them is not really a duty, but rather a law of physical reciprocity that the White World has betrayed. This attitude seems to say: "By obeying the law, you do yourself good, so I don't have to thank you."

The money thus earned by begging is used by them to buy food for the return because, in the Tarahumara forest, it is hard to see what the money would be used for.

This law of physical reciprocity that we call charity, the Indians practice naturally and without pity. Those who have nothing, because they have lost their harvest, because their corn burned, because their father did not leave them anything, or for any other reason, without needing to justify themselves, arrive at dawn at the houses of those who have something. Immediately, the mistress of the house brings them everything she has. No one looks at each other, neither the one who gives, nor the one who receives. After having eaten, the beggar leaves without saying thanks or looking at anyone.

※

The entire life of the Tarahumara revolves around the erotic rite of Peyote.

The Peyote root is a hermaphrodite. It has, as is well known, the form of the sex of the man and of the woman in copulation. In this rite resides the whole secret of these savage Indians. The force seemed to me symbolized by an rasping stick, a kind of piece of curved wood covered with incisions on which, for whole nights, the Peyote sorcerers rhythmically rattle their sticks. The strangest thing is the way wizards are recruited. One day, an Indian feels *called* to handle the rasping stick. He goes to look for it in a sacred corner of the mountain, where for thousands of years an incredible collection of rasping sticks that other sorcerers buried has been sleeping. They are made of wood, of warm earth wood, they say. The Tarahumara is going to spend three years on this rasping stick plantation and, after the third year, he returns master of the essential rite.

This is the life of this strange people on which no civilization will ever have influence.

JOURNEY TO THE LAND OF
THE TARAHUMARA

THE MOUNTAIN OF SIGNS

The land of the Tarahumara is full of signs, of forms, and of natural effigies that in no way seem the result of chance, as if the gods, whom one feels everywhere here, had chosen to signify their powers by means of these strange signatures wherein the figure of man is hunted down on all sides.

Of course, there are places on the earth where Nature, moved by a kind of intelligent whim, has sculptured human forms. But here the case is different, for it is over *the whole geographic expanse of a race* that Nature *has chosen to speak*.

And the strange thing is that those who travel through this region, as if seized by an unconscious paralysis, close their senses in order to ignore everything. When Nature, by a strange whim, suddenly shows the body of a man being tortured on a rock, one can think at first that this is merely a whim and that this whim signifies nothing. But when, in the course of many days on horseback the same intelligent charm is repeated, *& when Nature obstinately manifests the same idea*; when the same pathic forms recur; when the heads of familiar gods appear on the rocks, and when a theme of death emanates from them, a death whose expense is obstinately borne by man, — when the dismembered form of man is answered by the forms *become less obscure*, more separate from a petrifying matter, of the gods who have always tortured him; — when a whole country of stone develops a philosophy parallel to that of its men; when one knows that the first men utilized a language of signs, and when one finds this language formidably expanded on the rocks; surely, one cannot then continue to think that this is a whim, & that this whim signifies nothing.

If the greater part of the Tarahumara race is autochthonous, and if, as they claim, they fell out of the sky into the Sierra, one may say that they fell into a *Nature that was already prepared*. And this Nature chose to think like a man. Just as she *evolved* men, she also *evolved* rocks.

This naked man who was being tortured, I saw him nailed to a rock and worked on by forms, made volatile by the sun; but by I know not what optical miracle the man up there remained whole, although he was in the same light as the rocks.

Whether the mountain or myself, I cannot say what was haunted, but, in this journey through the mountain, I saw a similar optical miracle present itself at least once a day.

I may have been born with a tormented body, as rigged as the immense mountain; but a body whose obsessions are useful: and I noticed in the mountain that it is useful to have *the obsession of counting*. There was not a shadow that I did not count, when I felt it turn around something; and it was often by adding up shadows that I found my way back to strange hearths.

I saw in the mountains a naked man leaning out of a large window. His head was but a large hole, a sort of circular cavity in which, alternately and according to the time of day, the sun or the moon appeared. He had his right arm extended like a bar and the left like a bar too, but shrouded in shadow and bent.

You could count his ribs, which numbered seven, on each side. In place of the navel glittered a shiny triangle, made of what? I could not possibly say. As if Nature had chosen this piece of the mountain to expose its hidden flints.

Now, although his head was empty, the carvings in the rock all around imposed a precise expression on him, which the light made more nuanced from hour to hour.

This right arm extended forward and bordered by a ray of light did not indicate an ordinary direction . . . And I was looking for what it was proclaiming!

It was not quite noon when I encountered this vision; I was on horseback and I was moving quickly. However, I was able to observe that what I was seeing was not sculptured forms, but a certain phenomenon of light, which was *superimposed* on the relief of the rocks.

This figure was known to the Indians; it seemed to me by its composition, by its structure, to obey the same principle that underlay the whole of this mountain of truncated forms. In the line of the arm there was a village surrounded by a girdle of rocks.

And I saw that the rocks all had the shape of a woman's chest with two perfectly delineated breasts.

I saw repeated eight times the same rock that projected two shadows on the ground; I saw twice the same animal's head carrying in its jaws its effigy, which it devoured; I saw, dominating the village, a kind of enormous phallic tooth with three stones at its summit and four holes on its outer face; and I saw, from their beginning, all these shapes pass gradually into reality.

I seemed to read everywhere a story of childbirth in war, a story of genesis and of chaos, with all these bodies of gods which were carved out like people; and these truncated statues of human forms. Not one shape that was intact, not one body that did not look as if it had emerged from a recent massacre, not one group in which I was not forced to read the struggle that divided it.

I discovered drowned men, half eaten away by the stone, and on rocks above them, other men who were struggling to keep them down. Elsewhere, an immense statue of Death held in its hand a small child.

There is in the Cabala a music of Numbers, and this music, which reduces the chaos of the material world to its principles, explains, by a kind of astounding mathematics, how Nature is ordered and how she directs the birth of the forms that she extracts from chaos. And everything I saw seemed to correspond to a number. The statues, the forms, the shadows always presented the recurring numbers 3, 4, 7, 8. The broken-off busts of women numbered 8; the phallic tooth, as I said, had three stones and four holes; the forms that became volatile numbered 12, etc. I repeat, if someone says that these forms are natural, I shall not argue; but it is their repetition that is not natural. And what are even less natural are the forms of the landscape, which are repeated by the Tarahumara in their rites and in their dances. And these dances are not the result of chance, but obey the same secret mathematics, the same concern for the subtle relations of Numbers that govern the entire Sierra region.

Yet, this inhabited Sierra, which exhales a metaphysical thinking in its rocks, the Tarahumara have sown it with signs, perfectly conscious, intelligent, and concerted.

At every bend in the road one sees trees that have *deliberately* been burned in the form of a cross, or in the form of creatures, and often these creatures are double and face each other, as if to manifest the essential *duality* of things; and I have seen this duality reduced to its principle in a sign in the shape of an H closed by a circle, which appeared to me branded with a hot iron on a large pine tree; other trees bore spears, trefoils, or acanthus leaves surrounded by crosses; here and there, in places with steep embankments, narrow passageways between rocks, lines of Egyptian anserated crosses grew into processions; and the doors of the Tarahumara houses displayed the sign of the Maya world: two facing triangles with their points connected by a bar; and this bar is the Tree of Life which passes through the center of Reality.

Thus, as I travel through the mountain, these spears, these crosses, these trefoils, these leafy hearts, these composite crosses, these triangles, these creatures facing each other and opposing each other to mark their eternal conflict, their division, their duality, evoke in me strange memories. And I suddenly remember that there were Sects in History which inlaid these same signs on the rocks, whose men carried these signs on them, carved in jade, beaten or chiseled into iron. And I find myself thinking that this symbolism conceals a Science. And I find it strange that the primitive people of the Tarahumara, whose rites & whose thought are older than the Flood, already possessed this science well before the appearance of the Legend of the Grail, or the founding of the Sect of the Rosicrucians.

THE PEYOTE DANCE

The physical hold was still there. This cataclysm that was my body... After twenty-eight days of waiting, I had not yet come back into myself, or I should say: *exited* into myself. Into myself, into this dislocated assemblage, this piece of damaged geology.

Inert, as earth with its rocks can be; — and all these crevices that run in sedimentary layers piled on top of each other. Friable, of course, I was, not in fragments, but as a whole. From my first moment of contact with this terrible mountain that I am sure had raised barriers against me to prevent me from entering. And, since I was up there, the supernatural no longer seems to me something so extraordinary that I cannot say that I had been, in the literal sense of the word: *bewitched*.

To take a step was for me no longer to take a step, but to feel *where* I was carrying my head. Can you understand this? Limbs which obey one after the other, and which one moves forward one after the other, and the vertical position above the earth that must be maintained. For the head, overflowing with waves, the head that can no longer control its whirling, the head feels all the whirling energies of the earth below, which bewilder it and keep it from remaining erect.

Twenty-eight days of this heavy captivity, this ill-assembled heap of organs that I was & which I had the impression of witnessing, like an immense landscape of ice on the point of breaking up.

The hold was therefore upon me, so terrible that to go from the house of the Indian to a tree located a few steps away required more than courage, required summoning the reserve forces of a truly *desperate* will. For to have come this far, to find myself at last on the threshold of an encounter and of this place from which I expected so many revelations, and to feel so lost, so abandoned, so deposed. Had I ever known joy, had there ever in the world been a sensation that was not one of anguish or of irremissible despair; had I ever been in a state other than that cracking pain that every night pursued me? Was there anything for me that was not at the gate of agony, and could there be found at least one body, a single human body that escaped my perpetual crucifixion?

It required, of course, an act of the will for me to believe that something was going to happen. And all this, for what? For a dance, for a rite of lost Indians who no longer even know who they are or where they come from and who, when you question them, answer with tales whose connection & secret they have lost.

After an exhaustion so cruel, I repeat, that I can no longer believe that I was not in fact bewitched, that these barriers of disintegration & of cataclysms that I had felt rising in me were not the result of an intelligent & organized premeditation, I had reached one of the last places in the world where the dance of healing by Peyote still exists, or, at least the place where it was invented.

And what was it then, what false presentiment, what illusory & artificial intuition caused me to expect some sort of liberation for my body and also, and above all, a force, an illumination throughout the reaches of my inner landscape, which I felt at that precise minute to be beyond any kind of dimensions?

Twenty-eight days since this inexplicable torment had begun. And twelve days since I had come to this isolated corner of the earth, in this tiny compartment in the immense mountain, waiting on the good will of my sorcerers.

Why was it that each time, like at this moment, I felt myself touching on a vitally important phase of my existence, I did not come to it with a whole organism? Why this terrible sensation of loss, of a void to be filled, of an event that aborts? To be sure, I would see the sorcerers carry out their rite; but in what way would this rite profit me? I would see them. I would be rewarded for this long patience that nothing until then had been able to discourage. Nothing: neither the terrible road, nor the voyage with a body that was intelligent, but dissonant, & which had to be dragged, that had to be almost killed to prevent it from revolting; nor nature with her sudden storms that surround us with their nets of thunder; nor that long night filled with spasms, wherein I had seen a young Indian scratch himself in a dream with a kind of hostile frenzy in exactly the places where those spasms seized me, — & he said, he who scarcely knew me from the day before: "Ah, let him suffer all the evil that may befall him."

Peyote, as I knew, was not made for Whites. It was necessary at all costs to prevent me from obtaining a cure by this rite that was created to act on the very nature of the spirits. And a White, for these Red men, is one whom the spirits have abandoned. If it was I who benefited from the rite, it meant so much lost for themselves, with their intelligent sheathing of spirit.

So much lost for the spirits. So many spirits that could not be utilized again.

And then, there is the matter of *Tesgüino*, that alcohol which requires eight days of fermentation in jars; — & there aren't that many jars or that many arms ready to grind the corn.

Once the alcohol has been drunk, the sorcerers of Peyote become useless and a whole new preparation becomes necessary. But a man of these tribes had died when I arrived at the village, and it was necessary that the rite, the priests, the alcohol, the crosses, the mirrors, the rasping sticks, the jars, and all that extraordinary paraphernalia of the Peyote dance be requisitioned for the benefit of the man who had died. For now that he was dead his double could not wait for these evil spirits to be neutralized.

And after twenty-eight days of waiting, I now had to endure, throughout one long week, an unbelievable comedy. All over the mountain there was a hysterical coming and going of messengers who were presumably being sent to the sorcerers. But after the messengers had left, the sorcerers would arrive in person, amazed that nothing was ready. And I discovered that I had been tricked.

They brought me priests who heal with dreams, & who speak after they have dreamed.

— "Those of *Ciguri* (Peyote dance) not good," they said. "They do not *work*. Take these." And they pushed toward me some old men who suddenly broke in two, clicking their amulets strangely under their robes. And I saw that they were not sorcerers but magicians. And I learned, moreover, that these false priests were intimate friends of death.

One day this commotion died down without protests, without arguments, without fresh promises on my part. As if all this had been part of the rite and as if the performance had lasted long enough.

Undoubtedly, I had not come to the heart of the mountain of these Tarahumara Indians to look for memories of painting. I had suffered enough, it seems to me, to be rewarded with a little reality.

However, as the daylight faded, a vision confronted my eyes.

I saw before me the Nativity of Hieronymus Bosch, with everything in order and oriented in space, the old porch with its collapsing planks in front of the stable, the flame of the Infant King glowing to the left amid the animals, the scattered farms, and the shepherds; and, in the foreground, other animals bleating; and, to the right, the dancer kings. The kings, with their crowns of mirrors on their heads and their rectangular purple cloaks on their backs, to my right in the painting, like the Magi of Hieronymus Bosch. And suddenly, as I turned around, doubting to the last minute that I would ever see my sorcerers arrive, I saw them coming down the mountain, leaning on huge staffs, their women carrying huge baskets, the servants armed with bundles of crosses, in bulk like bundles or trees, and mirrors that glittered like segments of sky amid all this apparatus of crosses, pikes, shovels, and tree trunks stripped of their branches. And all these people were bent under the weight of this extraordinary apparatus, and the wives of the sorcerers, like their men, were also leaning on huge staffs a head taller than they were.

Wood fires rose on all sides toward the sky. Below, the dances had already begun; and at the sight of this beauty at last realized, this beauty of glowing imaginations, like voices in an illuminated dungeon, I felt that my effort had not been in vain.

Above, on the slopes of the immense mountain that descended toward the village in tiers, a circle had been drawn on the ground. Already the women, kneeling in front of their *metates* (stone basins), were grinding the Peyote with a kind of scrupulous brutality. The priests began to trample the circle. They trampled it carefully and in all directions; and in the middle of the circle they kindled a fire that the wind from above sucked up in whorls.

During the day, two young goats had been killed. And now I saw on a branchless tree trunk, which had also been carved in the shape of a cross, the lungs & hearts of the animals trembling in the night wind.

Another tree trunk had been placed near the first, and the fire that had been lit in the middle of the circle drew from it at every moment innumerable flashes of light, something like a fire seen through a pile of thick glasses. When I approached in order to discern the nature of this burning center, I perceived an incredible network of tiny bells, some of silver, others of horn, attached to leather straps that were also awaiting the moment for their ritual use.

On the side where the sun rises they drove into the ground ten crosses of unequal size but arranged in a symmetrical pattern; and to each cross they attached a mirror.

Twenty-eight days of this horrible waiting after the dangerous withdrawal were now culminating in a circle peopled with Beings, here represented by ten crosses.

Ten, of the Number of 10, like the Invisible Masters of Peyote, in the Sierra.

And among these ten: the Male Principle of Nature, which the Indians call *San Ignacio*, and its female, *San Nicolas!*

Around this circle is a zone of moral abandonment in which no Indian would venture: it is said that, in this circle, the birds, who stray there, fall, and that pregnant women feel their embryos rot inside them.

There is a history of the world in the circle of this dance, compressed between two suns, the one that sets and the one that rises. And it is when the sun sets that the sorcerers enter the circle, and that the dancer with the six hundred little bells (three hundred of horn and three hundred of silver) utters his coyote's howl, in the forest.

The dancer enters and exits, and yet he does not leave the circle. He moves forward deliberately into evil. He immerses himself in it with a kind of terrible courage, in a rhythm that above the Dance seems to depict the Illness. And one seems to see him alternately emerging and disappearing in a movement that evokes one knows not what obscure tantalizations. He enters and exits: "*leaves the daylight, in the first chapter,*" as is said of Man's Double in the *Egyptian Book of the Dead*. For this advance into the illness is a voyage, a *descent to* REEMERGE INTO THE DAYLIGHT. — He turns in a circle in the direction of the wings of the Swastika, always from right to left, and from the top.

He leaps with his army of little bells, like an agglomeration of dazed bees, caked together in a crackling & tempestuous disorder.

Ten crosses in the circle and *ten* mirrors. *One* beam with *three* sorcerers on it. *Four* desservants (*two* Males and *two* Females). The epileptic dancer, and *myself*, for whom the rite was being performed.

At the foot of each sorcerer, *one* hole, at the foot of which the Male and Female principles in Nature, represented by the hermaphroditic roots of the Peyote plant (Peyote, we know, has the shape of the male and female sexual organs combined), lie dormant in Matter, that is, in the Concrete.

And the hole, with a wooden or earthen basin inverted over it, represents rather well the Globe of the World. On the basin, the sorcerers grate the mixture or the dislocation of the two Principles, and they grate them in the Abstract, that is, in Principle. While below, these two Principles, incarnated, rest in Matter, that is to say in the Concrete.

And all night long the sorcerers reestablish the lost relationships with triangular gestures that strangely cut off the spatial perspective.

Between the *two* suns, *twelve* tempos in *twelve* phases. And the circular movement of everything that swarms around the fire, within the sacred limits of the circle: the dancer, the rasping sticks, the sorcerers.

After each phase, the sorcerers were eager to perform the physical proof of the rite, to demonstrate the effectiveness of the operation. Hieratic, ritual, sacerdotal, there they stand, lined up on their beam, rocking their rasping sticks like babies. From what idea of a lost formality do they derive the sense of these bows, these nods, this circular movement in which they count their steps, cross themselves before the fire, salute one another, and leave?

So they get up, perform the bows I have mentioned, some like men on crutches, others like truncated robots. They step outside the circle. But once they have left the circle, before they are a yard outside of it, these priests who walk between two suns have suddenly become men again, that is, abject organisms that must be cleansed, whom this rite is designed to cleanse. They behave like well-diggers, these priests, some kind of night laborers created to piss & to relieve themselves. They piss, fart, & relieve themselves with terrible thunderous noises; and to hear them one would think that they had set out to level the real thunder, to reduce it to *their need* for abjection.

Of the three sorcerers who were there, two, the two smallest and shortest, had had the right to handle the rasping stick for three years (for the right to handle the rasping stick is acquired, and in fact this right determines the nobility of the caste of the Peyote sorcerers among the Tarahumara Indians); and the third had had the right for ten years. And I must admit that it was the one most experienced in the rite who pissed the best and who farted the loudest & most expressively.

And a few moments later the same man, with the pride of this manner of crude purgation, began to spit. He spat after drinking the Peyote, as we all did. For after the twelve phases of the dance had been performed, and since dawn was about to break, we were passed the ground Peyote, which was like a kind of muddy gruel; & in front of each of us a new hole was dug to receive the spit from our mouths, which contact with the Peyote had henceforth made sacred.

"Spit," the dancer told me, "but as deep in the ground as possible, for no particle of *Ciguri* must ever emerge again."

And it was the sorcerer who had grown old in the harness who spat most abundantly and with the largest as well as the most compact gobs. And the other sorcerers and the dancer, gathered in a circle around the hole, had come to admire him.

After I had spat, I fell to the ground, overcome with drowsiness. The dancer in front of me passed back and forth endlessly, turning and crying *unnecessarily*, because he had discovered that his cry pleased me.

"Get up, man, get up," he shouted each time he passed me, with diminishing effect.

Aroused and staggering, I was led toward the crosses, for the final cure, in which the sorcerers shake the rattle on the very head of the patient.

Thus I took part in the rite of water, the rite of the blows on the skull, the rite of that kind of mutual cure that the participants give each other, the rite of immoderate ablutions.

They uttered strange words over my head while sprinkling me with water; then they sprinkled each other nervously, for the mixture of corn liquor & Peyote was beginning to make them wild.

And it was with these final movements that the Peyote dance ended.

The Peyote dance is contained in an rasping stick, in this wood steeped in time that has absorbed the secret salts of the earth. In this wand that is held out and withdrawn lies the curative power of this rite, which is so remote and which must be hunted down like a beast in the forest.

There is an out-of-the-way spot in the high Mexican Sierra where these rasping sticks seemingly abound. They sleep there, waiting for the Predestined Man to discover them, and bring them *into the light of day*.

When a Tarahumara sorcerer dies, he takes leave of his rasping stick with infinitely more sorrow than he feels in leaving his body; and his descendants and intimates take the rasping stick away and bury it in this sacred corner of the forest.

When a Tarahumara Indian believes that he is called upon to handle the rasping stick and distribute the cure, he goes to spend a week in the forest at Easter time every year for three years.

It is there, they say, that the Invisible Master of Peyote speaks to him, with his nine advisers, and that he passes the secret on to him. And he emerges with the rasping stick properly macerated.

Carved out of the wood of a tree that grew in warm soil, grey as iron ore, it carries notches on its length and signs at its two extremities, four triangles with one point for the Male Principle and two points for the Female of Nature, made divine.

One notch for every year the sorcerer was alive after he had acquired the right to handle the rasping stick and had become a master capable of performing those acts of exorcism that tear the Elements apart.

And this is precisely the aspect of this mysterious tradition, which I did not succeed in penetrating. For the Peyote sorcerers seem truly to have gained something at the end of their three years' retreat in the forest.

There is a mystery here that the Tarahumara sorcerers have until now jealously guarded. Of what they have acquired in addition, what they have *recovered*, if you will, no Tarahumara Indian, who is not a member of the aristocracy of the sect, seems to have the slightest idea. And as for the sorcerers themselves, on this point they are resolutely silent.

What is the singular word, the lost word that the Master of Peyote communicates to them? And why does it take the Tarahumara sorcerers three years to be able to handle the rasping stick, with which, it must be admitted, they perform some very curious *auscultations*?

What is it, then, which they have wrested from the forest, and which the forest *yields to them so slowly*?

In short, what has been communicated to them that is not contained in the external apparatus of the rite, and which neither the piercing cries of the dancer, nor his dance, which goes back and forth like a kind of epileptic pendulum, nor the circle, nor the fire in the middle of the circle, nor the crosses with their mirrors in which the distorted heads of the sorcerers alternately swell and disappear into the flames of the fire, nor the night wind that speaks and blows on the mirrors, nor the chant of the sorcerers rocking their rasping sticks, that astonishingly vulnerable and intimate chant, can succeed in explaining?

They had laid me on the ground at the foot of that enormous beam on which the three sorcerers were sitting during the dances.

On the ground, so that the rite would fall on me, so that the fire, the chants, the cries, the dance, and the night itself, like a living, human vault, would turn over me. There was this rolling vault, this physical arrangement of cries, tones, steps, chants. But, above everything, beyond everything, the impression, which kept recurring, that behind all this, greater than all this, and beyond it, there was concealed something else: *the Principal*.

I did not renounce as a group these dangerous dissociations which Peyote seems to provoke and which I had pursued for twenty years by other means; I did not ride a horse with a body extracted from itself, and which the suppression, to which I had abandoned myself, henceforth deprived of its essential reflexes; I was not that man of stone whom it required two men to turn into a man on horseback: and who was mounted on and dismounted from the horse like a distraught automaton, — and, once I was on the horse, they put my hands on the reins, and it was necessary, moreover, to close my fingers on the reins because, alone, it was too obvious that I had lost the use of them; I had not conquered by force of mind that invincible organic hostility in which it was *I* who no longer wanted to function, only to bring back a collection of outworn imageries, from which the Age, faithful to its own system, would at most derive ideas for advertisements and models for clothing designers. It was now necessary that what lay hidden behind this heavy grinding that reduces dawn to darkness, that this thing be drawn out, and that it *serve*, that it serve precisely by *my crucifixion*.

To this I knew that my physical fate was irrevocably bound. I was ready for all the burns, and I awaited the first fruits of the fire, in view of a conflagration that would soon be generalized.

LETTERS (1937)

TO JEAN PAULHAN

Paris
4 February 1937

Dear friend,

Arriving at the very heart of the Tarahumara mountain, I was overwhelmed by physical reminiscences so urgent that they seemed to recall direct personal events; everything: the life of the earth and of the grass, below the breaks of the mountain, the special forms of the rocks, and above all the dusting of the stepped light in the always incomplete perspective of the peaks, one above the other, each further and further away in an unimaginable distance, everything appeared to me as the representation of a lived experience, now past by, now within me, & not as the discovery of a strange but new world. All this was not new. But if the impression of what has already *been seen* is vague, I mean *without a date*, mine was perfectly situated; well, this lived organic experience reminded me of another, with which I felt indirectly linked perhaps, but always by material threads.

They were historical reminiscences that came to me, rock by rock, grass by grass, horizon by horizon. I have not invented the appearance of the Three Wise Men: this was *meticulously* imposed on me by a country made up like landscape paintings, which really do not appear out of nothing. I do not believe in absolute imagination, that is to say, the one that creates something out of nothing, there is no mental image that does not seem to me to be the separate member of an image acted out and lived somewhere. And in turn these immense, uninhabited images reminded me of others that were inhabited in the past, and their life seemed to me to extend precisely on an unusual plan; I have not been the one who invented the tradition of magickal signs, and it is a fact that this mountain was obsessed with them; I have drawn their nomenclature in one of the articles I sent you, but after all stone by stone & at the end of the journey I had the impression of having recorded them all: from / which is cut in //, divided in the middle by a bar Ⓨ that has in front of it the same right bar that came from it Ⓗ ; & it is not my fault if this form of H which seems to emerge is the central figure on which Plato relates that the Atlanteans had built their cities, it is childish if you will, but it exists in the Sierra Tarahumara and in Plato; I have seen a striated rock with three vertical bars, 3, and on this rock another smaller one striated with a single bar; I saw the huge phallic tooth that I had already told you about that has three stones on its head and four holes on its face; I have seen in a perforated rock a circular head of man exactly where the disk of the Sun is inserted at dawn, and above the body of the man prolonged *in shadows* and the right arm extended like a bar of light, and the left like the same bar, but also *in shadow*, and withdrawn; I have seen the figure of death as if *torn* from the surrounding rocks, carrying a little boy in his enormous left hand; I am not talking about all the images and all the similarities that I have seen, which drew a forgotten fauna from nature; similar to those ancient myths where the *tamed* man converses with the Kingdoms that have defeated him; and if the universal world of the Jews is represented by two interpenetrating triangles, the world of all the races of red extraction is represented by two opposite triangles I have seen hundreds of times on the rock, arising from I don't know what surprising chance of nature; in the trees: printed by the same hand of men; and wherever I found that famous ✋, the H of the generation, I actually saw exits and as if *extracted* from the trees that had been burned from top to bottom to highlight their figures, I saw a figure of a man and a woman facing each other and the man had the erect penis; how many times have I rediscovered the small world of the earth represented by a circle, and around that circle, the vastest of the indeterminate Universe; how many times have I found the cross of the Rosicrucian tradition; four triangles oriented toward the four cardinal points and all centered around one point; I have seen that sign! What is my fault if it conforms to the Rosicrucian tradition, if this is how they reveal to us that the Rosicrucians formed their cross, and that symbol would be repeated thousands of times, not only in the middle of nature, but on the doors of houses built with a single plank, on the walls, in the shade of the roofs; I have seen houses whose facades responded to each other by squares or points, and sometimes by some kinds of rectangles placed one on top of another and seeming to add up; & have I not been told there on the mountain that those scattered geometric figures were not scattered but gathered together and that they constituted the signs of a language based on the very shape of the breath when it is divided into sonorities; universal magick is not based on many more elemental signs than what I found live & on nature on a mountain that even without those signs has the light of haunted countries? For novelists and poets, much less has been needed to find and specify myths that they invented with their own imagination; in describing my journey, I have not intended to write a doctoral dissertation, rediscovering the path of a safe tradition, and providing corroborating evidence. It doesn't matter whether the conclusions you want are drawn from all these encounters; it matters very little to me to believe that the Three Wise Men, upon returning to their country, took a detour through the uninhabited mountains of Mexico; but I know that when I got up there and dominating almost infinite kilometers of landscapes, I have felt reminiscences and unusual images stirring inside me that nothing would have made me suspect when I left. And seeing those mountains encrusted with figures, more figures than those of the divinities that adorn the walls of certain temples in India, seeing men pass by with ribbons, men clad in cloaks adorned with embroidered triangles, with crosses, dots, circles, tears and lightning bolts; and those crosses, those dots, those circles, those rectangles, those tears, those lightning bolt stripes were not placed at all as decorative figures, keeping a symmetry that would have stripped them, but I never saw two cloaks bearing the same signs and each one of them suited the color of the *uneducated* faced man who wore it; seeing those men pass by, apparently ignorant of the symbolism in which his life seemed bathed, I could not believe that this one represented a calculation or any investigation on his part, was the result of a conscious & awakened premeditation; they did all this because their parents, they claimed, did it; and I wonder where those customs that came from generation to generation could come from; the least willing brain would have demanded where those vestiges had come from and what more than human tradition revealed their presence.

Are not green and yellow the opposite colors of death? — green for resurrection, yellow for decomposition, decay, & if the coincidences meant something, you will allow me, to finish, to call your attention to the fact that I am going to relate to you.

I arrived at twilight in one of those towns dominated by phalluses, those phalluses engraved with figures & which seem to have been planted by natural chance;

I don't know who was whistling an air of a Tarahumara dance, with 5 high-pitched measures that suddenly rush a hundred stories and as if a voice responded in the abysses; a boy approached us all alone, naked under a grey cloak and his face literally gnawed at with pus; a kind of greenish network on the forehead bone seemed to replace the course of a vein; he greedily ate the food that was offered to him, although he always kept a respectful distance; I had thought I noticed a red triangle on the front face of the cloak with the point drawn upwards, and when he turned around I saw a teardrop on his back, an enormous embroidered teardrop that covered everything, had the point pointing upwards and turned toward the left;

I shrugged at the image that tear evoked. I made an effort to stop my ever-ready imagination; and yet from the image that appeared to me at that moment, I cannot affirm that I have not thought about it; and I am going to tell you about this imagination ready for you to shrug your shoulders as I did before; I thought of the *FIAT LUX* of God, and of the way in which Robert Fludd imposes, in his *Theater of Eternal Wisdom*, the original movement of creation; this tear, this bent bladder, is the way he draws the light that coming out of the void bends little by little and encloses the darkness that it is going to replace; the tear itself was perhaps nothing; but the red tear, with the red triangle, meant a rather unique comparison; several weeks passed after that, I penetrated into the interior of the mountain, I saw the scattered Peyote priests who during whole nights grind the mixtures of the first principles on their rasping sticks, and I took the road back.

I passed through the town of the phalluses again & around noon I asked for asylum in a impoverished house from which I saw an Indian come out entirely wrapped in an enormous cloak despite the torrid heat. I had already seen strange cloaks all over the mountain: but this one had four white triangles that seemed to be strangled and which occupied its entire height; the edges had a line of green crosses on one side, yellow on the other, and was made up of those four triangles I told you about; the Indian greeted us without saying a word, with a slow but intelligent smile, and the woman hurried on. While she was arranging the corn and the herbs, my attention was caught by a false braid that she had tied to her hair; in that braid a woolen thread was knotted alternately green & yellow, the same color as the crosses; she also wore a necklace of green beads, & yellow stones hung from her ears. Inside the house the children were fighting, yelling shrilly, and I saw come out a very small boy with a huge belly and a mouth surrounded by abscesses, & behind him another older boy in whom I recognized the one in the grey cloak embroidered with the triangle & the teardrop; I didn't see anything unusual inside the house except a cross in one corner, the point of which was made of spear iron and with arms shaped like shamrocks. The Indian, questioned, remained perfectly silent.

So, dear friend, I wanted to tell you again what I saw without drawing any kind of conclusion from it, you will see that the facts and things speak for themselves, & undoubtedly more strongly than I made them speak, but evidently in the same sense. Perhaps one day I will have fun retelling it, or I will retell it without amusing myself, the world into which all these things made me dream that I was entering and into which I have the impression that there is much to enter. I do not want to place myself in the point of view of the picturesque to recount that trip, but from the point of view of efficiency.

Yours with all my heart,

ANTONIN ARTAUD

I would have liked you to tell me that it is the occult thesis itself that you do not like; however, in all the darkness in which poetry and modern language are enveloped, there are many fewer ideas than in all of this.

I really care *a lot* about this idea of the three Wise Men who appear at the origin of several essential stories, and of an entire tradition. My paper is not confusing;

it is terribly concentrated and elliptical due to the immense topic that I wanted to stress. This theme is fundamental to me and I will return to it elsewhere; for the moment let's stick to the combination that you proposed to me.

Yours very affectionately,

ANTONIN ARTAUD

TO JEAN PAULHAN

Saturday, 27 February 1937

Dear friend,

I am writing ahead of a terrible but *necessary* upheaval. You have SAVED me. I *know* now not only by intuition, but by precise Ways, I would say mathematics, that sensational things are being prepared of which this experience was the beginning.

 I had started writing *The Peyote Dance* before coming here: it has been impossible for me to finish it. It is only NOW when *I glimpse* what I wanted to say and that it is so far from what I wrote before entering here; ——— which is *myself*, the rest was barely caricature, except in quick moments of clarity!!! A letter full of things that I wrote to you, wouldn't it be in some of its fragments, some of those clear visions, and couldn't we add some part of it to the *Journey*? Specifically that part where I refer to the festering child. I think so ————

 What do you think?

 I don't ask you to write to me: I'll come see you when you leave.

 Affectionately yours,

ANTONIN ARTAUD

TO JEAN PAULHAN

Saturday, 13 March 1937

Dear friend,

Here is one of the first jobs I have dedicated myself to since I left the Maison de Santé.

I have long wanted to write an *explanatory* article regarding astrology today. A message that I talk about in the article gives me the opportunity (for the *tone of the month*?) since it is topical.

I really hope you can publish it in April.

You can see that it is a serious, researched article, but on the other hand it seems to have RECOVERED my personal tone. In another letter I also send the first part of *The Peyote Dance*.

Affectionately yours,

ANTONIN ARTAUD

TO JEAN PAULHAN

[*Paris*] *28 March 1937*

Dear friend,

At LAST I am sending you the final part of *The Peyote Dance*.

A general conclusion is still missing, but I believe it is enough for the choice of fragments that should appear in the magazine. Since they are the fragments of a *Journey to the Land of the Tarahumara*.

Furthermore, this would disproportionately lengthen my text, which as it is now is twice as long as *The Land of the Magi*, which I have suppressed.

You now have something concrete & you can judge it.

The entire *Peyote Dance* has been *rewritten* according to the spirit and emotion with which I corrected and recast *The Mountain of Signs* that you liked so much. I hope and wish that the dance as it is now written you will like it all the same. Write me in any case, as quickly as possible, to reassure me. But this time tell me *directly* what you think.

I think I have said exactly what I have seen in *The Dance* and I have expressed it point by point. I have also described my personal impressions point by point. There is no longer anything theoretical or arbitrary or preconceived or gratuitous, but a mysterious thing where what appears is only the allusive clothing, if I can say so, of something else infinitely more important and *absolutely* important in itself. It seemed to me that it was something serious, something essential. And so it will appear in my complete book about that *Journey*, which I *cannot doubt*, dear Jean Paulhan, & I say it with absolute faith, conviction, and sincerity that it was led by the *Invisible*, just as I feel that my entire current life is led. That is why these extracts seem to me an important introduction to an action that will take place shortly after I have fully regained my strength, and that is why it is so important to me that it appear without much delay before the *end of Spring* so that it can truly be what it is, the opening toward other things.

Forgive me this enigmatic language.

You cannot know to what extent it is true and how grateful I am to you for having served by your double intervention in what will come out of all this.

Yours affectionately,

ANTONIN ARTAUD

TO JEAN PAULHAN

Sceaux, 13 April 1937

Dear friend,

No news from you. I confess that I am impatient to see the *Journey* appear. Didn't you receive my last long letter in which I give all sorts of details about the mood in which *The Peyote Healing Dance* was written? I am very confident that you have thoroughly enjoyed this text & that you can see what I wanted to say — and that it is for me of special importance.

I received the proofs of *The Theater & Its Double*. It is very important to me that the Preface be printed in italics. I'm *rewriting it* anyway. Could you also find the variants to certain texts that I sent you in letters and which do not appear in the proofs sent to me?

See you soon then and yours very affectionately,

ANTONIN ARTAUD

TO JEAN PAULHAN

[*Paris, 27 or 28 May 1937*]

Dear friend,

See what strange sign my Destiny and my whole life are under.

Everything is falling to pieces with these wedding plans. And that's fair!

I am not made for such compromises — whatever the artifices by which I may hope to save them. So.

My destiny is cruel for an even crueler purpose for which *I know* it is preparing me. And I will SOON be prepared.

Your friend,

ANTONIN ARTAUD

P.S. — I decided *not to* sign *Journey to the Land of the Tarahumara*. My name must disappear.

TO JEAN PAULHAN

[*Paris, early June 1937*]

Dear friend,

Even initials aren't necessary. Remember. The correspondence with Rivière had appeared with 3 Stars & of everything that I wrote that is perhaps all that will remain. After 13 years it seems like I'm returning to the same point but the tour I took was a spiral: it took me higher.

The same kind of confession appears in the *Peyote Dance*, but this time with the *acceptance that* restores this torment to everyone. Even initials would limit the action. This is the last satisfaction that I ask of you, to remove everything that would recall my name. Many are terribly moved by what I am doing. A reminder of my name would disappoint them and disappoint *me*. In a short time I will be dead or in such a situation that I will not need a name. So I'm counting on you for the 3 Stars.

Your friend,

ANTONIN ARTAUD

LETTERS (1937)

TO JEAN PAULHAN

[Paris, end of June 1937]

Dear friend,

Those who know me will recognize me, but how many are there. They also recognize me when they see me & I talk to them. Since I'm still here.

What matters in all this is the affirmation of anonymity & not that I hide myself from those who have always seen me and there are those who have never seen me and who will never know me and in ten years or in six months it will perhaps be everyone.

I no longer want to sign at any price
 & am eternally your friend, to both you & your wife.

ANTONIN ARTAUD

LATER WRITINGS ON THE TARAHUMARA

TWO LETTERS

TO HENRI PARISOT

Rodez, 10 December 1943

Dear Sir,

I have written a *Journey to Mexico* of which the most important part is the *Journey to the Land of the Tarahumara*. But the text of the *Journey to the Land of the Tarahumara* is complete. As for that *Journey to Mexico*, it constitutes a book of 200 pages or more, which I wrote in eight months, from November 1936, the date of my return from Mexico, to August 1937, the date of my departure for Ireland; that book is not completely finished.

It happens that from September 1937 to the present date, I have been arrested, imprisoned in Dublin, deported to France, interned in Le Havre, transferred from Le Havre to Rouen, from Rouen to Sainte-Anne in Paris, from Sainte-Anne to Ville-Evrard, from Ville-Evrard to Chezal-Benoit and from Chezal-Benoit to Rodez. All my belongings were confiscated by the police, and all my papers were lost. I have absolutely nothing of what I possessed: a certain number of manuscripts, a wallet and, *above all*, a dagger from Toledo, 12 centimeters long, fixed with three hooks and given to me by a black man in Cuba. The Governor of Dublin Prison himself has returned all my belongings to me. Still in Le Havre, where I was particularly mistreated, the dagger was returned to me together with the red leather case that enclosed it. Still in Sainte-Anne, I had my brown crocodile wallet with my initials and the small red leather case that contained the sacred dagger, an object known to all initiates; but since Ville-Evrard I have not heard more about what has happened to those objects. As for my personal papers and manuscripts, I have lost track since I landed on French soil & to rewrite this *Journey to Mexico* and finish it would take me about a year. For the rest, the atmosphere of confinement is not conducive to this type of work. To write you have to be free. However, I will try to add a few pages to that *Journey to the Land of the Tarahumara*. Dr. Ferdière, who enthusiastically encourages me to do so, will give me all possible facilities. He is the only doctor in my six years of captivity who has tried to be amiable to the best of his ability.

What I am sure of is that it was at Chezal-Benoit that the little red leather case containing the little dagger of Toledo was not returned to me.

As for my manuscripts, I last saw them on my *release* from Dublin prison. Then I lost track of them.

For the rest, we are living in a time of trials and misfortunes and I cannot work because I have not had enough bread for three years.

But I repeat it to you, I will make an effort to overcome these obstacles & I will especially pray to Jesuschrist, because He is the one who is spoken of throughout my *Journey to Mexico* and He is the Word of God whom the Tarahumara adore as I have been able to warn in the *Tutuguri* Rite that is officiated when the sun rises.

They recognized it themselves and told me when they were shown two imprints of the Face of christ. One on the Canvas of Saint Veronica, the other on an Image taken at another moment of her Passion. And His True Face is perfectly recognized. The priestly class of the Indian Priests of the Sun is considered as an earthly emanation of his Virtue & his Force, and each priest is like an identification of his Rays. It is necessary to see the senseless energy through which each priest projects himself onto the earth at the precise moment in which in the solar home, which has never ceased to be free, is detached before the Indian conscience from the prison of darkness of the night. It is necessary to see how each priest reproduces through the place in which he knows how to place himself, together with the others, his brothers, the extraordinary distribution of that home. But above all, one must listen to the Words that are transmitted from one to the other through signs that seem to have been extracted from the very limbos of Eternity and which have been created to support and manifest something, & this something is the Spirit of the Word which rolls like a ball of flames before the mouth of the Lord God and of the one that they, the Tara-Humaras, remember, as they say, having been & being their Will & its reflections.

At that moment they all began to cry because, as they told me: "This Will of God of which we were the Angels, that is to say the Rays, behold, we are almost no longer so because Evil has descended too much upon us. The fight between Evil & God is not yet over and for the Kingdom of God to come upon earth we must be chaste. We are chaste to the extent possible. But the men who inhabit the expanse of the earth are not chaste in any absolute way. And now is the moment in which they have to return to complete chastity. For things are made by the Sun & like the sun, they are made like this" — those priests told me with the sign of the arms & the body which constitute the most extraordinary Religious Dance attitudes that I have ever seen.

Among these signs was the Sign of the Cross as catholics make, but there was an infinity more. It is about all this which I spoke of in my manuscripts, which I will now try to rewrite.

Waiting for you, believe in my warmest feelings,

ANTONIN ARTAUD
1, Rue Vieux-Sens
Rodez,
Aveyron

P.S. My best regards to Robert J. Godet to whom all of this is of special interest.

TO DOCTOR GASTON FERDIÈRE

Rodez, 11 December 1943

Very dear doctor & friend,

I wrote to Jean Paulhan to send me a copy of the August 1937 issue of the N.R.F. containing the *Journey to the Land of Tarahumara* in order to recall the tone & thus be able to make the connection, because the rest of the manuscript of my *Journey to Mexico* has been lost. Moreover, the *Journey to the Land of the Tarahumara* is complete as it appeared in the *N.R.F.* The additional text that Henri Parisot spoke to you about actually belongs to the rest of this *Journey to Mexico* that constituted a manuscript of nearly two hundred pages written in Paris between the month of November 1936, the date of my return from Mexico, and the month of August 1937, the date of my departure for Ireland. You know that I was thrown into prison in Dublin, that I spent 6 days there, that I was then deported to France, detained in Le Havre without explanation upon my arrival on French soil & without having been examined by a doctor, transferred from Havre to Rouen, from Rouen to Sainte-Anne, from Sainte-Anne to Ville-Évrard, from Ville-Évrard to Chezal-Benoît, and finally from Chezal-Benoît I came here. I had all my things with me & I don't know where they disappeared to because the last time I saw them was when I *left* Dublin Prison where

Governor de Soto gave them to me himself by hand. — To rewrite this *Journey to Mexico* & finish it completely would now take me close to a year. Because the 200-page manuscript written in Paris between November 1936 and June 1937 still needed around fifty pages to reach its definitive length. And there is one thing, that you feel as strongly as I do, Dr. Ferdière, since you have always done everything you could to ease my captivity: it is that in order to write you have to be free. What I lost was not lost for everyone but I want to add a few pages to this *Journey to the Land of the Tarahumara* because the Indian priests of the Sun who practice the Rite of *Tutuguri* explained to me a certain number of things about their priesthood which I did not talk about in the text published in the *N.R.F.* and which I want to write.

"The earth turns, they say, but the sun walks & carries it along. And those priests of *Tutuguri* are the Rays of this Sun who come to strike the earth at each dawn to command it to turn around and move forward. And they must be seen jump & spread to the four corners of space at the precise moment when the sun emerges & then rushes to the earth in accordance with its rays. — Because, the priests of Indian consciousness, they have the responsibility of these rays & it is up to them to dig out their place in the darkness of the expanse. They know, they say, by tradition & by instinct *where* the Sun must pass so that the human soul is happy and it is He who one day told their fathers before man was born."

I then asked them what their Fathers were at that time since man did not yet exist.

"Our Fathers," they replied, "were his closest Rays, not created but generated. These are the first syllables of the Word of God. And the Sun is this Word, his Word in brief."

Now the Word of God is Jesus-christ for Christians, his Son. — These Indian priests were then presented with a reproduction of the Veil of Saint Veronica containing an imprint of the Figure of Jesus-christ. — They approached with respect to look at it and contemplated it for a long time, then they gathered together & began to confer with extraordinary animation. — I could not hear their language, but I saw them tremble and kneel and they made with their right arm a sign that was nothing other than the Sign of the cross itself. Moreover, you must remember that the circular space reserved for the Rite of *Tutuguri* is on the eastern side bordered by six wooden crosses.

They finally got up & came to tell me that the Figure that was reproduced on the Veil of Saint Veronica was incontestably that of the Spirit who commanded them, that is to say that of Jesus-christ.

This revelation gave great joy to Henri Goiran, Minister of France in Mexico, when I communicated it to him on my return to Mexico City.

It was after that that I was able to attend all the other Tarahumara dances and in particular the Peyote Dance called the *"Ciguri"* because the *Tutuguri* Priests passed the necessary orders to all their own by signs.

And they gave me the most disconcerting details about the commandments of this Spirit, & to make me understand them they drew on the ground with sticks signs that are found on all the pyramids of Mexico, and I recognized two or three of them for having seen them on the Pyramid of Tenayuca or the Pyramid of the Serpents which is at the very gates of Mexico.

This is what I would like to add to my *Journey to the Land of the Tarahumara*.

Believe, my very dear friend, in all my gratitude for the sympathy with which you continue to support me in my work.

With all my heart, yours.

ANTONIN ARTAUD

LATER WRITINGS

SUPPLEMENT TO THE JOURNEY TO THE LAND OF THE TARAHUMARA

The human conscience has the right to ask itself many questions, and I have asked myself many throughout the world, up to this extreme interrogation where there is no longer either conscience, or question, but an indescribable flame, unique, springing from the mind of God, whenever His Heart is alert.

Because for whoever pushes the mind of things with his heart, there is a point where, as in the Peyote of the Tarahumara, like a tissue all perception opens up like a cross, it cracks in such a way that one no longer knows whether it is from his own heart that this cross comes, or from the heart of this Other, which then is no longer the Other, *an* Other, but THAT ONE, the Unique Distributor of the Flames, whose tongue pierces and picks up the taste for the Word, when the heart which beat like a Double, recognizes its GENERATOR!

For then if there is no God or problem, then there is no heart either to perceive, or to tear the perception which pierces, & to tear *oneself* to pieces in the middle of the perception.

By dint of seeing men lying around me, lying about what makes an idea be, this imbecile refusal to go as far as ideas, I felt the need to leave man and go away, where I will finally be able to move forward freely with my heart, all this heart that before my attentive conscience picks up and clears away the emotions of images that come to it from the circular Absolute, this flow of fabric piercing my spine and which my heart rejects then toward my plexus with the spasm of a sea.

What the Self is, I don't know. Consciousness? a dreadful repulsion of the Nameless, of the badly plotted, for the I comes when the heart has finally knotted it, elected it, *pulled* it out of this and that, against this and *for* that, through the eternal calculation of the horrible, of which all the not-Is, demons, assail what will be my being which I do not cease before my eyes to see fail as long as God in my heart has not passed his key.

We see God when we want to, and to see God is not to be satisfied with the small enclave of earthly sensations that have only ever done a little more to open the hunger of a self & of an entire conscience, which this world does not stop murdering and deceiving.

One day I was far from God, but never again have I felt so far from my own consciousness, and I saw that without God there is no consciousness or being, and that the man who thinks he is still alive will never be able to return to himself.

This is how, pushing toward God, I found the Tarahumara.

The highest idea of human consciousness & of its corresponding universals: Absolute, Eternity, Infinity, still exists among this race of old Indians who claim to have received the Sun to transmit it to the deserving, & who in the Rites of Ciguri have preserved the organic door of the proof, by which our being, which the impure assembly of the rejected beings knows that it is related to this beyond of the corporeal perceptions where the Heart of the Divine is consumed to call us.

I don't know how many, all the initiatory doctrines of the earth, of which I know the unique source is called JESUS CHRIST, claim to have known suns, from the first to the sixth, but it would be said that the Tarahumara of Mexico have not yet descended from the first because they have preserved themselves the image of that fountain that they call the Son of God. — One day, say the priests of TUTUGURI, the Great Celestial Healer appeared as if he had been born from the half-open lips of the Sun, THE WISHING ONE, His Father in Eternity. And He was, Himself, that Sun with the First Cross in His hands and He gave the touch; and other Solar Crosses and Double Suns were born from Him and came out with each Syllable which that Mouth of Celestial Crosses printed in wafers of light in the immensity.

Six times the Cross of Light struck and the Sun bounced in the spaces. And the last one was inextinguishable and pure, and just as it is now seen on the sea and on the lands, but from the start even the night had returned to the light because the Son of the Desirous One, by climbing up to his Father, had recovered with Him his march in Eternity.

Well, that is the true Story of Jesus Christ as the doctrines of Christianity from the Catacombs have handed it down to us; and I wanted to see so much behind the sacred memory of the Rites that I don't know what hidden paganism the Tarahumara of our time would recognize in their Initiator.

And they were shown an engraving of the authentic figure of Christ, the same one that remains imprinted on the veil of Saint Veronique, during the march to Golgotha, and after having mysteriously agreed, the priests of the TUTUGURI came to tell me that that was indeed his face, & that, in another time, that was how the Son of God had appeared to his ancestors.

And in his travels, this Healer of the Infinite had given them a plant to reopen the doors of Eternity to the tempted & weary soul. And that plant is the CIGURI.

Because the soul, like the earth, goes from day to night; only the sun goes from light to light, for it there is only day; the night is what is always far from it. But who will say at night that there is no sun; who said when the skies are covered with clouds that no sun has ever crowned them? Today that is all that men say about someone I saw as truly as I see the sun; and I have no doubt on rainy days! Like me, everyone I love on earth has longed for and missed this Someone; and they and I have traveled around something immeasurable, as if following the lost orbit of a star, until the star exploded before the human eye and we saw it explode.

And whoever, among my friends & my brothers, saw that sun explode will end up remembering it and saying it; what a beautiful day that was! As for the others, they will have become too beastly to obfuscate the Truth.

— It often happens that night descends on the soul, in such a way that it, violated by temptations & fatigue, does not know very well where it comes from: from above or below, from light or from darkness. Then the Peyote supplied by Jesus Christ intervenes. He removes the soul from behind the back and places it again in the eternal light, as it came from the Spirit from above; and by making the soul remain in that Above, he teaches it to distinguish between itself & that unfathomable energy that is like the multiple infinity of its own capacities and that is born there where thousands upon thousands of so-called beings become extinct & dry up.

— As high as I have risen in the darkness of the mental, for this or for that, I am not always aware of having decided for the clearest reasons. — Between the I and the not-I there is a war that the centuries until now have not been able to settle. The Illusory, which I do not like, very often gives me the impression of occupying my consciousness with a much stronger seductive force than the Real. — It is that before me there is temptation: temptation to be this or that, like this or that, like this one or like that one. — It is the reason for that frightful combat that in the pre-consciousness of my Will and of my Acts I have waged with the one who is not me. — But who will tell me why I decided to choose my conscience. Man lives Good and Evil as if a force were dictated to him, but he has never seen himself in the Distributing Source of nameless impulses that lead him to judge and prefer. When he does Good, he judges it better, calming and preferable, but when he does Evil, or when he thinks about it for a moment, he wonders if by chance and for what reasons it would not be the best, for reasons that have just disappeared from his consciousness, that Evil has just obscured, the Good was conceived by him as Good and the Evil as bad, whereas God, to go a step further than he who does not pretend to believe himself to be alive, has never ceased to tell him so. But God is that which he never wanted to listen to.

— By accepting himself like this, without curiosity for God and without problem, man is nothing more than an inert automaton, a generator of tedium and madness, abandoned by all conscience, and from which the still pure soul has fled, because it senses that the moment is coming, that this Automaton is going to give birth to a Beast, and the Beast an obscene demon.

I therefore felt that it was necessary to go upstream and relax in my pre-consciousness until I saw myself evolve and *desire*. That's what Peyote did for me. — Led by it, I saw that it was necessary for me to defend what

I am before I was born, & that my self is nothing more than the result of the fight that I waged in the Supreme against the lie of bad ideas.

As much as the beings try to mumble that things are as they are & that there is nothing more to look for, I can clearly see that they have lost their footing, & that for a long time *they no longer know what they are saying*, for the states with which they stretch themselves above the flow of ideas, and where one takes words for talk, they no longer know from where they got them.

It is because for centuries their thinkers, like them, have abdicated before this effort of honor that one must make to earn one's conscience, when one knows *where* one must win it.

— The Unconscious does not belong to me except in dreams, and then all that I see in it and which lags behind, is it a marked form to be born, or some filth that I rejected?

The Subconscious is shaped by the premises of my inner Will, but I don't know very well who reigns there; and I believe it's not me, but the wave of enemy Wills which, I don't know why, think in me, and never had any other concern in the world or any other idea, than to take my place in myself, in my body and in my self.

In Pre-consciousness I see again all these ill wills launching their Temptations against me & striking me, but this time, armed with all my consciousness, I feel myself there.

Peyote will hold me in the Pre-conscious, & above the state of man I will know from where my Will was formed, and that it is this force with which it rejected itself on the side where Good appeals, against the Evil that pursued it.

Good & Evil, say the Priests of the Ciguri, as the Mystics of Jesus-christ later repeated, no longer in sensations and visions, but with the proof of martyrdom, & the experience of their wounds, Good & Evil are not two opposed tissues & two principles, Good is what does not exist & Evil what does not exist, what will not live and what will cease to be. The Self of man will not always believe. But it is necessary for it to attain that science.

And it seems that, originally, the object of the Peyote Dance, a sententious Rite of teachings on the Plant given to man by Jesus-christ, was to invite the human being to become aware of it. Because without help, he can't bring himself to do it.

The soul needed thousands of tests to recognize what it accepted or rejected in that outpouring of unbridled appetites in which consciousness never ceases to expiate & to be born above any figure of Purity or Sin.

I live and I was born with the illimitable temptation of being: what will become of me, where do I come from, where will I go and how? And I don't know if with death I will stop choosing, fighting, rejecting. — But why is it necessary that in all my impulses toward the beyond, toward the opening, toward proliferation, this suppuration of the infamous, these insinuations of an abject eroticism, do not cease interfering?

Never will I see things in the light of the chastity in which they were born. Why is this sordid longing to be only through and in Sin added to my pure temptation to be and to live?

Today man is dirty & impure. He puts the abject & the Sublime, eroticism & Poetry, on the same level.

One day I wanted to rebut this detestable yoke that I felt did not come from me, but which was imposed on me by the infernal coalition of beings that besieged & desecrated consciousness as they disordered Reality.

And I saw over the mountains of Mexico, above all human proof, shine the flames of a Great Bleeding Heart. — Taken, when going up, as by the arm of evil, I saw myself thrown out of conformity, not assured of things, and *exhibited* as myself, in the Truth of the Essential.

Behind Ciguri there is fullness, plethora, the plethora of satiety.

But at the bottom of Ciguri, and in that Flaming Heart, there is a Figure, in which I could not recognize JESUS-CHRIST: the full perception of the Unalterable whole, the Cross inevitably pointing out the Cardinal Points of all Satiety.

With JESUS-CHRIST — THE PEYOTE I had *heard* the human body, Spleen, Liver, Lungs, Brain, thunder in the four corners of the Divine Infinite. — And out of what extraordinary necessity their organic disposition sprang.

But internally returned to the stature of my members, I saw the Cross of Calvary appear as a bloody tearing of organs that allowed human consciousness to reach the fords of Eternity through the virtues of that blood.

And that cross explained human consciousness to me. And because of Ciguri, I saw the original prototypes of every state and every form swell to the point of a terrible shudder in which the soul of man is dismembered at the very moment it imagines that it is going to fall into that opaque thing that has the form of Sin. — Because to take root in the conscience is to remain beyond Sin. — And it has no right to call itself conscience anymore than it has known never to leave the fords of Eternity. — Outside of there, the human being is going to sink so much that it believes it is still alive, when the Seers see it already saved.

With Ciguri-Jesus-christ, in the high clouds, I saw everything that is consciousness & being and, higher up, in the non-existent, that image in which the degraded conscience of man believed to mold sexuality. — Because this is the sin. — And to reach it is to flee from being to get lost in futility.

Thus the experience with Peyote separated me from futility and, after having traversed the cross of the spasm where my heart, bursting, changed, I went behind things, where the Virgin of the Eternal struck me, then sent me away, and I returned to earth as if thunderstruck in my thoughts.

Certainly, I had not reached God, because Divinity is not reached by means of an experimental, physical test; however, I understood one of the essential Laws, by which the Force of it, when transmitted, has regulated the level of Being, and that is it's tenor in Purity.

Among the Tarahumara of the mountain, I understood that one must be chaste or perish, which Evil had made them forget.

This Law is not just for me; it was written for all men, forever and ever. And I know that it will be seen again & that in the meantime it will not leave. — And that due to this Law, before leaving the earth, man will sweat blood.

As for God, All the Rigorous Height that nothing in the world can take away, is not found in the Irreal, but in the Real, far outside the ordinary consciousness in which his Reality resides. But the Supreme Divine Reality is at the bottom of the heart of every man for whom Love is *to love*. Love wholeheartedly; give without taking. — What the senses cannot do. — And what the world of terrestrial life has refused to do.

Those who say there is no God have forgotten the heart.

The infinite emulsion of the heart is what Evil wanted to annihilate in worlds. But this emulsion has many folds, many layers, many substances, and many patterns; each layer is an idea, the idea of a state of the heart, & a being with the soul of it; and each state of the sensible is a substance issued from God and the Source of all Substance in that Giving Heart, Distributor of substances of the being that gives the Being its substance in the Multiform of the Infinite. And the one who could not be killed, where would He die? Because as the Idea of the eternally Reborn, God is also Someone; & this Someone, the inexhaustible Active which, above all sleep & all dreams, accepts that which, in the furthest distance from Himself, later, He will give! Much later. In that later in which the Word has exploded, his Son, in Flames of Love, which will never be exhausted.

And the following year I went looking for this God of Eternal Charity among the Irish.

APPENDIX

Among the Ciguri Priests there is a strange doctrine that resembles in a strange way that of Grace which two hundred years ago caused some very bitter fights. But it has provoked worse fights, not in debates of conscience or in words, but in reality in the times after the death of Jesus-christ. But, those have been forgotten. And yet...

These priests of the Ciguri say that Peyote is not given to everyone and that to have access to it, it is necessary to be *Predestined*. Because Ciguri is a God who is jealous of his science & does not allow it to be forgotten. Well, the states that Peyote makes people go through are horribly severe vertigo. He who, when leaving, has lost something, can no longer have the right to the Word because without wanting it, he will lie about what is essential. And the Essential is the protection of God.

But Ciguri defends itself and he who has not entered with a very pure consciousness will return to the Infinite all the essential parts of his consciousness, as if he were unworthy of keeping them. As for the abject, it will stay at the door. And to enter Peyote with a sick conscience is to expose yourself to a horrible punishment.

LETTER TO HENRI PARISOT

Rodez
7 September 1945

My dear Henri Parisot,

Less than three weeks ago I wrote you two letters to ask you to publish the *Journey to the Land of the Tarahumara*, attaching another letter to put it in place of the *Supplement to the Journey*, in which I was foolish enough to tell you that I had converted to Jesus-christ, since christ is that which I have always abhorred, and that this conversion was nothing more than the result of a frightful bewitchment that had made me forget my own nature and that here, at Rodez, has made me swallow under the name of communion a frightful number of hosts fated to keep me as long as possible, & even eternally, within a being that is not mine. This being consists in ascending to heaven in spirit instead of descending more & more in the body toward hell, that is to say in sexuality, the soul of all life insofar as what is christ leads the being into the empyrean of the clouds & of the gases where it has been dissolving since eternity. The ascension of the one named Jesus-christ two thousand years ago has been nothing more than the ascension to an infinite vertical where one day he ceased to be & where everything that belonged to him fell into the sex of all men, as the basis of all libido. Like Jesus-christ, there will also be those who have never descended to earth, because man was too small for him, maintaining himself in the abysses of the infinite as a supposed immanence of the god who without fatigue, & similar to a Buddha in self-contemplation who awaits the day that BEING will be perfect enough for Him to descend into & settle there, which is equivalent to the infamous calculation of a coward & a lazy person who did not want to suffer the being, the entire being, but to make it suffer for another and then run to that other, to that one in pain, and return him to hell, when this suffering visionary would have made the being of his pain a paradise specially prepared for that gluttony of laziness and meanness called god & Jesus-christ. I am one of those in pain, I am that principal pain in which god intends to descend when I am dead, but I have three daughters who are also three in pain and I wish you to be so in soul as well, Mr. Henri Parisot, well next to god & christ there are angels who have the same pretense as him & have always sought to seize the consciousness of every being born, even when they believe they belong only to the innate. It is to tell you that it was not Jesus-christ that I went looking for among the Tarahumara but myself, Mr. Antonin Artaud, born on 4 September 1896 in Marseille at number 4 Rue Jardin des Plantes, from a uterus which I had nothing to do with & which I did not even have anything to do with before, because being copulated & masturbated for

9 months by the membrane is not a way of being born, the torn membrane that devours without teeth as the UPANISHADS say, and I know I was born differently, from my works and not from a mother, but the MOTHER wanted to take possession of me & you can see the result of my life. I was only born from my pain and I hope that you were able to do it too, Mr. Henri Parisot.

And this pain must be believed, that the uterus found it good 49 years ago now, because it has tried to seize it for itself & feed on it under the pretext of motherhood. And Jesus-christ is the one born of a mother who also wanted to take me for herself & that long before time & the world, and I did not go to the heights of Mexico except to strip myself of Jesus Christ as I hope one day to go to Tibet to empty myself of god and of the holy spirit. Would you follow me there?

Publish this letter *instead* of the *Supplement*, and please return the *Supplement* to me. With my friendship,

ANTONIN ARTAUD

INDIAN CULTURE

I came to Mexico to make contact with the Red Earth
and it stinks the same way that it embalms;
it smells good the same way that it stank.

Kaffir of urine from the slope of a tough vagina,
and which resists when one grabs it.

Urinary camphor from the protuberance of a dead vagina,
and which slaps us when we stretch it,

when one aims from the peak of the Clown Tower,
nail-studded tomb of the hideous father,

the hollowed hole, the acrid hollow hole, where the cycle
of red lice boils,
the cycle of solar red lice,
all white in the veined network of the one two.

Which two, and which of the two?
Who, both?
in the time
seventy times cursed
when man
          crossing himself
was born son
of his sodomy

on his own callused
ass.
Why two of them,
and why born of TWO?

Hideous clown of the pussy-peeping father,
filthy parasitical clown, in hollow mama-endpiece
                              [pulled out of the fire!

For the suns imbibed whole
are nothing next to the clubfoot,
of the immense articulation
of the old gangrenous leg,
old gangrenous ossuary leg,
where a shield of bones is ripening,

the warlike, underground uprising
of the shields of all the bones.

What does this mean?

It means that papa-mama no longer buggers
                              [the innate pederast,
the filthy tusk holes of Christian orgies,
interloper between ji and cri,
contracted into
              jiji-cricri,

and it means that war
will replace the father-mother
there where the ass made a barrier
against the nourishing plague
of the Red Earth buried
under the body of the dead
                warrior
for not wanting to pass
through the periplus of the serpent
who bites its own tail in front
while papa-mama
bloody his behind.

And if looking closely
into the tumified slice of the leg,
of the blotchy old femur
there fall
       it stinks
       and it stank;
and there resurges the old warrior
of insurgent cruelty,
of the unspeakable cruelty
of living and having no being
that can justify you;
and there fall
into the anchored hole
of the earth seen from above, and broached,
all the tips of the illuminated tongue,

and which one day believed themselves souls,
not even being wills;

there rise
all the coruscations
from the flogging of my dead hand,
against the objecting tongue,

and the sexes of will,

which are barely hurled words,
which could not take hold of being;

but fall better than rejected
suns,
into the cellar where they were killing each other
papa-mama
and pederast,
the son from before it stank.

When the solar donkey believed itself good!

And where was the sky in its round?

Where one was,
                    outside,
completely cunt
from feeling the sky
                    in his cunt,

with nothing to forge a barrier against the void,
where
no bottom
and no balance,
and no surface,
nor top,
and where everything draws you back to the bottom,
when one is all his length straight.

ANTONIN ARTAUD

THE PEYOTE RITE AMONG
THE TARAHUMARA

As I already said, the priests of Tutuguri were the ones who opened the path of the Ciguri for me, just as a few days before the *Chief of all things* had opened the path of Tutuguri for me. — The *Chief of all things* is the one who directs the external relations between men: friendship, mercy, charity, fidelity, devotion, generosity, work. His power stops at the door of what we in Europe understand by metaphysics or theology, but he goes much further in the field of inner consciousness than any European boss. No one in Mexico can be initiated, that is, receive the anointing of the priests of the Sun, the touch of immersion & incorporation of the Ciguri, which is a rite of annihilation, if they have not previously been touched by the sword of the old Indian chief who commands in peace and in war, in Justice, in Marriage and in Love. Apparently, he has in his hands the power that makes men love each other or go mad, while the priests of Tutuguri raise with their mouth the Spirit that engenders them & arranges them in the Infinite, where it is necessary for the soul to collect them and reclassify them in its self. The action of the priests of the Sun surrounds the entire soul and stops at the limits of the personal self, where the *Chief of all things* comes to collect the resonance. And the old Mexican chief struck my soul in order to open my conscience again, because

I was not born to understand the Sun; in addition, the hierarchical order of things requires that once one has passed the ALL, that is, the multiple, one returns to the simple Unit, which is the Tutuguri or the Sun, so that one is then dissolved & resurrected through this operation of mysterious reassimilation. I mean, of dark reassimilation that is contained in the Ciguri, like a myth of recollection, their extermination, & finally resolution in the riddle of supreme expropriation, as its priests do not stop clamoring & affirming it in the Dances of all the Night. Because the Dance takes all night, from sunset to dawn, but the dance takes the night and squeezes it as the juice is extracted from a fruit right up to the source of life. And the extirpation of property goes up to god & surpasses him; because god, and above all god, cannot take what in the self is authentically the very strong self, even if he has the foolishness to abandon himself.

It was a Sunday morning that the old Indian chief opened my conscience with a blow of the glaive between the spleen & the heart: "Have confidence," he told me, "don't be afraid, I won't do you any harm," and he quickly backed up three or four steps, & after drawing a circle with the glaive in the air at the height of my thigh and from behind, he rushed at me with all his might as if he wanted to annihilate me. But the tip of the glaive barely broke my skin and a small drop of blood gushed out.
— I did not feel any pain, but I felt as if I had awakened to something, to which up to that moment I had been

a bastard & to which I had been led on the wrong side, & I felt flooded with a light that I had never possessed. — It was a few days later, that one morning at dawn, I entered into relations with the priests of the Tutuguri & two days later, I was finally able to meet the Ciguri again.

"You join the entity without God that assimilates you and engenders you as if you created yourself, and as yourself in Nothingness and against Him, at all times, you create yourself."

These are the words of the Indian chief and I am only quoting them, not as he told me, but as I have *reconstructed* them under the fantastic illuminations of the Ciguri.

If the Priests of the Sun behave like manifestations of the Speech of God, or of his Word, that is to say of Jesus-christ, the Peyote Priests have made me attend the Myth of Mystery itself, plunge into the original mystical arcana, enter through them into the Mystery of Mysteries, see the figure of the extreme operations by which THE MAN FATHER, NEITHER MAN NOR WOMAN, created everything. In truth, I did not realize all this at once and it took me some time to understand it, and many of the dance gestures, attitudes, or figures that the priests of the Ciguri traced in the air, as if they imposed them in the shadows or pulled them out of the den of night, they themselves no longer understood, and they did nothing more than obey a kind of physical tradition on the one hand and, on the other, respond to the secret mandates that the Peyote dictated to them, the extract of which they drank before starting to dance to experience trances by calculated methods. — I mean that they do what the plant tells them to do, moreover, that they repeat it as a kind of lesson that their muscles obey, but which they do not understand in the spasms of their nerves, neither more than their fathers nor more than the fathers of their fathers. Because in the same way the role of every nerve is overrated. This did not satisfy me, and when the Dance was over I wanted to know more about it. — Because before attending the Ciguri Rite as the current Indian priests perform it, I had interrogated many Tarahumara from the mountains & spent an entire night with a very young couple whose husband was an initiate of this rite & knew, it seems, many secrets. — And from him I received marvelous explanations & extremely precise clarifications of the way in which Peyote resurrects, along the entire path of the nervous self, the memory of the sovereign truths by which human consciousness, I was told, never loses, but rather, on the contrary, regains the perception of the Infinite. "In what these truths consist," this good man told me, "it is not for me to show you. But it is I who makes them reborn in the spirit of your being. — The spirit of man is tired of God, because being mean & sick, we're the ones who have to make him hungry. But we find that, meanwhile, Time itself denies us the way. — You will be made to see tomorrow what we can still do. And if you want to work with us, perhaps with the help of the Good Will of a man who came from the other side of the sea & who is not of our Race, we will be able to break one more resistance." — CIGURI is a name that Indian ears hardly like to hear pronounced. I had a mestizo guide with me who also served as an interpreter among the Tarahumara and who had warned me not to speak to them about Ciguri, except with respect & caution because, he told me, *they fear it*. — Yet I realized that, if there is a feeling that these people may find strange, it is fear; but on the contrary, that word evokes in them the sense of the sacred in a way that the European conscience no longer knows, and in this lies their misfortune because here man no longer respects anything. And the series of attitudes that the young Indian demonstrated before my eyes when I pronounced the word CIGURI taught me several things about the possibilities of human consciousness when it has preserved the feeling of God. A terror, I must say, was indeed emanating from his attitude, but it was not his attitude because it covered him as if with a shield or a cloak. To himself, he seemed as happy as he is only in the peak moments of existence, his face overflowing with joy & adoration. It is thus that the First-born of a humanity still in labor had to behave at the moment in which the spirit of the UNCREATED MAN rose in flaming thunder over the disemboweled world; this is how the skeletons in the catacombs should pray, to which it has been told in the books that MAN himself appeared.

He clasped his hands and his eyes lit up. His face petrified and closed. The deeper he went into himself, the more I had the impression that an unusual and readable emotion objectively radiated from him. — He moved from one place to another two or three times. And each time his eyes, which had become almost fixed, turned to isolate a point next to him as if he wanted to become aware of something to be feared. But I realized that what he could thus fear was to fail by some negligence in the respect he owed to God. Above all, I verified two things: the first is that the Tarahumara Indian does not give his body the value that we Europeans give it and that he has another notion of it. — "It is not me at all," he seems to say, "that am this body," — and when he turned to look at something next to him, it was his own body that he seemed to scrutinize and watch. — "There where I am & what I am, *Ciguri* tells me and dictates to me, and you lie and disobey. What I feel in reality you never want to feel and you give me the opposite sensations. You don't want anything I want. And what you offer me most of the time is Evil. — You have been for me only a transitory test & a burden. One day I'll order you to go away when *Ciguri* himself is free, but, he said suddenly, crying, you won't have to let go entirely. — After all, it was *Ciguri* who made you, and many times you served me as a refuge against the storm *because Ciguri would die if he didn't have me.*"

The second thing that I verified in the middle of this prayer — because this series of movements before himself and as if next to himself that he had just witnessed and that took much more time to elapse than to relate, were the improvised prayers of the Indian to the evocation of the name of *Ciguri* —, the second thing that impressed me is that if the Indian is an enemy to his body, it also seems that he sacrificed his conscience to God and that the Peyote habit guides him in this work. The emotions that radiated from him, that passed one after the other across his face, and that one read, *were evidently not his own*; he did not adopt them, he no longer identified with what for us is a personal emotion, or at least he did not do it in our way, based on a choice and an immediate flashing incubation as we do. — Among all these ideas that go through our heads, there are some that we accept and others that we reject. — The day when our self and our consciousness are formed, a distinctive rhythm & a natural choice is established in this ceaseless movement of incubation, which makes only our own ideas float in the field of consciousness, the rest vanishing automatically. Maybe we need time to carve in our feelings and forge our own body, but what we think of things in general is like the *totem* of an indisputable grammar that scans its terms word for word. And our self, when questioned, always reacts in the same way: as someone who knows that it is he who answers and not someone else. With the Indian it is not like that.

A European will never accept the thought that what he has felt and perceived in his body, that the emotion that has shaken him, that the strange idea he has just had and that has excited him because of its beauty was not his, and that another has felt and lived all this inside his own body, or else he would think himself crazy and one would be tempted to say that he has become a madman. — The Tarahumara, contrarily, systematically distinguishes between what belongs to him and what belongs to the Other in everything he thinks, feels, and makes. But the difference between him and a madman is that his personal consciousness has developed in this task of internal separation *&* distribution, to which the Peyote has led him, and which reinforces his will. — If he seems to know much better what it is not than what it is, on the other hand he knows what it is and that it is much better than we ourselves know what we are *&* what we want. — "There is," he says, "in every man an old reflection of God in which we can still contemplate the image of that infinite force that one day threw us into a soul and that soul into a body; and it is in the image of this Strength that Peyote has led us because Ciguri calls us toward him."

What was observed in this way in this Indian who had not taken Peyote for a long time, but was one of the initiates in its Rites, because the Rite of the Ciguri is the highest of the religion of the Tarahumara, inspired me with great envy to see closely all the Rites *and to reach and participate in them.* — That was the difficulty.

The friendship that this young Tarahumara had shown me, who was not afraid to pray a few steps from me, was already a guarantee that certain doors would open for me. And furthermore, what he had told me about the help that was expected of me made me think that my admission to the *Ciguri* Rites depended in part on the initiatives that I took in the face of the obstacles that the Tarahumara currently encounter in exercising their rites by the mestizo government of Mexico. The Mestizo government is pro-Indian because those who govern are more red than white. But they are unequally so, and their leaders in the mountains are almost all of mixed blood. — And they consider the beliefs of the Ancient Mexicans dangerous. — The present government of Mexico has founded indigenous schools in the mountains where the children of the Indians are given an education modeled on the French communal schools. The Minister of Public Education of Mexico, from whom the French Minister made me obtain the circulation permit, made me stay in the buildings of the indigenous school of the Tarahumara. — Consequently, I entered into contact with the director of that school, who, moreover, was in charge of order in the entire extension of the Tarahumara territory, and under whose command was a cavalry squadron. — Without any provision having been made up to then on this matter, I knew that it was a question of preventing the next Peyote festival that was to take place in a few days. Apart from the great Racial

Festival in which all the Tarahumara people participate and which takes place on a fixed date like Christmas here, the Tarahumara also have a certain number of particular rites around Peyote. And they had agreed to show me one. In addition, there are other festivals in the Tarahumara religion such as here we have Easter, the Ascension, the Assumption, and the Immaculate Conception, but not all concern Peyote; and the Great Festival of the *Ciguri* does not take place, I think, more than once a year. — In said festival, Peyote is taken according to all the traditional millennial rites. Peyote is also taken at other festivals, but only as an occasional adjunct that no longer concerns itself with grading the force or the effects. — When I say that it is taken, it would be better to say that it was took, because the Mexican government does everything possible to take Peyote from the Tarahumara and to prevent them from abandoning themselves to its effect, and the soldiers sent to the mountains have the mission of preventing its cultivation. And I found the Tarahumara in despair, when I arrived in the mountain, at the recent destruction of a Peyote field by soldiers from Mexico.

I had a long conversation about this matter with the director of the indigenous school where I was staying. — The conversation was lively, painful, and disgusting at times. The mestizo director of the Tarahumara indigenous school was much more concerned with his sex, which he used every night to possess the teacher of the school who was a Mestizo like him, than with culture or religion. But the Mexican government has made the return to indigenous culture the basis of its program, and the mestizo director of the indigenous school of the Tarahumara was equally repulsed by spilling indigenous blood. "CIGURI," I told him, "it's not a plant, it's a man whose limb you have severed by blowing up the Peyote field. And of that mutilated red limb that sings: green, white, purple, everyone wants to ask you for an account. And they see it." I noticed, when passing through several Tarahumara villages, that with the appearance of the red member, a wind of rebellion was blowing over the village. The Director of the indigenous school was not unaware of this, but he was hesitating about the means that he should employ to restore tranquility among the indigenous people. "The only way," I told him, "is to win their hearts. — They will never forgive you for this destruction, but show them by a contrary action that you are not the enemy of God. You are only a handful, and if should they decide to revolt, it would be necessary for you to make war on them, and even with your weapons, you will not be able to subdue them. — And besides, the Ciguri Priests have caves that you will never be able to enter."

"And what would become of Mexico's return to Indian culture in the face of such a war, when it was civil war that you would've started there? — You must authorize this Feast now if you want the Tarahumara to stay with you, and you must also give the tribes facilities so that they feel that you are favorable to them."

—It's that, when they have taken Peyote, they no longer obey us.

— Peyote has something in common with everything human. It is a marvelous magnetic & alchemical principle, if you know how to take it, that is, in the desired doses or according to the desired amount. And definitely don't take it casually & without purpose. — If, after having taken Peyote, the Indians go crazy, it is because they abuse it until they reach that point of disorderly drunkenness in which the soul is no longer subjected to anything. By doing so, it is not you who they disobey, but *Ciguri* himself, because Ciguri is the God of the Presence of Justice, balance, and self-control. He who has *truly* drunk Ciguri, the true degree & measure of Ciguri, MAN and not an indeterminate GHOST, knows how things are made and can no longer lose his reason, because it is God who is in his nerves and from there he leads him.

"But drinking Ciguri is precisely not to exceed the dose, because Ciguri is the Infinite, and the mystery of the therapeutic action of the remedies is linked to the proportion that our organism absorbs. To exceed what is necessary is to RUIN the operation.

"God, the Tarahumara priestly traditions say, disappears immediately when one gets too close, and in his place comes the Evil Spirit.

— Tomorrow night you are going to get in touch with a family of Ciguri Priests, the director of the indigenous school told me. — Tell them what you just told me and I'm sure we'll see, this time at least, and perhaps more than on previous occasions, that the consumption of Peyote should be regulated, and also tell them that this Feast will be authorized & that we're going to do everything possible to provide them with what they need to meet and that we will supply them with the horses & the food that they require."

So I spent the night of the next day in the little Indian village where I had been told the Peyote Rite would be shown to me. — It took place at midnight. The Priest arrived with two helpers, a man and a woman, and two small children. He drew on the ground a kind of semicircle within which the games of his assistants were to take place, and he closed the semicircle with a thick wooden beam on which I was allowed to sit. To the right, the arc of the circle was limited by a kind of sanctum in the shape of an 8 that I understood that for the Priest constituted the Holy of Holies. To the left was the Void: and there remained the children. In the Holy of Holies the old wooden vase containing the Peyote roots was placed, because the Priests do not have the whole plant for their particular rites, or at least they no longer have it.

The Priest had a cane in his hand and the children small sticks. — The Peyote is taken after a series of dance movements & when his followers have obtained the religious fulfillment of the Rite, it is then that Ciguri wants to enter into them.

I verified that the assistants had a hard time getting moving and I had the impression that they were not going to dance or that they would dance badly if they had not known that Ciguri wanted to descend on them at that moment. — Because the Rite of Ciguri is a Rite of Creation and that explains how things *are* in the void and this in the Infinite, and how things sprouted from the Infinite to Reality and were made. The Rite ends at the moment in which, under the order of God, they have taken Being in a body. — That is what the two helpers danced, but all this did not go without a long discussion.

— We can't understand God if he hasn't touched our soul before, and our dance would be no more than a grimace, and the GHOST, they shouted, the GHOST that chases the CIGURI will be reborn here again.

The Priest took a long time to make up his mind, but finally he took out a little bag from his chest and poured into the hands of the Indians a kind of white powder that they immediately consumed.

Then they began to dance. Seeing their faces, after they took that Peyote powder, I understood that they were going to show me something that I had never witnessed. And I gave them my full attention so as not to lose anything of what I would see.

The two helpers lay down on the ground and faced each other like two inanimate balls. — But the old Priest must have taken some powder as well, because an inhuman expression came over him. — I saw him lie down and stand up. His eyes lit up and an expression of unusual authority began to take possession of him. — He gave two or three dull taps on the ground, then entered the 8 he had drawn to the right of the Ritual Field. Then the assistants seemed to come out of their position of their inanimate ball. The man first shook his head and touched the earth with the palms of his hands. The woman moved her back. — Then the Priest spat: not saliva but breath. He exhaled noisily between his teeth. And under the action of this concussion of the lungs, the man and the woman, at the same instant, perked up and stood upright. From the way they stood, facing each other, from the sure way each remained in space as if held in the pocket of emptiness and in the incisions of infinity, one understood that those who were there were not a man and a woman, but two principles: the male, mouth open, with chattering, red, inflamed, bloody gums, as if lacerated by the roots of the teeth, translucent at that moment, like commanding tongues; the female, a toothless larva, with her molars pierced by a file, like a rat in its cage, overcome by a rut, fleeing, turning before the hirsute male; and that they were going to collide, to plunge frantically, one into the other, like things, after having looked at each other for a while and waged war, finally intertwine before the *indiscreet & guilty* eye of God, which their action must gradually supplant. "Because *Ciguri*, they say, was *THE MAN*, THE MAN, as HIMSELF, HIMSELF in the space THAT HE *was building* himself, when God murdered him."

This is exactly what happened.

But one thing, above all, caught my attention in his way of threatening, eluding, attacking, to ultimately agree to walk in pairs. It is that those principles were not in the body, they did not come to touch the body, but remained obstinately suspended like two immaterial ideas outside of Being, in perpetual opposition to IT, which also made *their own body*, a body in which the idea of matter is volatilized by Ciguri. Looking at them, I remembered everything that poets, professors, and artists of all kinds that I had met in Mexico had told me about Indian religion and culture, and what I had read in the books that they lent me there about the metaphysical traditions of the Mexicans.

— The Evil Spirit, the initiated Priests of the Ciguri say, has never been able or wanted to believe that God is not accessible *&* exclusively a Being, and that there is something more than a Being in the inscrutable essence of God.

This was precisely what this Peyote Dance was showing me.

Because I thought I saw in this Dance the point where the universal unconscious is sick. And that it is outside of God. — The Priest touched now his spleen, now his liver with his right hand, while with his left he struck the ground with his staff. — Each of his blows was answered by a distant attitude from the man and the woman, sometimes one of desperate and haughty affirmation, other times of furious refusal. But responding to some hasty blows from the Priest, who was holding the staff with both hands, they rocked rhythmically against each other, elbows apart and hands joined in two triangles that would come to life. At the same time, the feet drew two circles on the ground and something like the limbs of a letter, an S, a U, a J, a V. Figures in which the form 8 appeared mainly. Once, twice, they did not come together, but they passed each other with a kind of greeting. The third time the greeting was more pronounced. On the fourth, they held hands, circled around each other, and the man's feet seemed to search the ground for the places where the woman's had trodden.

They did so eight times. But after the fourth, their countenances, which had a lively expression, did not stop radiating. For the eighth time, they looked to the side of the Priest, who then assumed a position with an air of domination and threat at one end of the Holy of Holies, there where things are in contact with the North. And with his cane he drew a large 8 in the air. But the cry he gave at the same moment revolutionized *the funereal anguished labor of the deceased black man from his old sin*, as the ancient lost poem of the Maya of Yucatan says;

and I do not remember in my life having heard anything that indicated in a more resounding and evident way to what depths the human will descends to raise its presence from the night. — And it seemed to me that I saw in the Infinite & as in a dream the way in which God created Life. — That shout from the Priest was given as if to prop up the drawing of the staff in the air. Shouting, the Priest jumped and drew an 8 with his whole body in the air and with his feet on the ground until he closed it on the South side.

The dance was going to end. The two children, who during all this time were on the left of the circle, asked if they could leave & the Priest with the staff signaled for them to leave and disappear. But neither of them had taken Peyote. They sketched what seemed to be a dance gesture and then gave up & withdrew like one who returns home.

※

I already said it at the beginning of this relationship: all this was not enough for me. And I wanted to know more about Peyote. I approached the Priest to question him:

"Our last Festival, he told me, couldn't take place. We are discouraged. We no longer take Ciguri in the Rites but as a vice. Soon our entire Race will be sick. Time has become too old for the Being. He can no longer sustain us. What to do, what are we going to do? Already our people no longer love God. Me, who am a priest, I have not been able to feel it. You see me completely desperate."

I told him what I had agreed to with the director of the indigenous school and that the next important festival could take place this time.

I also told him that I had not come among the Tarahumara out of curiosity, but to find a Truth that eludes the European world & that his Race had preserved. — This immediately put him at ease and he told me marvelous things about Good & Evil, about Truth & about Life.

— Everything I just said comes from *Ciguri*, he told me, and it is He who taught it to me.

"Things are not as we see & experience them most of the time, but as *Ciguri* teaches us through the centuries. They have been taken over by Evil, the Evil Spirit, and without *Ciguri*, it is not possible for man to return to the Truth. — At first they were true, but the older we get, the more they become false because Evil intrudes more. In the beginning the world was completely real, it sounded in and with the human heart. Now the heart is no longer in the truth, neither is the soul, because God withdrew. To see things was to see the Infinite. Now when I look at the light, I have a hard time thinking about God. — However, it is He, *Ciguri*, who did it all. But Evil is in all things, and I, man, can no longer feel pure. — There is something terrifying in me that rises and that does not start from me, but from the darkness that I carry in me, there where the soul of man does not know where *I* begin, or where I end, nor what made it begin, as it is seen. And this is what *Ciguri* told me. With Him I no longer know lies, and I no longer confuse *what he truly desires* within every man with what he does not desire but he pretends to desire to be of ill will. And soon this will be all there will be, he said, backing up a few steps: this obscene mask of the one who sneers between sperm and dung."

These words of the Priest that I have just referred to are absolutely authentic: they seemed to me too important and too beautiful for me to allow myself to change anything, and if they are not his, word for word, they should hardly differ from them, because it must be understood that they amaze me and my recollections on this point have remained extremely precise. — Also, I repeat, he had just taken Peyote & I was not surprised by his lucidity.

When this conversation was over, he asked me if I would like to try Ciguri & thus get closer to the Truth that I was looking for.

I told him that that was my greatest desire, and that I did not believe that without the help of Peyote we could achieve everything which eludes us and from which time and things take us further and further away.

He poured into my left hand a quantity, about the volume of a green almond, "enough," he said, "to see God two or three times, because God can never be known. To get into his presence it is necessary to put yourself at least three times under the influence of Ciguri, but each dose should not exceed the volume of a little pea."

I stayed one or two more days among the Tarahumara to get to know Peyote well; it would take many pages to describe everything I saw and experienced under his influence & everything that the Priest, his assistants, and his families also told me on this subject. — But a vision that I had and that impressed me was declared *authentic* by the Priest and his family; it seemed to correspond to what should be *Ciguri* and to what is God. — But one does not arrive at it without first having experiencing laceration & anguish, after which one feels as if returned and *thrust* to the other side of things & one no longer understands the world that one has just left.

I said: *thrust* to the other side of things; and as if a terrible force had given one a being *restored* to what exists on the other side. — One no longer feels the body that one has just abandoned and that inspired security in its limits, instead, one feels much happier to belong to the unlimited than to oneself, because one understands that what was oneself came from the head of this limitless, the Infinite, and that one is going to see it. One feels as if in a gaseous wave that radiates everywhere in an incessant sizzle. Things that came out of what was the spleen, the liver, the heart, or the lungs were detached incessantly and exploded in this atmosphere which oscillated between gas & water, but which seems to attract things toward itself and commands them to reintegrate.

What came out of my spleen or my liver had the shape of the letters of a very ancient and mysterious alphabet chewed by a huge mouth, but horribly compressed, proud, *illegible*, jealous of its invisibility; and these signs spread in all directions, while it seemed to me that I was going up into space, but not alone, but helped by an unusual force. But much freer than when I was alone on earth.

In an instant something like a wind rose and the spaces receded. On the side where my spleen was, an immense void hollowed out & turned grey and pink like the shore of the sea. And at the bottom of that hole appeared the shape of a deracinated root, a kind of J that would have had three branches on its crest crowned with a sad & bright E like an eye. — Several calls came out of the left ear of the J and passing behind it, seemed to push everything to the right, toward the side where my liver was, but well behind it. — I didn't see more & everything vanished, or I vanished when I came back to ordinary reality. In any case, I saw, apparently, the Spirit of Ciguri itself. And I believe that this should objectively correspond to a *painted* transcendental representation of ultimate & highest realities; and the Mystics must pass through similar states & images before reaching, according to the form, the supreme conflagrations & tearings, after which they fall under the kiss of God like prostitutes no doubt in the arms of their pimps.

This inspired in me a number of reflections on the psychic effect of peyote.*

The Peyote returns the self to its true origins. — Coming out of such a visionary state, one can no longer confuse the lie with the truth as before. — One has seen where it comes from and who it is, and one no longer doubts what it is. There is no longer any emotion or external influence that can divert it.

And the whole series of lustful phantasms projected by the unconscious can no longer interfere with the true breath of MAN, for the good reason that Peyote is MAN not born, but innate, & that with him the entire atavistic and personal consciousness is alerted and defends itself. — It knows what is good for it and what is of no value to it: and therefore the thoughts and feelings that it can receive without danger and *with profit*, and which are harmful to the exercise of its freedom. — Above all, it knows how far its own being goes, & how far *it has not yet gone*

---

* I want to say that if they return one last time to impose themselves on my thought, the Peyote, HE, does not lend itself to these fetid spiritual assimilations, because MYSTICISM has never been more than the copulation of a very wise & very refined hypocrite against which the PEYOTE protests because with it, MAN is alone and desperately strumming the music of his skeleton, without father, without mother, without family, without love, without God or society.

   And without beings to accompany him. And the skeleton is not bones, but skin, like skin that marches. And it marches from the equinox to the solstice, closing the ring on his humanity.

OR HAS NO RIGHT TO GO WITHOUT CAPSIZING INTO IRREALITY, ILLUSION, THE UNDONE, THE UNPREPARED.

Taking your dreams for reality is what Peyote will never let you sink into. — Or confusing perceptions borrowed from the fleeting, uncultivated, not yet walled, not yet lifted depths of the hallucinatory unconscious with the images, the emotions of the real. — For there is in consciousness the *Marvelous* with which to go beyond things. And Peyote tells us where it is and after what unusual concretions of an atavistically repressed and *closed* breath can form the Fantastic & renew its phosphorescence, its dust cloud in consciousness. And this Fantastic is of a noble quality, its disorder is only apparent, it actually obeys an order that is elaborated in a mystery & on a Plane that normal consciousness does not reach, but which *Ciguri* allows us to reach, & which is the mystery itself of all poetry. — But there is in human being another plane, dark, formless, where consciousness has not entered, but which surrounds it like an unilluminated extension, or as with a threat, depending on the case. And that also produces bold sensations, perceptions. These are the shameless specters that attack the sick conscience. It is abandoned & completely melts down if it finds nothing to stop it. And Peyote is the only barrier that Evil finds on this horrible side.

I also had sensations, false perceptions in which I believed. In the months of June, July, August, and until last September, I believed myself surrounded by demons and I seemed to perceive them, to see them take shape around me. — I did not find anything better to scare them away than to make signs of the cross every moment on all the parts of my body & the space where I thought I saw them. I wrote also on, it did not matter what piece of paper, or on the books that I had at hand, conjurations that were worthless, neither from the literary point of view, nor from the magickal point of view, because things written in that state are nothing more than the residue, the deformation, or rather the *falsification* of the highlights of LIFE. By the end of September, those haunting perceptions, in themselves illegitimate, began to disappear; in October, they were almost nonexistent. After 15 or 20 November, I felt energy and clarity return to me. Above all, I finally felt my consciousness to be free. No more false feelings. No more bad perceptions. — Meanwhile, day by day, slowly but surely, a feeling of security, of inner certainty, took possession of me.

If in recent times I made gestures that resembled those of certain sick victims of *religious mania*, they were nothing more than the residue of lamentable habits that I acquired in the face of beliefs that did not exist. As the receding sea leaves a mixed deposit on the sand that the winds come to sweep away. — I put, after several weeks, all my willpower into getting rid of this small residue. And I affirm that, day by day, they left.

Well, there is one thing that the Peyote priests of Mexico helped me to notice and the little Peyote that I took opened my consciousness. That in the human liver where this secret alchemy is produced and this work through which the I of every individual chooses what suits him, adopts or rejects it, among the sensations, the desires which the unconscious forms and which make up their appetites, their conceptions, their true beliefs and their *ideas*. — It is there that the Self becomes conscious and that its power of appreciation, of extreme organic discrimination, manifests itself. — Because that is where *Ciguri* works to separate what exists from that which does not exist. The liver seems to be the organic filter of the *Unconscious*.

I found similar metaphysical ideas in the works of the old Chinese. And according to them the liver is the filter of the unconscious, but the spleen is the physical responder of the infinite. But that is another question.

But for the liver to be able to fulfill its function, the body must at least be well nourished.

One cannot reproach a man, locked up for six years in a lunatic asylum and who for three years has not had enough to eat, of an occult weakening of the Will. Sometimes I go for months without eating a piece of sugar or chocolate. As for butter, I don't know how long it's been since I've tasted it.

I never get up from the table without feeling hungry because the rations, as is well known, are scant.

And the bread is especially insufficient. Apart from the piece of chocolate they gave me yesterday, it had been eight months since I had eaten any. I am not a man who allows himself to be diverted from fulfilling his duty for whatever reason, unless I am reproached for the lack of energy in a time like this in which the essential elements for the restoration of energy do not exist in the food that is given to all of us. And above all, they no longer force me to undergo electroshock for deficiencies that one well knows are not beyond the control of my own will, of my lucidity, of my intelligence. Enough, enough, and enough of this punishing trauma.

Each dose of electric shock plunged me into a terror that each time lasted for several hours. And I did not see each new application coming without despair, because I knew that once again I would lose consciousness and I would see myself suffocated for a whole day, without even recognizing myself, knowing perfectly well that I was somewhere, but the devil knows where, and as if he were *dead*.

With all this we are far from being cured by Peyote. Peyote, according to what I saw, *fixes consciousness* and prevents it from going astray, from indulging in false impressions. The Mexican Priests showed me, on the liver, the exact point where *Ciguri*, where the Peyote produces that synthetic concretion which lastingly sustains in the consciousness the feeling *&* the desire for the truth. And that it gives them the strength to abandon themselves there, automatically discarding the rest.

"It is like the coming skeleton that returns," the Tarahumara told me, "from the DARK RITE, THE NIGHT THAT MARCHES OVER THE NIGHT."

POST-SCRIPTUM

The Peyote Rite *was written in Rodez, the first year of my arrival in this asylum, already after seven years of confinement, three of which have been in secret, with systematic and daily poisonings. It represents my first effort to re-enter myself after seven years of estrangement and castration from everything. It is a recently poisoned, kidnapped, and traumatized one who recounts his memories of himself before death. That is to say, that the text cannot be but stuttering. I add that this text was written in the stupid mental state of the* convert *that the spells of the cleric, taking advantage of his momentary weakness, kept in a state of servitude.*

Ivry-sur-Seine, 10 March 1947

I wrote The Peyote Rite *in a state of conversion, & already with one hundred & fifty or two hundred recent hosts in my body,*
    hence my delirium about christ & the cross of Jesus Christ.
    Because nothing seems to me now more funereal and mortally ominous than the stratifying and limited sign of the cross,
    nothing more erotically pornographic than christ, ignoble, sexual concretization of all the false psychic enigmas, of all the bodily rubbish passed on to the intelligence as if it had nothing else to do in the world than to serve as material for a rebus, & whose lower magick masturbation maneuvers produce electric shock.

Paris, 23 March 1947

A NOTE ON PEYOTE

I took Peyote in Mexico in the mountains & I had a package that lasted two or three days among the Tarahumara; I thought then, at that moment, to be living the happiest three days of my existence.

I had ceased to get bored, to look for a reason for my life and I ceased having to carry my body.

I understood that I was inventing life, that it was my function and my reason for being and that I was bored when I had lost my imagination and the Peyote gave it to me.

A being stepped forward & with a blow made the Peyote come out of me.

With it I made real minced meat, and the carcass of a man was torn to pieces and found torn to pieces, somewhere.

rai da kanka da kum
a kum da na kum vönoh

Since this world is not the inverse of the other and much less its half,

this world is also a real machinery whose lever of control I own, it's a real factory, whose key is humor-born.

sana tafan tana
tanaf tamafts bai

TUTUGURI
THE RITE OF THE BLACK SUN

And below, as at the base of the bitter,
cruelly desperate slope of the heart,
the circle of the six crosses opens,
                entrenched,
as if entrenched in the mother earth,
disentrenched from the foul embrace of the mother
                who slobbers.

The earth of black coal
is the sole humid site
in this vent of rock.

The Rite is that the new sun which passes through
    seven points before exploding at the earth's slit.

And there are six men,
one for each sun,
and a seventh man
who is the sun entirely
           raw
dressed in black & red flesh.

Yet, this seventh man
is a horse,
a horse with a man leading him.

But it is the horse
that is the sun
and not the man.

On the rending of a drum and a
    long, strange
trumpet,
the six men
who they were placing down,
curled up at ground level,
spring forth successively like sunflowers;
not suns,
but turning soils,
lotuses of water;
and to each upspring
corresponds the increasingly gloomy
                and *suppressed* gong
                of the drum
until suddenly we see approaching at full gallop,
    with dizzying speed,
the last sun,
the first man,
the black horse with a
                naked man,
                absolutely naked
                and *virgin*
                on it.

Having pounced, they advance following circular
 meanders
and the horse of bloody meat goes mad
and caracoles without stopping
at the top of its rock
until the six men
they have finished encircling
completely
the six crosses.

Yet, the major tone of the Rite is precisely

> THE ABOLITION OF THE CROSS.

Having ceased turning
They uproot
the crosses of earth
and the naked man
on the horse
parades
an immense horseshoe
that he has tempered in a cut of his blood.

TUTUGURI

Dedicated to the external glory of the Sun, *Tutuguri*
   is a black rite.
The Rite of the black night and of the *eternal* death
   of the Sun.
No, the sun will not return
and the six crosses of the circle that the star has
   to traverse
are not really there but to stop you on your way.
Since not enough is known, no one knows at all here
   in Europe how the cross is a black sign,
not enough is known about *"the salivary power of the
   cross,"* & as the cross is an ejection of saliva cast
   on the words of thought.
In Mexico the cross and the sun go hand in hand,
   and the jumping sun is in this revolving phrase
   that takes six times to get up to date,
the cross is an abject sign and it is necessary that
   the matter burn,
because it is abject,
because the tongue that salivates the sign is abject,
and why does it salivate the sign?
To anoint it.
There is no holy or sacred sign if it is not anointed.
And the tongue at the moment of anointing it,
   doesn't it put itself on point?
is it not placed between the four cardinal points?

It is necessary then that the rising sun jump
 the six points of the abject phrase that must
 be saved, with which it will make a kind of
 translation in the lightning plane.
For the sun truly appears flush with the crosses
 but like the ball of a spark,
the one we know it won't forgive?
What will you not forgive?
The sin of man and of the neighboring town,
 and therefore for several weeks before the rite
 the Tarahumara race can be seen dressing in
 clean white garments, washing and purging.
And the Day of the Rite & of the meteoric apparition
 has finally arrived.
Then six men lie down on the ground with their
 white dresses, the six men considered the purest
 of the tribe.
And each is considered to have wed a cross.
One of those crosses made with two linked buttons
 of a dirty rope.
And there's a seventh man standing carrying a cross
 on him tied to his hip, and between his hands a
 strange musical instrument, made of lamellæ of
 wood superimposed, one on top of the other, and
 that produce a sound between a bell and a barrel.
And one day, at dawn, the seventh Tutuguri begins
 the dance by hitting one of the lamellas with a
 very black iron mallet.

Then the men of the crosses are seen, as torn from
> the ground; they advance and jump & stand in
> a circle and each must encircle his cross seven
> times without breaking the full circle.

I don't know if the wind is rising

or if a wind rises from this music of yesteryear that
> persists for a day, but one feels as if whipped by
> a hot flash of night, by a breath which rises from
> the caves of a humanity abolished & come here
> to show its face here,

a painted face,

a sneering and ruthless face.

Ruthless because the justice it brings
> is not of this world.

Be pure and chaste, it seems to say.

Be a virgin too.

Or I open my gehenna to you.

And gehenna half-opens too.

The tympanum of the seventh Tutuguri has become
> an excruciating pang: it is the crater of a volcano
> at its point of eruption.

The lamellæ seem to break when heard like a forest
> collapsed under the blow of a fantastic woodcutter.

And suddenly what was expected happens:

sulfurous, *lilaceous* vapors, arise en bloc
> from a point on the circle

that the six men
> > > have traced,

than the six crosses
>> they have closed,
and under the vapors a flame, an immense flame
>> suddenly
has lit,
this immense flame *boils*.
It boils making an *unheard* noise. Your interior
is filled with stars, of incandescent corpuscles;
as if the sun upon arrival brought with it a
celestial system.
And behold, the Sun has aligned.
It has taken shape in the middle of the celestial system.
It has been swiftly placed as in the center of a
formidable blow.
Because the flaming corpuscles have been thrown
about over others, like the soldiers of an army
at war and they explode.
So the Sun has become round. And you see an
igneous ball in the same axis of the natural Sun,
since it is the aurora, and that axis rises & jumps
from cross to cross.
The six men have opened their arms, not to make
the cross, but with their hands forward as if they
wanted to receive the ball, & this, turning around
each sown cross, does not cease to reject them.
Because the tympanum is a wind, it has become like
the Sun of a wind where an army might well
advance.

And indeed.
There is at the borders of noise and nothingness,
 because the
noise is so strong
that it only summons
nothingness ahead of it,
so there is an intense trampling. Split rhythm of a
 marching army, or gallop of a maddened charge.
The fireball has burned all six crosses; the six men
 with their hands forward and who saw the thing
 coming, they are all
  exhausted & drooling.
And the noise of the gallop is exacerbated.
And we perceive crosses on the horizon like a horse
 with a naked man on it because the beat of the
 rhythm was 7.
Yet there are only six crosses.
And on the wooden tympanum of the seventh Tutuguri
always an introduction of nothingness,
always this introduction out of the blue:
this hollow time,
a hollow time,
a kind of exhausting void between the lamellæ
 of the wood that he cuts,
nothing that claims the trunk of man,
the body imprisoning a piece of the man
in the fury (no: in the fervor)
of the things inside.

There, where below nothing
        elects itself
the noise of the great bells in the wind,
the tearing of the marine cannons,
the barking of the waves in the storms of the Autans;
in brief the horse advances carrying the trunk on
   itself of a man,
of a naked man & who brandishes
not a cross,
but a staff of iron wood,
bound to a gigantic horseshoe
that covers the entire body,
his body sculpted in a gash of blood,
and the horseshoe is there,
like the jaws of an iron collar,
that the man would have taken
to the gash of his blood.

Ivry-sur-Seine, 16 February 1948

NOTES

Antonin Artaud's writings are available in French in the 26 volumes of his *Œuvres Complètes*, published by Gallimard between 1956 and 1994, edited and exhaustively annotated by Paule Thévenin, as well as several additional volumes of letters, drawings, and notebook writings. Eight of the 26 volumes have been reissued in revised and expanded editions. Hereafter we refer to Artaud's *Œuvres Complètes* as OC followed by the volume (year) & page numbers.

In 2004, Gallimard also published *Œuvres*, a volume in its Quarto series, edited, introduced, and annotated by Évelyne Grossman. *Œuvres* presents a vast selection of Artaud's writings, including letters and notebook writings, in a single enormous volume that also includes illustrations & a detailed chronology of his life. Hereafter we refer to *Œuvres* as *Quarto* followed by a page number.

The French texts of many of Artaud's most important writings are also available in more accessible editions. These include editions of *Messages Révolutionnaires & Les Tarahumaras*, the contents of which appear in this volume.

The purpose of the notes that follow is to aid the reader in understanding the composition of & the relationships among these texts. Artaud wrote restlessly throughout his life. Some of his writing was intended for public consumption, other writings were intended for more limited forms of circulation, from the private notebook to the personal letter to pieces of writing intended to be heard by a small audience. His writing has also enjoyed — or perhaps suffered — a number of afterlives: from pieces published in small editions in France & elsewhere to the various volumes of his sprawling *Œuvres Complètes*.

These notes provide the sources for the texts translated in the present collection while also permitting the reader to follow some of the principal peregrinations of the texts from their composition to their initial publication, whether in newspapers, journals, and books, in some cases in Spanish translation, and thereafter through various volumes, in French, both during Artaud's lifetime and after his death.

THE CONQUEST OF MEXICO

The Conquest of Mexico (La Conquête du Mexique). OC 5 (1964) 21–29. Written circa January 1933. First published by André Breton in his *L'Almanach surréaliste du demi-siècle,* a special issue of the journal *Le Nef* No.

63–64 (Éditions de Sagittaire, mars–avril 1950). Artaud mentions this scenario in a letter he sent to Jean Paulhan on 22 January 1933. He included sections of the text in his "Second Manifesto" for the Theater of Cruelty, initially printed in 1933 as a separate brochure, but later incorporated into *The Theater and Its Double*. He read from the text at the home of Lise Deharme on 6 January 1934, along with an act from *Richard II*, as part of his efforts to secure funding for his theater projects. He proposed this scenario as the first production for the Theater of Cruelty.

PREPARATORY WRITINGS

The Awakening of the Thunder-Bird (Le Réveil de L'Oiseau-Tonnerre). OC 8 (1980) 407–14 and *Quarto* (2004) 671–6. First published in *La Bête noire* No. 6 (1 novembre 1935). The short-lived journal *La Bête noire* was founded in 1935 by Maurice Raynal and Michel Leiris and edited through its run of eight issues by Raynal and Efstratios Tériade, who had previously co-edited *Minotaure &* would later edit *Verve*. Artaud had previously published "The Theater and Culture" (Le Théâtre et la culture) in *La Bête noire* No. 5 (1 octobre 1935). That essay would later become the preface to *The Theater and Its Double*.

Mexico and Civilization (Le Mexique et la civilisation). OC 8 (1980) 127–32 and *Quarto* (2004) 677–80. Written in 1935. First published by Serge Berna in his anthology of texts by Artaud, *Vie et Mort de Satan le Feu,* suivi de *Textes Mexicains pour un Nouveau Mythe* (Éditions Arcanes, 1953), reprinted in *Les Tarahumaras* (Éditions l'Arbalète, 1955). This is an unfinished draft of a lecture written in Paris prior to Artaud's journey to Mexico.

Serge Berna was a member of Isidore Isou's Lettrist Movement. He participated in the "Notre-Dame Affair" of 1950. On Easter Sunday, Berna and three other Lettrists, Michel Mourre, Ghislain Desnoyers de Marbais, and Jean Rullier, disrupted the services at Notre-Dame Cathedral in Paris. Dressed as a Dominican priest, Mourre mounted the pulpit in place of the actual priest and proceeded to harangue the congregation with a profoundly anti-Catholic diatribe that had been written by Berna. Mourre was chased from the church by an incensed mob. All four of the Lettrists were arrested during the incident, which echoed through the press, in defense and denunciation, over the following weeks.

A few years later, Berna came upon a cache of Artaud's manuscripts by chance. They had apparently been left in an apartment by Cécile Schramme, the young woman to whom Artaud had been engaged in 1937. The manuscripts included drafts of letters & private notes, notes on religion and culture, texts written in preparation for the journey to Mexico, and texts written during and immediately subsequent to that journey, all of which could have been left with Schramme by Artaud in 1937. Berna published the material in *Vie et Mort de Satan le Feu,* suivi de *Textes Mexicains pour un Nouveau Mythe* (Éditions Arcanes, collection *Voyants*, 1953) before sharing some of it with Marc Barbezat for publication in *Les Tarahumaras* (L'Arbalète, 1955) and, later, Paule Thévenin for publication in Artaud's *Œuvres Complètes*. For Thévenin's account of Berna and his discovery of these manuscripts, see OC 8 (1971) 398–400.

The Eternal Treason of the White Man (L'éternelle trahison des blancs). OC 8 (1980) 133–6, and *Quarto* (2004) 681–3. First published in *Cartelas* (Havana, 1 Noviembre 1936), tr. from Spanish into French by Marie Dézon (Paule Thévenin) and Philippe Sollers.

Artaud's boat to Mexico stopped in Havana, Cuba, on 30 January 1936, remaining there until 2 February. During these few days Artaud met with Cuban writers and artists recommended to him by Alejo Carpentier, who had known for several years in Paris. He arranged for the publication of some of the writings he hoped to complete in Mexico, of which "The Eternal Treason of the White Man," is one. A few others, including previous writing related to the Theater of Cruelty, were also published, along with his photograph. For an account of Artaud's time in Havana as well as Spanish versions of a few additional writings published there, see Pedro Marqués de Armas, *Artaud en la Habana* (Richmond, VA: Casa Vacía, 2019).

While in Cuba, Artaud attended a voodoo ceremony and was given a small dagger that would become an important talisman for him.

Notes on Cultures (Notes sur les cultures). OC 8 (1980) 122–26. Written circa 1935–1936. Artaud read widely, particularly in historical and comparative cultural & religious studies, including the religious and philosophical classics of Asia and South Asia, such as the *Upanishads*, the *Vedas*, and the *Tibetan Book of the Dead*, as well as Greek, Roman, & Christian thinkers. Paule Thévenin presented a selection of the notes he took from these readings, from roughly 1933 to 1937, in OC 8 (1980) 101–126. See also her notes on Artaud's extensive research for *Héliogabale, ou l'Anarchiste couronné* (Denoël, 1934) in OC 7 (1967) 379ff. The selection of notes presented here is focused on Mexican cultures.

LETTERS (1935–1936)

To the International Congress of Writers for the Defense of Culture (Au Congrès international des écrivains pour la défense de la culture) (end of June 1935). OC 8 (1980) 278–81 and *Quarto* (2004) 497–99. Unfinished draft.

LETTERS (1935–1936)

Paule Thévenin notes that the manuscript of this draft includes a number of corrections, indicating its importance to Artaud, who also references it in the letter he wrote to Jean Paulhan on 19 July. Though this is an unfinished draft, based on Artaud's subsequent references, it seems that a finished copy of the letter was in fact sent.

The International Congress of Writers for the Defense of Culture was convened at the Palais de la Mutualité in Paris from the 21st to the 25th of June 1935. The event was organized as a gathering of anti–fascist intellectuals by a committee consisting primarily of French communists that included René Crevel, Louis Aragon, Tristan Tzara, André Malraux, Jean Cassou, and Ilya Ehrenburg, among others. As a heat wave gripped Paris, 3,000 delegates and spectators attended the opening speech by André Gide. Additional speakers over the next five days included E.M. Forster, Julien Benda, Robert Musil, Aldous Huxley, Heinrich Mann, Isaac Babel, Bertolt Brecht, Max Brod, Paul Nizan, Henri Barbusse, and many others.

The outpouring of anti-fascist rhetoric had little impact aside from one indisputably tragic event. René Crevel had hoped that the Congress might serve to reconcile his former colleagues in the Surrealist group with the more orthodox members of the Communist party. The event served however to deepen those divisions, ultimately provoking a despairing Crevel to take his own life in the days immediately prior to the Congress.

A few months later, in November 1935, André Breton published the speech that Paul Éluard had delivered at the Congress on his behalf — Breton had been forbidden to speak — in *The Political Position of Surrealism,* a volume that also included an announcement of the forthcoming publication of the *Cahiers de 'Contre-Attaque,'* a projected series of pamphlets representing the views of that nascent and ultimately abortive collaboration between Breton, Georges Bataille, and their respective allies. On *Contre-Attaque*, see Artaud's lecture "Surrealism and Revolution," in this volume.

Jean Paulhan, 19 July 1935. OC 8 (1980) 285–8 & *Quarto* (2004) 659–61.

Jean Paulhan, 6 August 1935. OC 8 (1980) 288–90.

Jean Paulhan, 15 August 1935. OC 8 (1980) 290–1.

To the Minister of Foreign Affairs (Au ministre des affaires étrangères), August 1935. OC 8 (1980) 291–3. Unfinished draft, originally published in *Vie et Mort de Satan le Feu* (Arcanes, 1953).

To the Minister of National Education (Au ministre de l'éducation nationale), August 1935. OC 8 (1980) 293–5. Unfinished draft, first published in *Vie et Mort de Satan le Feu* (Arcanes, 1953). The Minister of National Education at this time was Philippe Marcombes and he did, in the end, grant Artaud the mission that he had requested, though this only amounted to a title granted by the Ministry of Education rather than financial support. See the following letter to Paulhan.

Jean Paulhan, September 1935. OC 8 (1980) 297. This letter references a section of the chapter "On the Balinese Theater," from *The Theater and Its Double,* which Artaud hoped to see printed in the *NRF*. The first part of the chapter had been published in the *NRF* No. 217 (octobre 1931). The second section, written as a letter to Paulhan, had yet to be published. For an English translation of the material in question, see Artaud, *The Theater and Its Double* (Grove Press, 1958) 57–60.

Madame Germaine Paulhan, September 1935. OC 8 (1980) 298.

To the General Secretary of l'Alliance française, 14 December 1935. OC 8 (1980) 299–300. Unfinished draft, first published in *Vie et Mort de Satan le Feu* (Arcanes, 1953).

Jean Paulhan, 6 January 1936. OC 5 (1964) 266–67.

Doctor Allendy & Miss Colette Nel-Dumochel, 10 January 1936. OC 8 (1980) 302–303.

Jean Paulhan, 25 January 1936. OC 5 (1964) 272–73 & *Quarto* (2004) 662.

Jean Paulhan, 31 January 1936. OC 5 (1964) 272–73 and *Quarto* (2004) 662–3.

Jean-Louis Barrault, 31 January 1936. OC 8 (1980) 305.

Balthus, 31 January 1936. OC 8 (1980) 304–305.

René Allendy, 7 February 1936. OC 8 (1980) 307–8.

Jean Paulhan, 26 March 1936. OC 8 (1980) 308–10. Artaud hoped that "The Theater of the Séraphim" and "An Affective Athleticism" would be published in *Mesures,* a quarterly literary journal published by the American Expatriates Henry and Barbara Church. Paulhan was on the editorial committee along with Henri Michaux, Bernard Groethuysen, and Giuseppe Ungaretti. "An Affective Athleticism" would later appear as chapter 12 of *The Theater and Its Double*. Although Artaud intended for "The Theater of the Séraphim" to be included in that book, in the end it was omitted.

René Thomas, 2 April 1936. OC 8 (1980) 310–1.

Jean Paulhan, 23 April 1936. OC 5 (1964) 276–83 and *Quarto* (2004) 663–7.

Jean Paulhan, 21 May 1936. OC 5 (1964) 284–88 and *Quarto* (2004) 667–9. Artaud sent Paulhan the texts of the three lectures he presented at the University of Mexico on 26, 27, and 29 February 1936. See "Surrealism and Revolution," "Man Against Fate," and "Theater and the Gods," in this volume.

Jean-Louis Barrault, 17 June 1936. OC 8 (1980) 312–3.

Balthus, 18 June 1936. OC 8 (1980) 313–4. This letter included a clipping of the article Artaud wrote on Balthus for *El Nacional Revolucionario*, "Young French Painting and Tradition," included in this volume.

Jean-Louis Barrault, 10 July 1936. OC 8 (1980) 314–5. Bernard Palissy (c. 1510–c. 1589) was a French scientist and ceramicist, famous for his ornately decorated platters and for the particular style of pottery that he invented, now known as "Palissy Ware." In his autobiography, he recounts burning his furniture and even the floorboards of his house in his furnaces, while his family lived in poverty and often went hungry, as he sought to perfect his ceramics.

REVOLUTIONARY MESSAGES

Artaud proposed the title *Revolutionary Messages* for a collection of his writings from Mexico in a letter to Jean Paulhan written on 21 May 1936 (included in this volume). He did not specify the precise contents of the collection, since he was in fact still writing the lectures and essays that it would contain. At a minimum, it would include the essays he had already written and that he intended to publish in various newspapers, journals, and reviews in Mexico, as well as the texts of lectures that he delivered there. He told Paulhan that a publisher in Mexico was interested in a collection of his "texts on the autochthonous culture of Mexico" as all as various texts on the theater. The resulting volume would thus have included essays and lectures from both *Revolutionary Messages* and *The Theater and Its Double*. Nothing came of this proposal.

Though Artaud had begun writing about pre-Columbian and indigenous Mexican cultures prior to his departure from France, he devoted himself to this task when he arrived in Mexico. He was however also asked to write about contemporary theater, art, and politics in France. These articles, published for the most part in *El Nacional Revolucionario*, were his primary source of income. That in mind, their subject matter probably includes topics that his editors believed would interest readers in Mexico, as well as topics that interested Artaud. The pieces were written and translated on the fly, mostly in cafes, where Artaud collaborated with his translators, who included Luis Cardoza y Aragón, José Ferrel, José Gorostiza, Enrique O. Henríquez, Samuel Ramos, and others, and who, by and large, devoted themselves to the task out of friendship for Artaud rather than professional obligation or financial remuneration.

When Artaud was preparing to return to France in October 1936, he left copies of the essays that he had published in Spanish translation in the care of Gorostiza in hopes that he could later see them into print as a book. Gorostiza was unsuccessful in this endeavor and, worse, the copies of the texts were lost.

In 1962, Luis Cardoza y Aragon, another one of Artaud's friends and translators, made a systematic search for texts published by Artaud during his journey to Mexico and assembled the results of that search in a volume entitled *México*, published by the Universidad Nacional Autónoma de México. The volume included the contexts of *Revolutionary Messages* as well as some essays, originally published in Spanish newspapers, which would later be collected with Artaud's writings on the Tarahumara. These include "The Mountain of Signs," "The Land of the Magi," "A Principle Race," and "The Rite of the Kings of Atlantis" (they are included in this volume). Since they rightly belong with the other writings on the Tarahumara, Thévenin included them along with those writings in her editorial schema for Artaud's *Œuvres Complètes*.

Artaud sent only a few manuscripts back to France during his sojourn in Mexico. These were pieces that he hoped Paulhan would publish as soon as possible in the *NRF*. The original French manuscripts for the remainder of Artaud's writings from Mexico were lost. Luis Cardoza y Aragon's edition of Artaud's writings from Mexico published the translations that had been originally produced in 1936.

In assembling these writings for inclusion in Artaud's *Œuvres Complètes*, Thévenin enlisted the aid of

Philippe Sollers, the writer and editor of *Tel Quel*, and the two transcribed the Spanish texts and translated them into French. Thévenin used the pseudonym Marie Dézon for these translations.

The title *Revolutionary Messages* derives from at least two sources. The messages are revolutionary because they promote revolutionary ideas but also because many of them were published in a government-sponsored newspaper, *Él Nacional Revolucionario*.

UNIVERSITY OF MEXICO LECTURES

Artaud delivered the following three lectures on 26, 27, and 29 February 1936 in the Bolivar amphitheater of the Escuela Nacional Preparatoria, part of the Universidad Nacional Autónoma de México. He had arrived in Mexico only on 7 February, but he had begun writing the texts of these lectures prior to his departure from France.

Surrealism and Revolution (Surréalisme et Révolution). OC 8 (1980) 141–50 and *Quarto* (2004) 685–92. A review of this lecture was published in *Él Universal* (28 February 1936). The details of the review suggest that Artaud spoke extemporaneously rather than strictly reading his prepared text. The review mentions a discussion of Philippe Soupault, who is not mentioned in the text.

Artaud joined the Surrealist group in October 1924 and quickly became one of its core members. Only a few months later he was asked to take charge of the nascent Surrealist Research Bureau and given editorial control of the third issue of *La Révolution surréaliste,* which was published in April 1925. Within two years however the relationship had soured. Artaud's ties to the worlds of theater and film had deepened to the degree that he co-founded the Alfred Jarry Theater, while André Breton and other members of the Surrealist group sought to bring the movement into collaboration with the revolutionary agenda of the Communist Party. Artaud was effectively expelled at a meeting held on 23 November 1926. The date for this meeting that he gives here, 10 December 1926, is incorrect. Artaud's acrimony spilled over into a pamphlet, "In Total Darkness, or The Surrealist Bluff," which he printed at his own expense in June 1927 (See Artaud, *Selected Writings*, 139–45). Breton reciprocated by attacking Artaud, among many others, in his *Second Surrealist Manifesto*, in 1930. Breton's flirtation with the Communist Party was however also short-lived, primarily due to his unwillingness to subordinate himself to another cause.

A few years later, in the fall of 1935, following the debacle surrounding the International Congress of Writers for the Defense of Culture, Breton was still looking for a vehicle for his political purposes. He brought the Surrealist group into collaboration with Georges

Bataille and several former members of Boris Souvarine's Democratic Communist Circle to form Contre-Attaque. This unstable union held a few organizational meetings and published a single issue of its journal along with a number of broadsides & calls for action before it too dissolved. By subsuming Contre-Attaque within Surrealism, as only its latest attempt at political activism, Artaud illustrates, with unintended irony, the tensions between Breton and Bataille that foundered the group. Bataille, for his part, went on to co-found Acéphale over the late spring and summer of 1936, and, the following year, the College of Sociology. See Stuart Kendall, *Georges Bataille* (Reaktion Books, Critical Lives, 2007) 118ff.

Artaud's quotation from Théodore Jouffroy (1796–1842), author of *Du problème de la destinée humaine* (1830) — "In suicide what kills is not identical to what is killed" — appears in *La Révolution Surréaliste*, No. 2 (15 janvier 1925) immediately prior to Artaud's own contribution to that issue's questionnaire on suicide. For his part, Artaud rejected suicide on the grounds that it was only a hypothesis & something he doubted, as he doubted reality. A principal point of Artaud's is that he had already long been dead, that he had been suicided, and that he had no appetite for death, only for non-being (see Artaud, *Selected Writings*, 102–3).

Artaud also quotes from the Marquis Alexandre Saint-Yves d'Alveydre's *Keys to the Orient* (Clefs de l'Orient, 1877). Saint-Yves d'Alveydre (1842–1909) was a major figure in the 19th century French esoteric tradition, that of the Cabala in particular. He promoted understanding between Christians, Muslims, & Jews and was a significant influence on René Guénon, among others. The passage Artaud quotes appears in the final chapter of the book, which concerns the "mysteries of death."

While this lecture recounts Artaud's expulsion from the Surrealist group, it also signals his reconciliation with Breton. If the question of revolution is that of Surrealism *or* Marxism, Artaud and Breton are both Surrealists. Shortly after Artaud's return to Paris, he encountered Breton among friends in a café. Breton was fascinated to hear about Artaud's experiences in Mexico and he became a significant source of emotional and even occasionally financial support during the spring and summer of 1937, prior to Artaud's disastrous trip to Ireland. Artaud in turn inspired Breton to organize his own journey to Mexico, upon which he embarked on 2 April 1938. Regarding Breton's trip to Mexico, see André Breton, "Memory of Mexico," in Breton, *Free Rein* (1953), tr. Michel Parmentier and Jacqueline D'Amboise (University of Nebraska Press, 1995) 23–8.

Man Against Fate (L'Homme contre le destin). OC 8 (1980) 151–9 & *Quarto* (2004) 693–8. A Spanish translation of this text, "El Hombre contra el destino," was published in *Él Nacional* in four installments on 26 April, and 3, 10, and 17 May 1936. A review of the lecture appeared in *Él Universal* (29 February 1936).

The Theater and the Gods (Le Théâtre et les dieux). OC 8 (1980) 160–8 and *Quarto* (2004) 699–704. José Ferrel's Spanish translation of the first section of this text appeared in *Él Nacional* on 24 May 1936 under the title "El Teatro y los Dioses." The manuscript that Artaud sent to Jean Paulhan is dated 29 February 1936.

Artaud's reference to Emperor Julian here ("'There are three suns,' said the Emperor Julian, 'of which only the first is visible.'") is a paraphrase from his book *Heliogabalus, or the Crowned Anarchist* (1934), though he has reversed the order of the suns referenced in the passage. See Artaud, *Selected Writings*, 318.

MEXICO

This section gathers the majority of the texts Artaud wrote for publication in Mexico. Additional texts first published in Mexico appear in the section of writings devoted to the Tarahumara.

The Post-War Theater in Paris (Le Théâtre d'après guerre à Paris). OC 8 (1980) 171–85. This is the text of a lecture delivered at the Alliance Française on 18 March 1936.

The French Ambassador to Mexico, Henri Goiran, was in attendance. First published in Spanish translation as "El Teatro de post-guerra en Paris," in *Revista de la Universidad Nacional Autónoma de México* (junio 1936).

Open Letter to the Governors of the States of Mexico (Lettre ouverte aux gouverneurs des états du Mexique). OC 8 (1980) 186–9. First published in Spanish translation as "Carta abierta a los gobernadores de los estados" in *Él Nacional* (19 mayo 1936). Reprinted in Spanish in *Revista de la Universidad Nacional Autónoma de México,* Vol. XXII, No. 6 (febrero 1968).

Universal Foundations of Culture (Bases universelles de la culture). OC 8 (1980) 189–91 & *Quarto* (2004) 705–7. First published in Spanish translation as "Bases universales de la cultura" in *Él Nacional* (28 mayo 1936). Artaud references Hermann von Keyserling, *America Set Free* (Harper & Brothers, 1929); French translation by Germain d'Hangest, *Psychanalyse de l'Amérique* (Stock, 1930).

First Contact with the Mexican Revolution (Premier contact avec la Révolution mexicaine). OC 8 (1980) 192–6 and *Quarto* (2004) 707–10. First published in Spanish translation as "Primer Contacto con la Revolución Mexicana," in *Él Nacional* (3 junio 1936). Artaud may have presented this text as a lecture at the Liga de Escritores y Artistas Revolucionarios. See his letter to Paulhan from 26 March 1936.

A Medea Devoid of Fire (Une Médée sans feu). OC 8 (1980) 197–200 and *Quarto* (2004) 710–3. First published in Spanish translation as "Una Medea sin fuego," in *Él Nacional* (7 June 1936). The text is a review of Margarita Xirgu's production of Miguel de Unamuno's adaptation of Seneca's *Medea* at the Palais des Beaux-Arts. Margarita Xirgu Subirá (1888–1969) was of Catalan origin. She became famous in Spain for her staging of Federico Garcia Lorca's plays but was forced into exile by the Spanish Civil War in 1936. She enjoyed popular success in Spain prior to her exile and throughout Latin America thereafter.

Young French Painting and Tradition (La Jeune Peinture française et la tradition). OC 8 (1980) 201–5 and *Quarto* (2004) 713–6. First published in Spanish translation as "La Pintura francesa joven y la tradición," in *Él Nacional* (17 junio 1936).

French Theater Searches for a Myth (Le théâtre français cherche un mythe). OC 8 (1980) 206–8. First published in Spanish translation as "El teatro francés busca un mito," in *Él Nacional* (28 June 1936). Artaud's laudatory review of Jean-Louis Barrault's production of *Auteur d'une mère* was first published in *NRF* No. 262 (1 July 1935). It also appears in *The Theater and Its Double* (Grove Press, 1958) 144–6.

What I came to Mexico to Do (Ce que je suis venu faire au Mexique). OC 8 (1980) 209–14 and *Quarto* (2004) 716–20. First published in Spanish translation as "Lo que vine a hacer a México," in *Él Nacional* (5 julio 1936). Artaud references Alexis Carrel, *L'Homme, cet inconnu* (Plon, 1935).

The Eternal Culture of Mexico (La Culture éternelle du Mexique). OC 8 (1980) 215–9 and *Quarto* (2004) 720–3. First published in Spanish translation as "La cultura eterna de México," in *Él Nacional* (13 julio 1936).

The False Superiority of the Elites (La Fausse Supériorité des élites). OC 8 (1980) 220–4 and *Quarto* (2004) 723–6. First published in Spanish translation as "La falsa superioridad de las élites," in *Él Nacional* (25 julio 1936).

Eternal Secrets of Culture (Secrets éternels de la culture). OC 8 (1980) 225–8 and *Quarto* (2004) 726–8. First published in Spanish translation as "Secretos eternos de la cultura," in *Él Nacional* (1 agosto 1936).

The Occult Forces of Mexico (Les Forces occultes du Mexique). OC 8 (1980) 229–32 & *Quarto* (2004) 729–31. First published in Spanish translation as "Las fuerzas ocultas de México," in *Él Nacional* (9 agosto 1936).

The Social Anarchy of Art (L'Anarchie sociale de l'art). OC 8 (1980) 233–5 and *Quarto* (2004) 731–3. First published in Spanish translation as "La anarquía social del arte," in *Él Nacional* (18 agosto 1936).

I came to Mexico to Escape European Civilization... (*Je suis venu au Mexique pour fuir la civilisation Européenne...*). OC 8 (1980) 236–42 and *Quarto* (2004) 733–7. This is the text of a lecture, though it is unclear as to whether or not it was delivered, or even for whom it might have been intended. It was translated into Spanish by Alberto Ruz Lhuillier, who provided the text to Paule Thévenin, who in turn translated it into French.

FRANZ HALS — ORTIZ MONASTERIO — MARIA IZQUIERDO

Franz Hals. OC 8 (1980) 245–6. First published in Spanish in *Boletín mensual Carta blanca* (año III, No. V, julio 1936). Reprinted by Luis Cardoza y Aragón in *México*.

A Technician Who Works in Stone: Monasterio (Un technician du travail de la pierre: Monasterio) OC 8 (1980) 247–51. This text was translated into Spanish by Enrique O. Henríquez in 1936 but remained unpublished until it appeared in *Revista de la Universidad Nacional Autónoma de México* (Vol. XXII, No. 6, febrero 1968). Artaud wrote the text while in Mexico and gave it to the sculptor whose work it concerns, Luis Ortiz Monasterio (1906–1990). One of the principle Mexican sculptors of the 20th century, Monasterio is known for his monumental works, including the Monumento a la Madre in

Sullivan Park and the Nezahualcoyotl Fountain in Chapultepac Park, both in Mexico City. Monasterio's work combined Mayan & Aztec metaphysical concepts with ideas drawn from numerology & Pythagoreanism.

The Painting of Maria Izquierdo (La Peinture de Maria Izquierdo). OC 8 (1980) 252–55 and *Quarto* (2004) 738–40. First published in Spanish in *Revista de Revistas*, No. 1370 (agosto 1936); reprinted in *Revista de al Universidad Nacional Autónoma de México* Vol. XVII, No. 12 (agosto 1963). Artaud wrote this text on the occasion of an exhibition of paintings by Maria Izquierdo & sculptures by Eleanor Boudin at the Wells Fargo building in Mexico City on 10 August 1936. Translated into French by Marie Dézon (Paule Thévenin) & Philippe Sollers.

Maria Izquierdo (1902–1955) studied painting with Diego Rivera in the late 1920s before beginning a successful career as a painter. Her work incorporated traditional Mexican themes & motifs in a naïve but vivid modern style. She was the first Mexican woman to have a solo exhibition in the United States &, in the 1940s, was a cultural ambassador for Mexico, traveling throughout South America.

Three Notes (Deux Notes, Maria Izquierdo) OC 8 (1980) 256–7 and, in part, *Quarto* (2004) 740–1. The first note was published in the catalogue for the August 1936 exhibition of Izquierdo's works at the Wells Fargo building in Mexico City. The second note was written by Artaud on scrap of *Él Nacional &* kept by Izquierdo. The third of these notes was written at this same time. It was intended for a newspaper, but it is unclear whether or not it appeared. The French originals of the first and second notes were available for inclusion in Artaud's OC. The third note was translated into French by Marie Dézon (Paule Thévenin) *&* Philippe Sollers.

Mexico and the Primitive Spirit: Maria Izquierdo (Le Mexique et l'esprit primitif: Maria Izquierdo). OC 8 (1980) 258–64 and *Quarto* (2004) 742–5. First published in *L'Amour de l'art,* No. 8 (octobre 1937), illustrated with reproductions of four gouaches by Izquierdo. Artaud wrote this text following his return from Mexico as part of his effort to organize an exhibition of Izquierdo's paintings in Paris. The exhibition was held in January 1937 at the Galerie van der Berg on the Boulevard Montparnasse.

THE TARAHUMARA

Artaud returned to Mexico City from the Sierra Tarahumara on 7 October 1936. He immediately began publishing material related to his experiences in Él Nacional Revolucionario. "The Mountain of Signs" was the first of these articles, published on 16 October. The four essays that he published in Él Nacional form a series of essays on the Tarahumara. Since Artaud subsequently edited "The Mountain of Signs" prior to publishing it in *NRF* the following year, it appears later in this collection.

TEXTS PUBLISHED IN *ÉL NACIONAL* AND *VOILÀ*

The Land of the Magi (Le pays des rois mages). OC 9 (1979) 63–6 and *Quarto* (2004) 751–3. First published in Spanish translation as "El país de los 'reyes magos'" in *Él Nacional Revolucionario* (24 octubre 1936); this version was reprinted by Luis Cardoza y Aragon in *México* in 1962. It was first published in French in *Les Lettres nouvelles* No. 1 (March 1953), reprinted in *Vie et Mort de Satan le Feu* (Arcanes, 1953), and *Les Tarahumaras* (L'Arbalète, 1955). Artaud mailed the manuscript of this article, along with the manuscript for "The Mountain of Signs," to *Él Nacional* from Chihuahua prior to 6 October. Notes on the manuscript indicate that Artaud viewed this article as a continuation of "The Mountain of Signs" which is to say as the second part of "Journey to the Land of the Tarahumara." However, in a letter he sent to Paulhan on 28 March 1937, he tells him that he has "suppressed" this essay as a part of "Journey to the Land of the Tarahumara" in favor of "The Peyote Dance," an essay he wrote following his return to Paris.

Note (La nature a produit les danseurs...). OC 9 (1979) 67. This is a note written on a separate sheet of paper that was found accompanying the manuscript for "The Land of the Magi." It presumably also dates to October 1936.

A Principle Race (Une race-principe). OC 9 (1979) 68–71 and *Quarto* (2004) 753–6. First published in Spanish translation as "Una Raza-Principio" in *Él Nacional* (17 noviembre 1936). This version was reprinted by Luis Cardoza y Aragon in *Mexico* in 1962. Artaud retained a typed copy of the original French version. It was first published in *Les Lettres nouvelles* No. 1 (mars 1953), reprinted in *Vie et Mort de Satan le Feu* (Arcanes, 1953), & *Les Tarahumaras* (L'Arbalète, 1955). The manuscript indicates that this is the third part of the series of articles that constitute the "Journey to the Land of the Tarahumara."

The Rite of the Kings of Atlantis (Le rite des rois de l'Atlantide). OC 9 (1979) 72–6 and *Quarto* (2004) 756–9. First published in Spanish translation as "El rito de los reyes de la Atlántida" in *Él Nacional* (9 noviembre 1936). This version was reprinted by Luis Cardoza y Aragon in *Mexico* in 1962. The French original has not been recovered. Marie Dézon (Paule Thévenin) & Philippe Sollers translated the text into French from Spanish.

The Race of Lost Men (La race des hommes perdus). OC 9 (1979) 79–82. First published in *Voilà* 7 année, No. 354 (31 décembre 1937), attributed to John Forester.

Voilà was a weekly news magazine illustrated with photographs that were often very good. It paid contributors generously and the director, Florent Fels, was friendly with Artaud, whose work he had supported in the past. He published poems by Artaud in another magazine, *Action*, in 1921, and another essay in *Voilà*, "Galapagos, Les Iles du Bout du Monde" in issues 59 & 60 (7 & 14 mai 1932). Though the essay on the Galapagos was presented as a travel piece, it was in fact fiction. Artaud had never visited the Galapagos. He submitted another similarly fictional travel piece around the same time, in 1932, this one on Shanghai, though it was not published until after his death. See "L'Amour a Changhaï," in *Voir* No. 429 (21 décembre 1952). Both of these pieces are in OC 8 (1980) 23–46.

In her notes to OC 9 (1979), Paule Thévenin speculates that Artaud wrote "The Race of Lost Men" during the summer of 1937 while planning his trip to Ireland. During these months, he had also written to Paulhan asking that his name be removed from his forthcoming essays in the *NRF*. The pseudonym John Forester may have been adopted to accommodate a similar request made to Florent Fels. By the time this text was published, however, Artaud was interned at the Quatre-Mares psychiatric hospital.

NOTES

JOURNEY TO THE LAND OF THE TARAHUMARA

Journey to the Land of the Tarahumara (D'un voyage au pays des Tarahumaras). OC 9 (1979) 33–52 and *Quarto* (2004) 766–74. First published in *NRF* No. 287 (1 août 1937); reprinted in *Au pays des Tarahumaras* (Éditions Fontaine, collection l'Age d'Or, 1945) *& Les Tarahumaras* (L'Arbalète, 1955). The text is composed of two essays, "The Mountain of Signs" and "The Peyote Dance."

Artaud wrote "The Mountain of Signs" (*La Montagne des Signes*) while still in the Sierra Tarahumara. He sent the essay to *Él Nacional* where it was published in Spanish translation as "La Montaña de los Signos" (16 octubre 1936). The Spanish translation was reprinted by Luis Cardoza y Aragon in *México*.

Artaud mailed a typed copy of the text to Paulhan prior to his return to Paris in hopes that he would publish it in the *NRF* as soon as possible. Over the coming months, Artaud edited the text with care, as he discusses in his letter to Paulhan from 28 March 1937.

Artaud wrote "The Peyote Dance" (*La Danse du Peyotl*) in Paris during the spring of 1937. The text borrows elements from "The Land of the Magi" which had been rejected by the *NRF* in early February.

LETTERS (1937)

Jean Paulhan, 4 February 1937. OC 9 (1979) 101–6 & *Quarto* (2004) 760–4. First published in *NRF* No. 95 (1 novembre 1960), reprinted in *Les Tarahumaras* (L'Arbalète, 1963). Robert Fludd (1574–1637) was a well-known English doctor and philosopher. A follower of Paracelsus, he was an astrologer, cosmologist, mathematician, Cabbalist, and Rosicrucian who wrote prolifically.

Jean Paulhan, 27 February 1937. OC 9 (1979) 107. Artaud attempted another detoxification at the Centre français de médecine et chirurgie, 12, rue Boileau, Paris, from 25 February to 4 March 1937. The attempt was unsuccessful. He then attempted a second cure at another clinic, in Sceaux, from 14 to 29 April 1937. Paulhan arranged for both of these attempts at detoxification.

Jean Paulhan, 13 March 1937. OC 9 (1979) 108.

Jean Paulhan 28 March 1937. OC 9 (1979) 108–9 and *Quarto* (2004) 765.

Jean Paulhan 13 April 1937. OC 9 (1979) 110. An early version of what became the preface to *The Theater and Its Double* was published in *La Bête noire* No. 5 (1 octobre 1935). As this letter indicates, Artaud revised that text in April 1937, after his journey to Mexico, for inclusion in the collection. *The Theater and Its Double* would not however be published by Gallimard until February of 1938.

Jean Paulhan, 27 or 28 May 1937. OC 7 (1980) 223 and *Quarto* (2004) 804. Artaud was briefly engaged to a young Belgian woman, Cécile Schramme, during the spring of 1937. In May, he and Schramme traveled to Brussels where the couple stayed with Schramme's family and Artaud gave a lecture at the Maison d'Art on the "decomposition of Paris." The lecture, presented to 200 or 300 people, devolved into a ranting performance and, in the end, caused a scandal. His engagement to Schramme ended shortly thereafter.

Jean Paulhan, beginning of June 1937. OC 7 (1980) 226–7 and *Quarto* (2004) 805. Artaud's *Correspondence with Jacques Rivière* was first published in *NRF* No. 132 (1 septembre 1924). In the table of contents on the cover of the issue, the author's name was replaced with three stars. Artaud's name was however present as a signature for his letters in the exchange.

Jean Paulhan, end of June 1937. OC 7 (1980) 320 and *Quarto* (2004) 806.

LATER WRITINGS ON THE TARAHUMARA

TWO LETTERS

Henri Parisot, 10 December 1943. OC 9 (1979) 111–4. In October of 1943, while Artaud was still interned at the asylum at Rodez, the publisher Robert Godet wrote to him to propose the republication of the essays Artaud published on his journey to the land of the Tarahumara in the *NRF* in 1937 as an illustrated book. Henri Parisot was working with Godet at the time and he and Artaud entered into correspondence.

This letter references not only the two essays published in the *NRF* but also a much longer book, of 200 pages or more, entitled, *Journey to Mexico* (Voyage au Mexique) that Artaud claims to have written between his return from Mexico, in November 1936, and his departure for Ireland in August 1937. He claims to have lost the manuscript of this book along with his other manuscripts and belongings during the course of his arrest, deportation, and series of internments. The existence of this manuscript remains a question of speculation.

In her notes on this letter in OC 9 (1979), Thévenin suggests an explanation for Artaud's insertion of a hyphen in Tara-Humaras. She writes: "In Nahuatl, *Tarahumara* would mean running on foot (from *tārā*: foot, and *huma*, to run). But by decomposing this name into two elements, Antonin Artaud might have wanted to also recall the famous historic, almost mythic site, *Tara*, the site of the *High Kings* of Ireland. And *Humaras* sounds a little like the future form of the verb *humeras*, meaning to breathe or to smell. Nor should the Sanskrit term *tārā* be neglected: star, pupil."

Though Godet failed to publish the volume in question, Artaud's correspondence with Parisot resumed in July 1945 when Parisot himself undertook the task of publishing the book on the Tarahumara. As their correspondence continued, Parisot requested Artaud's permission to publish some of their letters as a book, permission which Artaud granted. A first collection of five of these letters was published as *Lettres de Rodez* by Guy Lévis Mano in February 1946 (though the book did not actually appear until April). The Tarahumara are mentioned several times during the correspondence, Artaud's 6 October 1945 letter is most directly related to the journey. See Artaud, *Selected Writings*, 451–6.

Dr. Gaston Ferdière, 11 December 1943. OC 9 (1979) 114–6. First published in *Nouveaux écrits de Rodez* (Gallimard, 1977).

LATER WRITINGS

Supplement to the Journey to the Land of the Tarahumara (Supplément au Voyage au Pays des Tarahumaras). OC 9 (1979) 83–94 and *Quarto* (2004) 929–35. Written in January 1944 but withheld. First published by Marc Barbezat in *Les Tarahumaras* (L'Arbalète, 1955). As noted above, Artaud wrote this text in response to a request from Henri Parisot, who was at that time working with publisher Robert Godet, to re-publish the texts Artaud published on the Tarahumara in the *NRF* in 1937 as a separate illustrated book. He initially wrote "The Peyote Rite among the Tarahumara" (included in this volume) in December 1943 but subsequently set that text aside. He wrote this "Supplement" the following month, but Godet failed to publish the planned volume.

A year and a half later, on 6 July 1945, Parisot, who was by then directing l'Age d'Or, a collection at Éditions Fontaine, requested Artaud's permission to publish the book in his collection. Artaud accepted this proposition. By this time, however, Artaud had renounced Christianity with a definitive virulence. He wrote a letter to Parisot on 7 September 1945, which he requested be printed in the book in place of the "Supplement," which Parisot did.

Au Pays des Tarahumaras was published in the l'Age d'Or collection directed by Henri Parisot at Éditions Fontaine with a cover by Mario Prassinos in November 1945. It contains "The Mountain of Signs," "The Peyote Dance," and the 7 September 1945 letter to Parisot.

Letter to Henri Parisot, 7 September 1945. OC 9 (1979) 51–2 and *Quarto* (2004) 935–36. First published in *Au pays des Tarahumaras* (Éditions Fontaine, L'Age d'Or, 1945). Artaud intended this letter to be published alongside the texts on the Tarahumara that he published in the *NRF,* "The Mountain of Signs" and "The Peyote Dance." Thévenin respected this intention in her ordering of Artaud's writings on the Tarahumara in OC 9. She placed the text immediately after "The Peyote Dance."

Indian Culture (La Culture indienne). OC 12 (1974) 69–75 and *Quarto* (2004) 1149–51. Written on 25 November 1946, published by K. Éditeur on 20 January 1948. Artaud wrote first drafts of both "Indian Culture" and "Here Lies" on 25 November 1946. The poems were later dictated to Thévenin and edited repeatedly through August 1947 prior to publication by K. Éditeur. Artaud read "Indian Culture" along with two sections from *Artaud the Mômo* and "Madness and Black Magic" at the Vieux-Colombier Theater on 13 January 1947, as part of his performance event, *The Story Lived by Artaud-Mômo.*

The Peyote Rite among the Tarahumara (Le Rite du Peyotl chez les Tarahumaras). OC 9 (1979) 9–32 and *Quarto* (2004) 1679–93. Written in December 1943, abandoned, then edited substantially in March 1947 prior to publication in *L'Arbalète* 12 (mai 1947). As noted previously, Artaud wrote this text in December 1943 when Parisot requested to re-publish Artaud's texts on the Tarahumara from the *NRF* as a separate illustrated volume. Having written the text, he did not however send it to Parisot. He deposited it with the secretary of Rodez for Dr. Ferdière to retain along with other letters and texts. Dr. Ferdière sent a copy of the text to Marc Barbezat, the publisher of *L'Arbalète*, in early 1947 so that it could be prepared for publication. Artaud edited the proofs substantially. He also added, as post-scripts, fragments of two letters to Barbezat written while correcting the proofs in March 1947. Barbezat told Thévenin that Artaud believed this text, in its revised form, should appear at the beginning of any collection of his writings on the Tarahumara. She followed this suggestion in her ordering of those writings in OC 9.

A Note on Peyote (Une note sur le peyotl). OC 9 (1979) 95–8. A note written in May 1947 on the occasion of the publication of "The Peyote Rite among the Tarahumara" in *L'Arbalète* No. 12.

Tutuguri, The Rite of the Black Sun (Tutuguri, Le Rite du Soleil Noir). OC 13 (1974) 77–9 and *Quarto* (2004) 1642–43. Written in October 1947, first published in *Pour en finir avec le jugement de dieu* (K. Éditeur, 1948). Following the publication of "The Peyote Rite among the Tarahumara" in *L'Arbalète* in 1947, Artaud proposed the publication of three pamphlets to Marc Barbezat, who, in addition to the journal, edited an associated series of books. The pamphlets would include a new edition of "Journey to the Land of the Tarahumara," "The Peyote Rite among the Tarahumara," and a new work that he had not yet written, "The Rite of the Sun" (Le Rite du Soleil). Barbezat suggested publishing these works together as one book, an idea that Artaud accepted. The contract for the book was signed on 22 June 1947. As the discussion progressed, the proposed book was to contain "The Mountain of Signs," "The Rite of the Sun," "The Peyote Dance," and "The Peyote Rite." Artaud intended to illustrate the volume with his own drawings.

Artaud did not write "The Rite of the Sun" until October 1947, at which point it became "Tutuguri, The Rite of the Black Sun."

A few weeks later, Fernand Pouey, the director of dramatic and literary programing at Radio Française, invited Artaud to prepare a program for a new series, *La Voix des poètes*. Artaud accepted the proposition and began assembling the elements of what would become *To have done with the judgment of god*. He decided to include "Tutuguri, The Rite of the Black Sun" in the broadcast. It was recorded along with the other texts at end of November 1947. The actress Maria Casarès performed this section of the recording. Artaud, Roger Blin, and Paule Thévenin performed the other sections. Additional recording & editing took place in January 1948.

On 1 February 1948, the day before the program was scheduled to be broadcast, Wladimir Porché, the head of the radio station, listened to the work, found it obscene and blasphemous, and banned it. A scandal ensued at the station and in the press. As the scandal played out, "Tutuguri, The Rite of the Black Sun," was published in *Combat* (13 février 1948) as representative of the recording as a whole. The recording nevertheless ultimately remained banned until 6 March 1973 when it was first broadcast by France-Culture.

At this same moment, Parisot, now publishing under the imprint K. Éditeur, which had previously published Artaud's *Here Lies preceded by Indian Culture* and *Van Gogh, The Suicide of Society*, proposed publishing the full text of the broadcast. It was released as a book at the end of April 1948.

Artaud most likely borrowed the terms "tutuguri" and "ciguri" from Carlos Basauri's writings about the Tarahumara. See Carlos Basauri, "The Resistance of the Tarahumaras," *Mexican Folkways*, Vol. 2, No. 4 (1926) and *Monografía de los Tarahumaras* (México, D.F.: Talleres Grafico de la Nación, 1929).

Tutuguri (Tutuguri). OC 9 (1979) 53–60 and *Quarto* (2004) 1694–7. Written 16 February 1948, first published in *Les Tarahumaras* (L'Arbalète, 1955). After deciding to include "Tutuguri, The Rite of the Black Sun" in *To have done with the judgment of god,* Artaud wrote this piece for the edition of his writings on the Tarahumara that he had previously agreed to publish with *L'Arbalète*. This was among Artaud's final works. He died on 4 March 1948.

ABOUT THE EDITOR

Stuart Kendall is a writer, editor, and translator working at the intersections of philosophy, poetics, media, & design. He is best known as the author of a biography of Georges Bataille, published in Reaktion Books' series Critical Lives, and as the editor and translator of seven volumes of Bataille's writings, including *Inner Experience, Guilty, On Nietzsche, The Unfinished System of Nonknowledge*, and *The Cradle of Humanity*. Contra Mundum published his *Gilgamesh* (2012; 2020) as well as his translation of *Phrases: Six Films* by Jean-Luc Godard.

ABOUT THE TRANSLATOR

Rainer J. Hanshe is a writer and the founder of Contra Mundum Press and *Hyperion: On the Future of Aesthetics*. He is the author of two novels, *The Acolytes* (2010) and *The Abdication* (2012), and the editor of Richard Foreman's *Plays with Films* (2013) and William Wordsworth's *Fragments* (2014). He is also the author of the hybrid entity *Shattering the Muses* (2016), a collaboration with Italian visual artist Federico Gori, *Closing Melodies* (2023), a phantomatic encounter between Nietzsche & Van Gogh, and *Dionysos Speed* (2024). Work of his has appeared in *Cæsura*, *Sinn und Form*, *ChrisMarker.org*, *Asymptote*, Black Sun Lit's *Vestiges*, and elsewhere. In 2016, Petite Plaisance published an Italian translation of his second novel, *The Abdication*. Shorter and longer works of his have been translated into other languages. His own translations include Charles Baudelaire's *My Heart Laid Bare* (2017; 2020), *Belgium Stripped Bare* (2019), and *Paris Spleen* (2021) and Évelyne Grossman's *The Creativity of the Crisis*, as well as longer and shorter works by other authors. His translation of Léon-Paul Fargue's *High Solitude* is due out in 2024. *Beyond Sense*, a vatic exploration of the aphasiac disintegration of Hölderlin, Baudelaire, Nietzsche, and Artaud, is forthcoming in 2025, *The Accumulating Wreckage: Poems, Essays, & Other Texts* in 2026, and *Paris Without End: Assorted Translations From Giacometti to Artaud: 1914–1964* in 2027. He is at work on a new book entitled *Humanimality*.

COLOPHON

JOURNEY TO MEXICO: REVOLUTIONARY MESSAGES & THE TARAHUMARA
was handset in InDesign CC.

The text font is *Migra*.

The display font is *Scala Sans*.

Book design & typesetting: Alessandro Segalini

Cover design: CMP

Image credit: Sanctuary tablet from the Temple of the Sun, Palenque, Mexico, ded. * 9.13.0.0.0 (692 CE).

JOURNEY TO MEXICO: REVOLUTIONARY MESSAGES & THE TARAHUMARA
is published by Contra Mundum Press.

Contra Mundum Press   New York · London · Melbourne

CONTRA MUNDUM PRESS

Dedicated to the value & the indispensable importance of the individual voice, to works that test the boundaries of thought & experience.

The primary aim of Contra Mundum is to publish translations of writers who in their use of form and style are *à rebours*, or who deviate significantly from more programmatic & spurious forms of experimentation. Such writing attests to the volatile nature of modernism. Our preference is for works that have not yet been translated into English, are out of print, or are poorly translated, for writers whose thinking & æsthetics are in opposition to timely or mainstream currents of thought, value systems, or moralities. We also reprint obscure and out-of-print works we consider significant but which have been forgotten, neglected, or overshadowed.

There are many works of fundamental significance to *Weltliteratur* (& *Weltkultur*) that still remain in relative oblivion, works that alter and disrupt standard circuits of thought — these warrant being encountered by the world at large. It is our aim to render them more visible.

For the complete list of forthcoming publications, please visit our website. To be added to our mailing list, send your name and email address to: info@contramundum.net

Contra Mundum Press
P.O. Box 1326
New York, NY 10276
USA

OTHER CONTRA MUNDUM PRESS TITLES

2012 *Gilgamesh*
Ghérasim Luca, *Self-Shadowing Prey*
Rainer J. Hanshe, *The Abdication*
Walter Jackson Bate, *Negative Capability*
Miklós Szentkuthy, *Marginalia on Casanova*
Fernando Pessoa, *Philosophical Essays*
2013 Elio Petri, *Writings on Cinema & Life*
Friedrich Nietzsche, *The Greek Music Drama*
Richard Foreman, *Plays with Films*
Louis-Auguste Blanqui, *Eternity by the Stars*
Miklós Szentkuthy, *Towards the One & Only Metaphor*
Josef Winkler, *When the Time Comes*
2014 William Wordsworth, *Fragments*
Josef Winkler, *Natura Morta*
Fernando Pessoa, *The Transformation Book*
Emilio Villa, *The Selected Poetry of Emilio Villa*
Robert Kelly, *A Voice Full of Cities*
Pier Paolo Pasolini, *The Divine Mimesis*
Miklós Szentkuthy, *Prae, Vol. 1*
2015 Federico Fellini, *Making a Film*
Robert Musil, *Thought Flights*
Sándor Tar, *Our Street*
Lorand Gaspar, *Earth Absolute*
Josef Winkler, *The Graveyard of Bitter Oranges*
Ferit Edgü, *Noone*
Jean-Jacques Rousseau, *Narcissus*
Ahmad Shamlu, *Born Upon the Dark Spear*
2016 Jean-Luc Godard, *Phrases*
Otto Dix, *Letters, Vol. 1*
Maura Del Serra, *Ladder of Oaths*
Pierre Senges, *The Major Refutation*
Charles Baudelaire, *My Heart Laid Bare & Other Texts*

2017	Joseph Kessel, *Army of Shadows*
	Rainer J. Hanshe & Federico Gori, *Shattering the Muses*
	Gérard Depardieu, *Innocent*
	Claude Mouchard, *Entangled — Papers! — Notes*
2018	Miklós Szentkuthy, *Black Renaissance*
	Adonis & Pierre Joris, *Conversations in the Pyrenees*
2019	Charles Baudelaire, *Belgium Stripped Bare*
	Robert Musil, *Unions*
	Iceberg Slim, *Night Train to Sugar Hill*
	Marquis de Sade, *Aline & Valcour*
2020	*A City Full of Voices: Essays on the Work of Robert Kelly*
	Rédoine Faïd, *Outlaw*
	Carmelo Bene, *I Appeared to the Madonna*
	Paul Celan, *Microliths They Are, Little Stones*
	Zsuzsa Selyem, *It's Raining in Moscow*
	Bérengère Viennot, *Trumpspeak*
	Robert Musil, *Theater Symptoms*
	Miklós Szentkuthy, *Chapter on Love*
2021	Charles Baudelaire, *Paris Spleen*
	Marguerite Duras, *The Darkroom*
	Andrew Dickos, *Honor Among Thieves*
	Pierre Senges, *Ahab (Sequels)*
	Carmelo Bene, *Our Lady of the Turks*
2022	Fernando Pessoa, *Writings on Art & Poetical Theory*
	Miklós Szentkuthy, *Prae, Vol. 2*
	Blixa Bargeld, *Europe Crosswise: A Litany*
	Pierre Joris, *Always the Many, Never the One*
	Robert Musil, *Literature & Politics*
2023	Pierre Joris, *Interglacial Narrows*
	Gabriele Tinti, *Bleedings — Incipit Tragœdia*
	Évelyne Grossman, *The Creativity of the Crisis*
	Rainer J. Hanshe, *Closing Melodies*
	Kari Hukkila, *One Thousand & One*

SOME FORTHCOMING TITLES

Rainer J. Hanshe, *Dionysos Speed*
Amina Saïd, *Walking the Earth*

AGRODOLCE SERIES Æ

2020 Dejan Lukić, *The Oyster*
2022 Ugo Tognazzi, *The Injester*

HYPERION
On the Future of Æsthetics   2006–PRESENT

To read samples and order current & back issues of *Hyperion*, visit contramundumpress.com/hyperion
Edited by Rainer J. Hanshe & Erika Mihálycsa (2014 ~)

CONTRA MUNDUM PRESS

is published by Rainer J. Hanshe
Typography & Design: Alessandro Segalini
Publicity & Marketing: Alexandra Gold

THE FUTURE OF KULCHUR
A PATRONAGE PROJECT

LEND CONTRA MUNDUM PRESS (CMP) YOUR SUPPORT

With bookstores and presses around the world struggling to survive, and many actually closing, we are forming this patronage project as a means for establishing a continuous & stable foundation to safeguard our longevity. Through this patronage project we would be able to remain free of having to rely upon government support &/or other official funding bodies, not to speak of their timelines & impositions. It would also free CMP from suffering the vagaries of the publishing industry, as well as the risk of submitting to commercial pressures in order to persist, thereby potentially compromising the integrity of our catalog.

CAN YOU SACRIFICE $10 A WEEK FOR KULCHUR?

For the equivalent of merely 2–3 coffees a week, you can help sustain CMP and contribute to the future of kulchur. To participate in our patronage program we are asking individuals to donate $500 per year, which amounts to $42/month, or $10/week. Larger donations are of course welcome and beneficial. All donations are tax-deductible through our fiscal sponsor Fractured Atlas. If preferred, donations can be made in two installments. We are seeking a minimum of 300 patrons per year and would like for them to commit to giving the above amount for a period of three years.

WHAT WE OFFER

Part tax-deductible donation, part exchange, for your contribution you will receive every CMP book published during the patronage period as well as 20 books from our back catalog. When possible, signed or limited editions of books will be offered as well.

WHAT WILL CMP DO WITH YOUR CONTRIBUTIONS?

Your contribution will help with basic general operating expenses, yearly production expenses (book printing, warehouse & catalog fees, etc.), advertising and outreach, and editorial, proofreading, translation, typography, design and copyright fees. Funds may also be used for participating in book fairs and staging events. Additionally, we hope to rebuild the *Hyperion* section of the website in order to modernize it.

From Pericles to Mæcenas & the Renaissance patrons, it is the magnanimity of such individuals that have helped the arts to flourish. Be a part of helping your kulchur flourish; be a part of history.

HOW

To lend your support & become a patron, please visit the subscription page of our website: contramundum.net/subscription

For any questions, write us at: info@contramundum.net

www.ingramcontent.com/pod-product-compliance
Lightning Source LLC
Chambersburg PA
CBHW021147230426
43667CB00006B/290